S. R.

M000033177

SIMILAR TRANSACTIONS

ISBN-10: 0996383700
ISBN-13: 978-0996383707

Editor: Clint Cargile
Cover Design: Andrew Higdon • www.thebrandhq.com
Book Design: Simpson Point Press

Images – Book One: *Dedication photos, next page, courtesy of family; Chapter 1, mug shot, courtesy of the Knoxville Police Department; Chapter 3, snapshot, courtesy of family; Chapter 4, flyer (minus authentic phone numbers), courtesy of family; Chapter 7, forensic photos & document, courtesy of Dr. Bill Bass; Chapter 11, mug shot, DeKalb County, Georgia court records; Chapter 15, WATV screen shots. Images – Book Two: Chapter 1, photocopy, Georgia Department of Corrections; Chapter 2, mug shot. Knoxville County Sheriff Department; Chapter 31, "Band of Sisters," photo by Herb Neu.*

Simpson Point Press (SPP)

This book is dedicated to Michelle and "Sara"

Michelle Anderson   "Sara" Smith

AUTHOR'S NOTE

This is a true story. Some names have been changed to protect and promote the privacy of those individuals. Names of some geographic locales have also been altered to aid in protecting certain identities. The name of Michelle Denise Anderson has not been changed, nor has that of Larry Lee Smith for reasons that will be obvious to the reader. The names of most officials have not been changed, as they are serving in a public capacity. There are no composite characters.

The narrative is based on many hours of interviews conducted over a number of years with the victims, their family members, friends, acquaintances, neighbors, and members of law enforcement. All events and dialogue not witnessed firsthand are based on personal accounts, published reports, court documents and transcripts. The author attended all related legal proceedings as allowed.

Contents

BOOK ONE

Part One – Nature of the Beast
1 – Near Saturn and Mars   3
2 – Psychogenic Amnesia   14

Part Two – Gone Missing
3 – 24 Hours   23
4 – Sightings   38
5 – The Interviews   52
6 – Captive Bride   63
7 – Walking the Dogs   74
8 – Atlanta Boogie   88

Part Three – Georgia Justice
9 – Friday the Thirteenth   97
10 – Matters of the Court   110
11 – State of Georgia vs. Larry Lee Smith   117
12 – Okay. Then What Happened?   129
13 – Ladies & Gentlemen   138
14 – Lies & Leniency   144

BOOK TWO

Part One – Picking Up a Cold Trail
1 – No Reason to Run Away   153
2 – Now I Just Wake Up Sad   163
3 – Anita and Doug   169
4 – York   174
5 – Investigating the Investigation   178
6 – Differing Detail   182
7 – The Survivors   193
8 – Steed   198
9 – Means, Motive & Opportunity   206
10 – Sara   212
11 – Release   218

Part Two – Connecting the Dots
12 – Tracking Larry Lee   223

13 – New Eyes   231
14 – The Lone Note   239
15 – Channel 6 News   245
16 – Joey   252
17 – Family Matters   267
18 – Ruby and Edsel Smith   274
19 – Caseload   279

Part Three – Beyond a Reasonable Doubt

20 – Can I Use Your Phone?   285
21 – What She Said Happened, *Happened*   294
22 – Eye to Eye   302
23 – Timeline   309
24 – Prior Bad Acts   315
25 – Oh, I'll Be There   324
26 – Band of Sisters   332
27 – Shades of Gray   338
28 – Theatre of the Absurd Part 1   350
29 – Theatre of the Absurd Part 2   359
30 – Think About It   372
31 – Something's Wrong Here   379
32 – In Closing   385

Epilogue & Acknowledgements

394

Monster: one who deviates from normal or acceptable behavior or character; a threatening force, a person of unnatural or extreme wickedness or cruelty.

Predator: an organism that lives by preying on other organisms; one that victimizes, plunders or destroys, especially for one's own gain.

BOOK ONE

Part One
Nature of the Beast

1. <u>NEAR SATURN AND MARS</u>

Larry Lee Smith of the County of Pinellas and State of Florida, and on the 12th day of July in the year of our Lord, one thousand nine hundred eighty-one did insert his penis into the vagina of Katherine McWilliams without the consent of Katherine McWilliams, and in the process thereof used physical force and violence likely to cause serious personal injury, to-wit did choke and strike the victim, thereby causing Katherine McWilliams to submit to said sexual battery.

State of Florida vs. Larry Lee Smith

He'd circled nearly-empty city blocks more than once, Katherine noticed, before the guy giving her a lift home, late on that summer Sunday evening, finally brought his small truck to a stop in front of an apartment building. Taking in elements of her surroundings, Katherine would remember the white picket fence and the rectangular shape of the four-plex: two units up, two units down, stairs running up the middle.

"Come up with me," Larry Lee urged his passenger as he reached for the door handle. "It'll just take a minute."

"That's okay," she replied agreeably. "I'll wait here."

"No, come with me. It'll be quick. I want you to meet some people."

She breathed a sigh of reluctant submission. "All right," she surrendered, hoping it would actually speed things along. She really needed to get home.

Fourteen-year-old Katherine McWilliams hadn't been living in Florida all that long prior to that July night in 1981. Her mother had moved there from New York, and Katherine—who'd admittedly become a somewhat difficult teen, playing her divorced parents against one another, moving back and forth between their homes in New York and Florida—had joined her about a month before.

Precocious and somewhat rebellious, the pixie-cute, brown-eyed Katherine had made some friends in her New Port Richey neighborhood, although they were three to four years older than her. She rode off with them on a Sunday afternoon excursion that continued into the evening. First the group of teens decided to drive down to Clearwater, twenty miles or so south, to catch a movie showing at a theater there. But when they arrived too late for the opening, they elected to travel a few miles farther west over the Clearwater Memorial Causeway to Clearwater Beach, a barrier island lying within the city domain. As a younger tag-along, Katherine's vote wasn't a deciding factor in the changed plans.

On the beach the kids hung out for a while, getting a little summer party going. The weather was ideal; from a high of ninety-five the temperature had dropped back into the eighties. A gentle breeze blew in off the gulf under the glow of a waxing moon, just six days away from making a full showing. Yet as the time got closer to Katherine's curfew, her thoughts were on her need to head back home.

She'd ridden to the beach party with a neighbor, Tom

Spiller, his brother and a few other older teens. Katherine spoke with Tom about leaving, explaining that she had a curfew, one she'd missed before; it was important to Katherine that she not do that again—not now.

"Yeah, I get that," sympathized Tom as they talked in the parking lot of the North Beach Pier. "It's a little early for me though. I'm not quite ready to leave." He hesitated. "Can you call your mother and tell her you'll be a little late?"

All Katherine could think of was how much she didn't want to call her mother and say, "I'm forty minutes away," knowing it was only ten minutes until her curfew. Katherine and her mother were working out some difficult issues. It was a challenging time. She didn't want to mess up. Not like this.

That's when they ran into Larry Lee Smith. He'd just gotten off work from his job as a cook at the Holiday Inn on the other end of the parking lot. Neither Tom nor Katherine had noticed the bushy-haired twenty-year-old, leaning against his small truck nearby, eavesdropping on their conversation. "Where do you live?" the stranger asked. "She lives in New Port Richey," Tom answered for her.

"I'm going that way," offered the friendly, soft-spoken guy. He was short, pudgy, with disarmingly blue eyes and a wide, pleasant grin. "I can give her a ride."

Katherine, feeling desperate to avoid a conflict with her parents, hesitantly agreed. *He seems harmless enough,* she thought. *Kinda cute.* Tom wrote down Larry Lee's license plate number from his Tennessee tag and told him to take Katherine directly home. Then Tom wrote his own phone number on the same piece of paper and handed it to Katherine, who deposited the note in her purse. Tom did not think to keep a copy of the stranger's plate number for himself. Larry Lee opened the passenger door, and Katherine climbed inside.

He maneuvered his truck past the palm trees to the other

end of the parking lot and over the causeway into Clearwater proper—the smallest of the three principal cities of the Tampa Metropolitan area. Then he informed his passenger that he needed to stop at a friend's apartment "for just a minute. No problem, right?" Larry Lee asked. "It'll be real quick."

"Yeah, sure," Katherine said. "No problem."

It was dark inside as Larry Lee held the door and Katherine walked behind him into the building. She detected a pungent, slightly moldy odor that lingered unpleasantly in her nostrils as she followed him upstairs toward apartment number four. He pulled the key from his pocket and led the way inside. The loud, echoed clicking of the door closing behind Katherine startled her. The apartment seemed empty. A mild sense of panic moved through her body. She glanced back at the door, and then toward this guy she'd just met as he walked ahead down a short hallway and motioned for her to follow.

"I want to show you something," Larry Lee said.

He stood facing an open doorway, perpendicular to Katherine as she advanced in his direction. When she got close enough that his right shoulder was just beyond her left, he swung his right arm up behind her, quick as a cobra's strike, and grabbed her forcefully by the back of her neck. He spun her around and pushed her into the bedroom. Katherine let out a scream. He wrapped his hand around her throat, squeezing, pressing his thumb against her trachea.

"Shut up or I'll beat the shit out of you!" Larry Lee growled. Then he punched her in the stomach and shoved her into the middle of the bed. "Take off your clothes. *Cooperate,* and you won't get hurt." He pulled at her clothes himself while he simultaneously shed his own.

As Larry Lee pushed Katherine's hand toward his exposed genitalia, indicating what he wanted her to do, her thoughts raced, and she moved as if in a dream, a nightmare. Realizing how utterly alone she was, the teen rapidly reasoned that if she appeared cooperative, submissive, she might get through this. Larry Lee climbed on top of her and shoved his erect member inside her adolescent body.

Time slowed down.

In an effort to speed things up and prevent her assailant from turning violent—to encourage his warped ego, his perverted sexual deviance—Katherine pretended to come around, to enjoy the activity, to be turned on by this creep in the process of raping her.

He seemed to fall for it. This was exactly what he wanted, to be in *control* of Katherine, to have her, to force her to *comply*. When he finally slid off, he informed her that she was going to take a bath. Then he ambled into the bathroom and filled the tub with warm water. His young victim would obediently wash away any evidence of his crime, he reasoned.

All in all, Larry Lee seemed pleased with himself, borderline excited. "I believe you liked that," he cooed from the bathroom doorway, a sly, crooked smile fixed upon his face.

Katherine kept her eyes on her rapist as she groped around for her clothes, then walked in his direction. She could feel that she was winning him over and surmised that if he was having her bathe, he might not be planning to kill her. "Yeah, sure I did," she replied, feeling her stomach tighten as she smiled uneasily back at him.

Larry Lee sat on the closed commode and watched her. While she lathered her petite, pubescent body, he warned her he would come after her and her family if she didn't keep her mouth shut. She absorbed his words in attentive silence, lifting her eyes briefly toward his. "No problem. It's cool. I'm not going to say anything."

While her brain felt like it was exploding inside her skull, Katherine managed to put on a small theatrical show, indulging her captor by listening to him brag about his dubious exploits all of which were exaggerated or completely untrue. He bragged about how much he could drink. (His alcoholic older brother, Brad, was the big drinker). He claimed he had a bullet in his ankle, a combat wound from his days in the marines. (Again, a story appropriated from Brad, only it was a lie on top of a lie; Brad, who had been a marine, was shot in the ankle while fleeing a police officer in Knoxville, Tennessee). Katherine pretended to be amused and impressed. *He's trying to come off as a bad-ass,* she thought in her masked, high-alert mode. But to Larry Lee, it seemed that Katherine might actually like him. His tone became warmer. She played along.

After she dressed, Larry Lee told her to give him the note from her purse, the one Tom had written the license plate numbers on. Then he walked her downstairs to his truck. "Slide down and cover your eyes," he instructed Katherine as she got inside, which prevented her from seeing the street names and landmarks as they drove out of the Clearwater neighborhood.

"Okay. You can sit up now," he said after a few blocks. Her eyes quickly focused on the unusual names of the streets. They were named after planets: Saturn, Mars—a detail that Katherine hoped would prove helpful.

Katherine couldn't tell Larry Lee how to get to her home from their location. She didn't know if New Port Richey was north or south of Clearwater on U.S. Route 19. So they pulled into the parking lot of a Waffle House. "Stay here and be quiet," Larry Lee warned her, and he went inside to ask for directions.

Inside her chest her heart pounded wildly. It occurred to

Katherine to get out of the truck and scream her head off, or to run inside and yell to the waitress that she'd been abducted, but it was very dark and very late and there appeared to be only one visible waitress in the Waffle House. Where was she, anyway? And how would this guy, whose name Katherine still did not know, react if she did tell? He'd already threatened to kill her and her family. Hard to know what to do. Katherine thought again: not safe. Stay put. She just wanted to make it home.

Larry Lee got back in the truck and pulled out of the parking lot, pointing his vehicle north. The drive took thirty-five minutes, during which time Larry Lee made flirty small talk. He informed her that he was apartment sitting where they'd just been. Katherine continued in her efforts to come across as relaxed and receptive.

"I just moved down here from New York," she responded. "Brooklyn." Larry Lee mentioned that he too had been living in Florida only a short time, just a few weeks. He didn't say from where he'd come, or why.

"You're pretty cute," he told her. "You know that?"

Katherine forced the corners of her mouth into the arc of a strained smile. "Thanks."

"How old are you?"

"Fourteen."

As they reached Katherine's neighborhood and then her street, she instructed her assailant to let her out in front of a house that was actually a half-block or so down from her own. "I was afraid," she later confided. "Afraid that he might remember where I live, and that he might come back."

Larry Lee stopped and Katherine climbed out without a word. She walked at a steady pace as his small truck continued down the street. When it turned out of sight, Katherine broke into a run. She raced down the block, sprinting under the pencil shadows of the tall palm trees that lined her street. The emotions she'd kept in check during the hours of suppressed terror now came spewing out as she burst through her front door.

"I've been raped!" she screamed through tears.

By now, Katherine was many hours past her curfew. In fact, the sun would soon make a showing. Her mother, Jane, had been pacing the floor, anxious, ready to lower the consequence boom upon her defiant daughter. Now she was stunned, shocked, reeling as she processed the details of Katherine's terrifying night.

As Katherine cried and talked, describing her predicament, her acceptance of a ride from a guy at the beach and the subsequent assault and rape, Jane's shock turned to rage, but now it was directed toward this man, this unknown predator.

She called the cops—the New Port Richey Police—who responded and took a report of the night's events. Yet they were initially cautious about buying into Katherine's story and questioned her mother about Katherine's behaviors and motives. Jane acknowledged that her feisty teen was a handful, but in this matter, the mother believed her daughter. Jane knew Katherine, and she knew her daughter had been traumatized. Besides that, bruises were now emerging along Katherine's neck where her attacker's choking hands had gripped her a few hours before.

A salty Florida breeze blew as the officers escorted Katherine and her mother to the local hospital emergency room. A rape exam seemed to corroborate Katherine's story. Inside her vaginal cavity Larry Lee's semen remained. A bath couldn't wash that away. One of his pubic hairs clung to her skin. Evidence obtained.

From the hospital Katherine and her mother were

directed to the police station for interviews and statements. An image composition book was placed before Katherine— one of those books with flipping pages of eyes, noses, mouths, and other features. Katherine was exhausted and choosing the right features seemed hard, but when she was done, the image was a dead-ringer for her assailant. She was amazed. "It looks just like him," she said.

Katherine had a copy of that sketch in her possession for a while. She took it out one day, months later, and stared into the eyes of her assailant. Filled with a sudden rage, she pressed a lit cigarette into each one, burning holes all the way through. Then she torched the entire image. "I really hate him for doing that to me," she admitted to a friend. "It was horrible."

From the Pasco County Sheriff's office, a gruff police officer—"Unnecessarily gruff," Jane recalled—drove Katherine and Jane around Clearwater in search of the fourplex apartment building where Katherine said she'd been taken. But Katherine was so exhausted by her ordeal that she was falling asleep in the car. Finally, Jane insisted that they be driven home.

The next day, the mother and daughter were told to report to the Clearwater Police Station, in adjacent Pinellas County, where the crime had actually taken place. There Jane and Katherine met with two detectives, and Katherine was instructed to draw from memory a picture of the apartment building. She complied, drawing a rectangular two-story dwelling, the white gate and fence in front, and the stairs leading up to them. Now the challenge would be for the police to find Katherine's assailant, somewhere out there in the community, with little precise information leading directly to him. But Katherine landed a special ally, a female officer who went out of her way in search of the structure, even looking in her off-duty hours. She'd been a sexual-assault survivor herself and felt great compassion for young Katherine. The female detective searched Clearwater neighborhoods, looking for a fourplex like the one drawn by Katherine, near a neighborhood with street signs named after planets.

The detective was determined to locate the building; then she found a structure that she thought might be the one. Katherine and her mother were driven to see it. Pulling up in front of the building, Katherine knew it matched her drawing, but in daylight the fourplex looked different. She wasn't completely sure it was the place until they walked inside. There it was: the smell. Unmistakable. Then she walked up to apartment four.

Jane waited in the police car while the detective walked Katherine to the entrance. She looked up at the building her daughter was being led into and observed the similarity to Katherine's drawing. When Katherine came walking back out of the house in tears, her mother knew it was the right place.

Three weeks after the kidnapping, assault and rape of fourteen-year-old Katherine McWilliams, Larry Lee Smith was arrested at his job at the Clearwater Beach Holiday Inn. He'd driven Katherine past the hotel on the night of her abduction and assault, but she hadn't known that he worked there.

Despite Katherine's ability to act cool and at times too old for her age, the sexual assault had shaken her badly. After Larry Lee's arrest, she wrote a poem blaming him for the walls she felt herself erecting in her instinctive need to protect herself from a now-scarier world. He'd stolen her ability to feel safe, to trust. For a while, Katherine lashed out at her mother; she felt the need to blame something or someone, so she blamed Jane for moving to Florida. If she'd been allowed to stay in New York, the hurt and rebellious teen accused her mother, none of this would have happened.

On July 16, 1981, twenty-year-old Larry Lee Smith was arraigned, charged with the kidnapping and rape of Katherine McWilliams. He was represented by attorney Douglas Prior, whose practice was based in Clearwater. The defendant pleaded "not guilty."

The Notice of Trial went out December 21, 1981. On January 5, 1982, Larry Lee changed his plea to "guilty" to the lesser charge of *involuntary sexual battery*—a deal had been struck—and he was sentenced by Judge Jerry R. Parker to five years in prison. He received credit for the one hundred fifty-seven days he had been incarcerated in the Clearwater jail since his July arrest.

As the Circuit Court for the Sixth Judicial District of Florida dispensed its justice for Larry Lee Smith, it advised the following: "In imposing the above sentence, the court further recommends that the defendant receive any psychiatric or psychological evaluation and treatment as available."

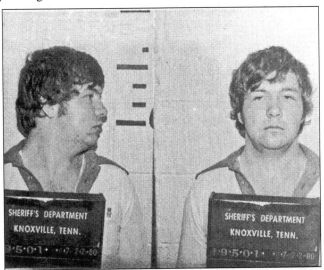

Larry Lee Smith, in Knoxville, 1980, shortly before leaving for Florida, where he would kidnap and rape Katherine McWilliams.

2. <u>PSYCHOGENIC AMNESIA</u>

Larry Lee Smith celebrated his twenty-first birthday in the same month and year, January 1982, in which he began serving his five-year prison sentence for the kidnapping and rape of fourteen-year-old Katherine McWilliams. During the three-and-a-half-hour ride from the Clearwater jail to the Florida Department of Corrections Reception and Medical Center (RMC) in Lake Butler, the shackled prisoner no doubt worried about what lay ahead.

Larry Lee wasn't a man's man; he wasn't tough, not really. He'd readily strike or choke a young woman to get what he wanted, to act out the deviant fantasies fermenting within his mind, but he would go out of his way to avoid a fight with a guy. His build was squat and thick, but that was mostly fat. At heart, Larry Lee was a pudgy mama's boy.

Born to Ruby Jane and Edsel Ray Smith on January 27, 1961, Larry Lee was their youngest by six years, although Edsel was gone from Larry Lee's life by age four and wouldn't meet him again until he moved to Florida at age twenty, just weeks before Larry Lee's assault of Katherine McWilliams. By all accounts, Ruby loved her baby boy—perhaps to a fault.

Everyone knew how much she spoiled him and made excuses for any questionable thing he did.

Secured in the back seat of a police cruiser, he gazed out the window at the lush, flat Florida terrain, probably mesmerized by the greenish-gray, lace-like Spanish moss draped from the many-limbed southern live oaks flashing by. Despite its name, Spanish moss isn't a moss at all, but a flowering epiphyte, an air plant, which absorbs nutrients from the air and moisture from the rain and hangs and sways in long, graceful, intertwined masses. These would make good pictures, Larry Lee might have noted, thinking back to the photography classes he'd enjoyed in high school before dropping out five years earlier.

The population of Lake Butler in rural Union County was under two thousand, barely outnumbering the captives held in the prison there. As the police vehicle carrying the new inmate turned up the entry road to the correctional facility, the flat-roofed structures of the compound came into view. Passing under the archway announcing *Reception and Medical Center* in large cutout metal letters, the cruiser rolled up to the cluster of white and tan concrete buildings, protected on all sides by razor wire-topped fencing.

The cruiser door opened to the sunny, winter Wednesday as Larry Lee swung his short legs out, hoisted himself up from the seat, shuffled in his chains, and was escorted inside. At RMC new inmates were processed into the correctional system and provided with medical care, including psychiatric evaluation and hospitalization as needed. The full intake and assessment phase—administering questionnaires and conducting evaluations—would take several months. Reports would be written and recommendations would be made. Metal bolts clanged loudly in the heavy locks as prison doors opened to admit Florida DOC inmate #081525, and then locked again behind him.

The first staff member to meet one-on-one with Larry Lee was the chaplain, whose job was to complete a spiritual assessment. Christian icons adorned the walls and shelves of his modest office, which was painted a pale blue. It would have been a welcome break from the bleak beige of Larry Lee's cell. "Come in. Take a seat," offered the chaplain, waving his hand toward a couple of wooden chairs as he reviewed Larry Lee's admission papers. He noted to himself that Larry Lee was serving time on a "morals" charge. "Tell me about yourself," the chaplain said. "Are you single or married?"

"I'm divorced," Larry Lee answered. Actually, he and his estranged teenage wife, Sara, were only separated. All of Sara's efforts to divorce Larry Lee had been successfully blocked (and would be blocked for years to come) by an attorney hired by Ruby, who was fighting for custody of Larry Lee and Sara's son, Joey. In response to the chaplain's inquiries, Larry Lee told him that he believed in God and daily prayer. Despite this declaration, he remained "noncommittal" about attending services in the prison chapel and declined to receive visits from the chaplain in his prison cell.

Prison psychologist Dr. Margaret Beatty administered a battery of tests to determine the prisoner's level of cognitive functioning and degree of emotional stability. In her "Psychological Screening Report," Dr. Beatty noted that Larry Lee had an IQ of 91, placing him smack in the middle of average, with a reading level of 6.6, slightly above mid-sixth grade. Larry Lee reported that he'd obtained a GED and had skills as a cook and a photographer. Dr. Beatty identified depression and an emotionally unstable personality as "special difficulties" that Larry Lee was dealing with at the time.

Yet little was real or honest in most things Larry Lee said and did. When the psychologist administered a test to determine

Larry Lee's personality makeup and psychopathology, Larry Lee deliberately chose answers that reflected mental or emotional illness. The test had been designed to catch such skewed responses. When the psychologist determined that Larry Lee had "faked bad" on his answers, she ruled the results "invalid."

Larry Lee had good reason to fake his evaluation. If he appeared more psychologically disturbed, he would have a greater chance to remain in a treatment setting and not in the general prison population. And if all went well, he could secure an early release.

After taking the evaluation, Larry Lee informed Dr. Beatty that he also wanted to consult with a psychiatrist. Soon after, Dr. Jose Ramirez, Psychiatric Services Coordinator at RMC, summoned Larry Lee to his office. A well-worn, green leather sofa with matching chairs formed a seating area in which Dr. Ramirez sat opposite Larry Lee.

"So, you asked to see me," Dr. Ramirez began.

"I think I have a sex problem," Larry Lee confessed, and told the psychiatrist that he wanted to understand why he was attracted to young girls. This was something that he'd never admitted to anyone. Then he confessed that he'd tried to rape his niece six years earlier when she was eight years old. (Six years earlier, the niece in question was actually six years old.) And he'd also tried to rape a fifteen-year-old friend of his wife. His wife, pregnant at the time, had rescued her friend from the assault.

Whether he truly wanted help or was just scheming to stay in a psychiatric setting, Larry Lee got what he wanted. Dr. Ramirez assessed the inmate to be clear of mind and emotionally stable at the time of the clinical interview, but with a fragile personality overall. He determined that Larry Lee most likely suffered from a personality disorder—a long-term, extremely dysfunctional pattern of relating to people and situations with ongoing, consequential mood changes. Dr. Ramirez did not prescribe any medications, but his "Psychiatric Consultation Report" concluded with the recommendation that Larry Lee be accepted by the Florida Department of Health and Rehabilitative Services (HRS) and placed in their program for the treatment of mentally disordered sex offenders. Larry Lee expressed agreement with this plan.

He spent three months at the RMC awaiting his transfer. During that time his ability to keep it together, to remain clear of mind and emotionally stable, became more challenged. Two months into his stay, RMC staff recorded an incident where he became visibly stricken with grief and anxiety after talking to his mother on the phone.

When Larry Lee was finally transferred, he was not immediately sent to the state hospital for admission into its sex-offender treatment program. He was first transferred to Sumter Correctional Institution in Bushnell, a small town in the Florida peninsula. It was there, in early June, less than five months into his sentence, that Larry Lee appeared to have a mental breakdown. His dorm officer found him crying in the corner of the room and talking to himself, unresponsive to the efforts of others to talk to him.

The babbling inmate was taken to the prison medical clinic where the staff psychiatrist assessed Larry Lee as appearing delusional, oriented to neither time nor place. He was talking about having been with his sister and mother just the night before. It was determined that he was suffering from separation anxiety related to his family, especially his mother and older sister, upon whom he was deemed "extremely dependent."

Although Larry Lee had seen two medical staff earlier that day, he denied any memory of these contacts. The doctor decided that his "amnesia" was most likely hysterical in nature, brought on by psychological stress, not physiological causes. Larry Lee was diagnosed as suffering from Psychogenic Amnesia and Passive-Dependent Personality Disorder. To rule out a more serious psychotic disorder, a call was made to Dr. Ramirez back at the RMC in Lake Butler. He authorized Larry Lee's transfer back there for further diagnostic evaluation and treatment.

In late July, after little more than a month back in the hospital at the RMC, Larry Lee's doctors determined that he was stable enough to enter the Dr. Geraldine Boozer Rehabilitation Program for Sex Offenders, a "self-help rehabilitation program" located at the twenty-five-year-old South Florida State Hospital, a mental institution where the halls and rooms were uniformly painted a pallid pea green.

Although a criteria of the program was that the patients could not be psychotic, the sex offender program was part of the forensic unit for the "criminally insane." After Larry Lee's transfer, the hospital's clinical psychologist administered another personality test. The test again revealed that Larry Lee had deliberately chosen answers he believed would portray a mental illness. The psychologist noted that despite Larry Lee's willingness to admit to at least some of his sexual offenses, he showed "little remorse" when discussing them. The clinical team described him as exceedingly immature, someone who continually seeks negative attention through defiant behavior. Staff complained that he was overly critical of fellow group members in sessions, yet he resisted all feedback given to him. Group members complained that he lied constantly and couldn't be trusted. During sessions, Larry Lee reported a history of heavy drinking and eventually claimed that he had a drinking problem and had been intoxicated when he'd kidnapped and raped Katherine McWilliams, something that neither party had reported at the time of the crime.

After a year at the state hospital, Larry Lee had received forty rules violations and failed to complete assigned therapeutic activities related to his treatment. He then requested to be discharged from the program and returned to the general inmate population. At that time, the psychologist administered a second personality test, and it was again flagged for deliberately false answers. Now that Larry Lee wanted to leave, he had picked answers he believed would reflect his improved mental health.

From the two tests given to Larry Lee at the South Florida State Hospital, the psychologist observed that a number of insightful conclusions could be drawn about his personality. He would likely have sudden mood swings and be prone to strong feelings of inferiority and hopelessness. He was an individual who was resentful, argumentative and overly sensitive to the demands of others, and he had difficulty trusting people, always keeping them at a distance, fearing emotional involvement. His primary defenses were likely to be projection (blaming others), rationalization (making excuses) and acting out.

The psychologist's report went on to say that while Larry Lee was capable of having positive social interactions with others, these interactions would likely be shallow, superficial, selfish and insincere; he would seek only to meet his own desires. The report claimed that such individuals are unpredictable and unable to express their emotions in a modulated, adaptive way. In fact, at the time of Larry Lee's request to be released from the treatment program, the psychologist observed that he appeared to have increased in his potential to act out aggressively.

Given Larry Lee's lack of progress and desire to leave,

the clinical team determined that there was nothing more they could offer him. In their final assessment and discharge summary, they noted that Larry Lee had requested to be discharged, demonstrated no desire to change, was unrehabilitated and remained potentially dangerous. His discharge diagnosis read: Mentally Disordered Sex Offender, Unimproved.

On April 17, 1984, eight months after asking to be discharged from the sex offender treatment program and two years and four months into his five-year sentence, Larry Lee Smith was paroled from the Florida prison. If early release had been his plan all along, then it worked. He was a free man again.

He remained in Florida until sometime in 1986, when he packed up his new girlfriend and her young son and returned to his hometown of Knoxville, Tennessee.

Part Two
Gone Missing

3. <u>24 HOURS</u>

It was a cold, gray Saturday morning, January 10, 1987, with temperatures below freezing and a thin layer of snow on the ground. The first inkling Anita Anderson had that something was amiss was when she woke with a start in the predawn hours and her daughter's bed was still empty. Sleep-stumbling through the rooms of the one-story house, Anita called out her name softly, "Michelle?" When she opened the bedroom door of her son, Doug, three years Michelle's senior, Anita heard him snoring lightly beneath a pile of covers. No one else was in there, or anywhere in the house; Michelle had not come home. That was a first. Although parenting her fifteen-year-old daughter had become increasingly challenging of late, this had not been part of the pattern.

It hadn't been Anita's intention to fall asleep. After Michelle had called the second time, saying she was finally on her way home, Anita, exhausted and having to work the next day, stretched out across her bed. *I'll just close my eyes and rest until she gets here,* she thought, but exhaustion overpowered her intention; Anita drifted into sleep.

Now, some hours later in the dark dawn of the morning,

she was awake, confused, a little worried, possibly annoyed, but not alarmed. Not yet. Michelle was no doubt at a friend's house, but for her not to call her mother regarding the change in plans was far from acceptable, and Anita would set her straight.

Anita phoned Michelle's best friend, Marci, who'd been at the house with Michelle the previous evening, but had declined to go out with her and some others to a party.

"Michelle didn't come home?" Marci said sleepily, Anita's call having pulled her out of bed.

Anita told her about Michelle's phone call, but then falling asleep and waking to discover that Michelle was not there.

"I haven't heard from her," Marci said, growing concerned, "but I'll call a few people."

Marci arrived at Anita's house soon after. She and Michelle were scheduled to visit Marci's younger brother, Tommy, at Taft Youth Development Center in Pikeville, something the two did each month. Anita had to leave for work but she called back to the house frequently to check in with Marci, who was calling everyone she could think of—with no luck. No one knew where her best friend was. Finally, she went into Doug's room. Throughout the morning's commotion, he had remained asleep. Now Marci shook him awake. "Michelle didn't come home last night," she said. Doug climbed out of bed and got ready to track down his little sister. He knew who he needed to talk to first.

With his Goth dress and his dark curls hanging over his eyes, Doug Anderson had adopted an air of defiance and mystery during this phase of his adolescence. At age eighteen, he was a bit of a wild child: partying, hanging out, no sense of where he was headed. Yet Doug had actually tried to prevent his younger sister from leaving with the group the night before. They'd had a heated exchange over it. Michelle's changing behavior concerned him, although in some ways, it seemed, she was following in his footsteps.

An olive-skinned beauty with dark, dancing eyes and wavy, mahogany-colored hair, Michelle Denise Anderson was going through a rebellious phase. "Choosing all the wrong friends," her mother later observed, though Anita didn't know the reasons. Parenting had seemed so much simpler when the children were small. Michelle had always been such a loving, compassionate kid, a reader, and, like her father and older brother, creative. In Ohio, where the family had lived when she was younger, Michelle played the flute and danced, and she liked to draw and paint.

After the move back to her mother's hometown of Knoxville, eleven-year-old Michelle earned a headline in the *Knoxville News Sentinel:* "Whittle Springs Student Wins Second Grand Prize in N-S Coloring Contest." As her prize, Michelle won tickets for the whole family to the 1982 World's Fair in Knoxville, with unlimited rides in the FunFair area and a river cruise on the *Becky Thatcher*.

Like her brother, she could be kind of shy. Anita's parents put in a pool the year Michelle turned thirteen. She loved to swim but was self-conscious about her body, so she'd cover up with a T-shirt and socks to hide her budding breasts and short toes. "Pretty little short toes," her mother said, "in a family dominated by long toes." In Michelle's self-conscious, pre-pubescent mind, her toes looked oddly different.

In recent months, however, since Michelle turned fifteen, she'd begun pushing against the rules, garnering increased scrutiny and interference from her mother. Sometimes she skipped school and had friends over while Anita was at work. Whatever the variables were in the equation of Michelle's changing teenage behaviors, the mild-mannered Anita was trying to determine how to regain control. She was working on a plan that included counseling, scheduled to begin later that month.

Despite Michelle's newfound rebelliousness, she had signed an attendance contract at school and brought up her grades. She'd also been saying she wanted to get back into soccer, a sport she'd played in Ohio when she was younger.

Between Michelle and Doug, Anita had her hands full, and she wasn't feeling all that strong herself, truth be told. For the past three years, since she and Doug Sr. divorced, Anita had been a single parent. After the split, he'd returned to his hometown, Miami, Florida, and Anita and the kids moved into a comfortable brick house closer to her parents in North Knoxville. They lived on a quiet, curvy, tree-lined street that winds to an end at Redwood Park on Redwood Avenue, behind a branch of the local library. It was a nice neighborhood, Anita thought, a good place for her kids, even if she didn't always approve of who they hung out with.

Anita felt guilty. On the previous evening, she herself had gone out for a few hours. The understanding when she left was that Michelle would stay at the house with Marci and Marci's boyfriend, Mike. But new plans evolved after Anita's departure. Eighteen-year-old Chas, a friend of Michelle's brother since tenth grade—and now Michelle's bad-boy boyfriend of a month or so—had also stopped by, as had Michelle's hard-partying friend Becka and a few others. Anita didn't approve of Becka, a particularly troubled and out-of-control young girl who was home on a weekend pass from her adolescent alcohol and drug treatment program. Anita had told Michelle that she preferred Becka not come around.

The assembled kids pooled their cash to buy alcohol and

got someone of age to purchase it. As the evening moved on and the booze ran low, some of the teens wanted to keep the party going. Becka called a friend who had his own apartment. Sure, he was open to the group moving over to his place. They wanted a lift in Mike's car, but he refused and he and Marci stayed behind. Marci remembered that Michelle was also reluctant at first, but Becka pleaded with her and she eventually gave in. Marci, Mike and Doug wanted her to stay put, but Michelle said she wouldn't be gone long. She changed into a pair of blue jeans and Marci's yellow and white striped sweatshirt and left with the group in a cab.

Doug went to bed and Marci and Mike remained at the house to update Anita when she arrived home, which was just a short time later. They told her about the kids dropping by and everyone going to Becka's friend's house, minus some details about the drinking that had gone on. Not long after that, Michelle called to check in. She told her mom that she would be home shortly. Anita offered to come pick her up, but Michelle said she had a ride.

Anita later acknowledged that if she erred in any of her parental persuasions, it was that she was too naïve and trusting, too laid back and lenient, too easy. It is in her nature to be easy. She sat at home and waited. Over an hour passed and Michelle called again, saying she was finally on her way. "Come on, young lady," Anita said firmly. "Now!"

Michelle's boyfriend, Chas, and his younger brother, Bobby, lived with their grandparents in a 1920's-style bungalow on Jefferson Street, off Cherry, in a section of East Knoxville that had once been comfortably middle class, but had since begun the descent into something less. Tall and rangy, Chas wore his curly brown hair long and tousled like the rock stars on MTV. His face was rugged and narrow, with a wicked, healed-over break in the bridge of his prominent nose. He'd considered Michelle his girlfriend for about a month, but he'd known her for years. His grandparents didn't have a phone, so when he wanted to call Michelle, he had to walk to a pay phone at the convenience store on Cherry Street.

That Saturday morning, while Anita was at work, she phoned a friend, Len, and asked him to pick up Doug and drive over to Chas's house to see what he knew about Michelle's whereabouts. Chas's grandfather answered the door. He let Doug in and woke his grandson. A groggy Chas, face swollen by alcohol and sleep, expressed surprise and confusion when told that Michelle never made it home. He filled Doug in on having met a guy who'd helped them buy more beer at a convenience store, then going back to his apartment with Michelle and Becka. Not long after, Becka left and Chas got into an argument with Michelle, so the guy took Chas home first, then drove off alone with Michelle, claiming he would take her home next. When pressed for details, Chas remembered that the guy had a yellow truck. "And his name was Larry Lee," Chas said. "Larry Lee Smith."

Chas climbed into Len's van with Doug and directed them to Larry Lee's place, located in the Western Heights public housing project west of Broadway. It was a plain brick unit, connected on both sides to ones just like it, a scaled-down, bare-bones version of connected townhouses. Although the place looked different in daylight, Chas was sure this was it. He got out, walked up to the building, and knocked on the doors and windows. No one answered, and the yellow truck was nowhere in sight.

They called Anita from a nearby pay phone. She agreed to meet them back at Larry Lee's apartment. She remembers the next events as a blur. As panic set in and her heart rate soared,

Anita didn't trust herself to drive, so a coworker chauffeured her to the site.

Len, Doug and Chas returned to Larry Lee's place to find the yellow truck now parked out front. They pulled up near it. When Anita and her coworker arrived, the guys were sitting in Len's van waiting for them. While they debated how to handle the situation, Larry Lee came bolting out of the apartment and made a beeline for his truck. He was *barefoot*, in January, with temperatures below freezing. He jumped into his truck, fired it up and tore off down the street.

The shocked group sprang back into their vehicles. Len shifted his van into gear and followed in close pursuit. As Len zoomed in close to Larry Lee's bumper, the guys could see him eyeing them in his rear-view mirror.

At a stoplight Larry Lee opened his truck door and cautiously stepped halfway out, one bare foot on the icy blacktop. He twisted around to look at the guys spilling out of the van behind him. "Why are you following me?" he called out, his anxious words giving rise to steam in the cold. He had a look of bewilderment on his face.

"What did you do with Michelle?!" Chas yelled, running at Larry Lee.

"I dropped her back near *your* house."

Chas lunged. There was a scuffle, but Larry Lee broke free, dove back inside his truck and gunned it. As the pursuit continued, Anita and her coworker honked their horn, signaling Len, Doug and Chas that they were pulling into a convenience store on the corner of Keith and Western to call the police. The guys pulled in behind them. "Why was he running like that?" Anita asked in alarm, an uneasy feeling forming in the pit of her stomach. From a pay phone she called the Knoxville Police Department (KPD).

In the meantime, Larry Lee flagged down a police car

of his own to report that he was being chased by some guys, but he didn't know why or what they were accusing him of. Those officers followed his truck into the same convenience store parking lot. When the second set of officers arrived in response to Anita's call, the two groups were separated into the two police cars while the officers took down their respective stories. Anita was assured that the report would be passed on, and that the KPD would look for Michelle. They told her to go to the station on Monday and fill out a missing person's report. To her shock, the officers then told everyone to go home. No more car chases tonight, they instructed. They let Larry Lee go without any further questioning.

It was now past five o'clock, dark, and beginning to snow again. Another inch of the white powder would fall on the city that night. Anita's party caravanned back to her house on Tacoma Trail. She called her parents, Charles and Marie, who lived just a few blocks away in the home where Anita and her two younger sisters grew up. They came over. Anita made a pot of coffee. Her panic was evolving into full-blown terror. Her mind began to explore every gruesome possibility.

While Michelle's family and friends talked over what they knew and offered each other moral support, some silently wondered about Chas. He was Michelle's boyfriend, after all, and the last person to see her other than—according to him—Larry Lee Smith. Anita asked him to walk her through the night's events one more time.

He recounted that he and two of the other kids walked from the party to the store for more beer, but they were underage and the clerk refused to sell it to them. Larry Lee was in the store at the time and had witnessed this interaction. He approached the teens and offered to buy the beer. As thanks, the kids offered to give him a few, but he invited himself to the party instead.

As the party wound down, Larry Lee told Chas, Michelle and Becka that he'd give them a ride home. Anita now realized that when Michelle had called and said she had a ride, that ride was with Larry Lee. After they had all piled into Larry Lee's truck, he suggested that he could get some more pot and alcohol and keep the party going. Chas could tell that twenty-six-year-old Larry Lee was hoping for some action with fifteen-year-old Becka. At the apartment, she began to feel uncomfortable with his leering and suggestive comments, so she asked to leave. Larry Lee agreed to take her home and Chas and Michelle rode along.

Once they'd dropped off Becka, Larry Lee invited Chas and Michelle back to his apartment. They said it was too late, almost two in the morning. "He insisted we had a bottle of champagne to finish," Chas claimed. "He said it was getting warm, and he needed help drinking it." So they returned with him. "We'd already had too much to drink," Chas then admitted.

The family mostly trusted him, but at this point, Chas's story became increasingly confusing to them.

Back at the apartment Michelle passed out, and Larry Lee took her upstairs and laid her down on one of the beds. Chas followed behind and was sitting on the edge of the bed. When he got up and walked to the stairs, Chas said, Larry Lee shooed him back into the bedroom again.

At that point, Michelle began to call for "Mike." Chas didn't know who *Mike* was, and in his intoxicated state he got angry. He admitted that he shook Michelle, "But only to awaken her," he said. Michelle, now fully conscious and extremely upset, pulled herself up from the bed and stumbled down the stairs and out of the apartment. Chas followed her outside where they got into a big argument. Larry Lee came out and said he needed to take them home. Michelle climbed into the cab of the truck, but when Chas went to get in beside her, Larry Lee yelled at him to sit in the back. Chas did as he was told and settled uncomfortably onto the cold metal bed of the truck in the subfreezing weather.

"Take us to her house," he called out to Larry Lee.

"No. She doesn't want you at her house," Larry Lee barked back. "I'm taking you home."

Chas shivered as they drove east on I-40 to the Cherry Street exit. He sat with his back against the cab, head folded down, knees drawn in as close to his chest as possible, arms wrapped tightly around his torso with each hand tucked into the cuff of the opposite sleeve. When he twisted around to look inside the cab, he could see Larry Lee and Michelle talking.

On the two-lane southbound side of Cherry Street, Larry Lee pulled his truck next to the median. This positioned the passenger side of the vehicle alongside the street, rather than next to the sidewalk. As Chas climbed out and walked toward the front, Michelle opened her door and stepped out onto the street to face him. She ripped Chas's crucifix from around her neck and hurled it at him. They yelled a few more accusations at one another before Chas picked up the broken necklace and threw it back at Michelle. She climbed back into the truck, slammed the door shut, and Larry Lee sped off. That was the last time Chas saw her. He walked to his grandparents' house and got something to eat.

Anita paced the floor, trying to process Chas's story amidst her growing fears. And that's when Larry Lee called the Anderson home.

Doug answered the phone. Larry Lee told him that he wanted to speak with his mother. Doug stretched the receiver across the kitchen table to Anita.

"Hello?" she said.

"Yeah," a nervous voice responded. "This is Larry Lee Smith. Listen, I don't want you to think I was running away because I did something, because I didn't. I was scared. Can you come back to my apartment? I want to explain what happened."

Anita was silent. She didn't know how to respond.

"But don't bring Chas or that other guy who got out of the van. They're *crazy!*"

"Just a minute." Anita pressed her hand tightly over the mouthpiece and told the others in a low voice what Larry Lee was requesting.

"I'll go with you," Doug said. "Did he say anything about me?"

"Well, I know I'm driving you there," Len said.

Anita removed her hand and spoke into the receiver: "I'm going to bring my son with me. He's the one with the dark, curly hair."

Larry Lee hesitated. "Okay. But that's all."

Anita hung up the phone and walked back to the kitchen table. Taking one last gulp of her barely warm coffee, she lit a cigarette and inhaled deeply. Then resting it on an ashtray, she closed her eyes and rubbed her fingertips over her temples as she anticipated the next scene in this surreal nightmare. "I just wonder what this guy is going to say," she said aloud to no one in particular.

While Anita had been talking to Larry Lee, Doug had a realization: that was not the first time he'd heard Larry Lee's voice. It was distinct: nasally, with an odd accent, not truly Southern but undefinable. Then it hit him. Larry Lee had called the house before.

There had been some kind of adolescent drama the previous summer. Michelle was visiting Marci while Marci's parents were away. Marci's brother Tommy was there, too. Tommy, however, had a crazy ex-girlfriend who was still in love with him. She also believed—rightly so—that Michelle had a crush on Tommy. When she found out that Michelle was at Tommy's house, she flew into a rage and asked her neighbor to give her a ride over to Tommy's so she could fight Michelle.

Her neighbor, Larry Lee Smith, didn't think that was such a hot idea, so he concocted a less violent scheme. More of a prank, really. He called Michelle's house. When Doug answered, Larry Lee told him that Michelle was at Tommy's house and Tommy was "having his way" with her. Doug at once told his mother, who drove straight over and picked up Michelle.

Doug never knew the identity of the prankster until that night. He immediately told Anita the connection.

What is going on? Anita thought.

Len drove Anita and Doug to Larry Lee's place. The apartment was actually leased to an absent ex-girlfriend, Maryanne. It opened directly into a small, stark living room, behind which was a kitchen and a back door. Opposite the front door were stairs leading to a second floor containing two bedrooms. One had been for Maryanne and the other for her young son.

When Anita and Doug arrived, they found a teenage girl in the apartment with Larry Lee. They soon learned that she was a neighbor Maryanne had sometimes used as a babysitter. Larry Lee explained that she was there as moral support and as a witness to their conversation. He then offered Anita and Doug a seat on the worn sofa, which they politely declined.

Right away Anita questioned Larry Lee about the phone

call Doug remembered from the previous summer. Larry Lee admitted to the call, saying it was a favor for his neighbor. He apologized, said he knew it was wrong. To Anita, Larry Lee seemed to be trying hard to turn on the charm, always responding with "Yes, Ma'am" and "No, Ma'am," often taken in the South as a sign of personal integrity, someone raised right, with respect and good manners.

He informed Anita that the police had already searched his messy apartment at his request. He then provided an account of what had allegedly transpired the night before. His story matched nearly perfectly with the one already given by Chas.

On the previous evening, he recalled, he'd encountered the kids at a convenience store on Cherry Street when he stopped there on his way home from work. He witnessed the interaction between the clerk and the underage teens and offered to buy them beer. As thanks, the kids invited him back to the party.

Later, as the party broke up, Larry Lee invited Chas, Michelle and Becka to go riding around in his truck and then over to his apartment, where they could drink and smoke pot. They all squeezed into the cab of his small, yellow truck, Becka in the middle and Michelle on Chas's lap by the passenger door.

After hanging out for a while, Becka said she needed to go home, so Larry Lee took her. He also took Chas and Michelle along for the ride. Once they'd dropped Becka off, he invited the couple back to his place.

At Larry Lee's apartment, Michelle passed out on the couch, and Larry Lee carried her upstairs to a bedroom, while Chas followed right behind. "So she would be more comfortable," Larry Lee told Anita.

He said Chas went into the room with Michelle and they

had some kind of fight. Michelle, visibly upset, stumbled out of the room, hurried down the stairs, and ran out of the apartment. Chas followed along right behind her. Outside, Chas and Michelle's voices grew loud, so Larry Lee suggested that he take them home. Michelle agreed. But Chas continued yelling at Michelle, so Larry Lee ordered him to sit in the bed of the truck while Michelle sat in the cab. Chas climbed into the back and Michelle said she didn't want him at her house, so Larry Lee decided to take Chas home first.

When they got to Chas's grandparents' house, Chas climbed out and walked toward the passenger door. Michelle threw open the door and the two immediately began arguing in the street. There was a lot of yelling before Michelle finally jumped back into the cab and slammed the door shut. Larry Lee then drove off. After this second altercation with Chas, Michelle wanted to talk. So she and Larry Lee rode around for a while. "Until it was very late," Larry Lee said. "Like maybe four or five in the morning." Then Michelle asked to be dropped off at the corner near Chas's, because now she wanted to talk to him. So Larry Lee obliged. Then he headed home and that was the last he saw of her.

"How could you just leave her there!?" Anita asked, incredulously.

"She insisted," Larry Lee claimed. He said she'd told him that Chas's grandparents' house was just three down from the corner on Jefferson Street and that she'd be all right.

Three down, thought Anita. *That detail is correct. Could this guy be telling the truth?* She was feeling so confused.

Then in a voice expressing equal parts panic and concern, Larry Lee added: "I was the last person to see her. If anything happened to her, it would be blamed on *me!*"

Larry Lee told Anita and Doug that he'd never had so much as a parking ticket, and that he was an alcoholic who watched what he drank. The kids had noticed the night before that while he was pushing the alcohol their way, he kept his consumption light. Larry Lee then invited Anita and Doug to look around the apartment before they left. He also gave Anita the name of his mother, Ruby, who lived on Fern Avenue in South Knoxville, and his girlfriend, Maryanne Parker, in whose apartment he was staying while she was "away" in Florida.

"Well, he was very cool and well mannered," Anita said to Len as she and Doug came out of his apartment and climbed back into the van. She was perplexed. Her gut didn't trust Larry Lee or his story. But she didn't know if she believed Chas either. She didn't know what to think.

When they got back to the house, she stared at the family sofa, where she'd last seen her lovely daughter twenty-four hours earlier, smiling, laughing, claiming she would be home all evening, safe in her own home. Anita turned to her mother. "Where do we go from here?"

Snapshot of Michelle, taken just weeks before her disappearance. She is wearing the yellow-and-white-striped sweatshirt she borrowed from her best friend, Marci.

4. <u>SIGHTINGS</u>

Downtown Knoxville is built on the banks of the mighty Tennessee River, which glides through the southern portion of the city and beyond for another six-hundred and fifty-two miles. Once known as the Cherokee, the mammoth river forms where the Holston and French Broad merge just east of the metropolis, having carved their way out of the Blue Ridge Mountains.

Angled a few city blocks north of the river, off Hill Avenue, is the Knoxville Police Department. Anita reported there, as instructed, on Monday, January 12, 1987, two days after Michelle went missing. Inside the industrial-looking yellow brick and concrete structure she rode the elevator up to the office of Detective Jerry McNair, who would be investigating her daughter's disappearance. McNair was an easygoing kind of guy: friendly, with a pleasant face, but requisite blank expression. He had many friends inside the KPD, where he'd spent his career. The affable detective greeted Anita, shaking her hand, sympathizing with her problem. "Please take a seat," he offered.

Anita recounted the events of the previous Friday night

when Michelle had failed to return home. She included Larry Lee's version of what had transpired after he'd driven off with her daughter.

McNair informed Anita that he had already talked with Larry Lee. He had looked around the messy public-housing apartment and checked into his local criminal history. "He's got an arrest record," the detective said flatly, "but it's not that bad." He was referring to Larry Lee's Knox County charges— possession of marijuana for resale, receiving and concealing stolen property, felonious assault. The detective had not uncovered Larry Lee's rape conviction in Florida, or the fact that he'd been paroled from a Florida prison just two-and-a-half years before.

After Detective McNair summed up his findings, he advised Anita that her daughter was—in his professional opinion—most likely a runaway. After all, Larry Lee said he'd dropped Michelle back off at the corner of Cherry and Jefferson—at her request. The detective then instructed Anita to file a report at the family court, from which a pickup order for Michelle would be issued.

"I don't think Michelle ran away," a perplexed Anita responded softly, blinking back tears. "She had no reason to. We were very close." Yet Anita was not inclined to argue or appear oppositional. McNair was a detective; maybe he understood something she didn't. Before she left the station, she asked him if she should put up flyers, leaflets. "Sure," he said. "That'd be fine."

Despite her doubts and misgivings and repressed intuitive alarm, Anita went through the steps, as instructed by McNair, and completed the paperwork at the Knox County Juvenile Court on Division Street. She answered the questions, filled out the forms, and provided a description of Michelle: wavy, below-the-shoulder mahogany hair, olive skin, large hazel eyes, five feet tall, one hundred and five pounds, last seen wearing size five Levi's and a yellow and white striped sweatshirt.

None of Michelle's friends thought she'd run away either. Not even her toothbrush was missing, let alone clothes or other belongings, and she was always careful about her appearance. All her good friends were accounted for, and no one knew where she was. Who was she supposed to have run away with?

* * *

REWARD
Missing Since January 10, 1987

MICHELLE DENISE ANDERSON

**15 yrs. old - Brown Hair - Hazel Eyes
5' Tall - 105 lbs.**

ANYONE WITH INFORMATION PLEASE CALL
(615)███ or (615)███

Michelle We Love You. Please Come Home or Call.

Flyers were posted by the family shortly after Michelle went missing and were updated until she was found.

Anita returned home from the juvenile court and stayed home from work for the next week. The Anderson house on Tacoma Trail had been hangout central for Doug, Michelle and their friends. In light of Michelle's disappearance, that function changed instantly and completely. It was now command central for any leads, any hope, any help—a shoulder to cry on. Flyers were printed and hung by the hundreds. Groups of family and friends manned shifts for weeks at the house, making calls, answering the phone and following up on leads generated by the leaflets or word of mouth.

The KPD did not publicize that a fifteen-year-old girl had gone missing in North Knoxville; even other divisions within the department knew nothing about the case. But calls and reported sightings generated by the posters came into Anita's house daily. Some were detailed. Many were from callers or witnesses who swore with absolute certainty that they'd seen Michelle. Most were false leads that brought on false hope.

Psychics offered insights. Would-be detectives offered their services. Anita realized that some people just liked to get in on the drama of a missing child. Despite these frustrations, Anita and her crew went out looking every day. They even staked out a few locations, sometimes for hours, sometimes in disguise. Chas participated in at least one of these stakeouts, eager to help find his missing girlfriend, the elusive, phantom, runaway Michelle.

The ongoing reports of sightings gave the fractured family reason to hope. Anita latched onto that hope, following leads for as long as she could, telling herself that if so many people claimed sightings of Michelle, she must be out there somewhere.

Anita focused on this thought every day, day by day, until the days grew into weeks, and still she had not pushed past her overwhelming fear to tell Doug Sr., her ex-husband, of their daughter's disappearance. It was killing her not to tell him, and yet she just couldn't bring herself to do it; she couldn't quite surmount that fear.

Doug Sr. had been the more authoritarian parent when the kids were young, keeping them tightly in line. Now he was more than seven hundred miles away, and had been for a couple of years. While the kids had adjusted to their transformed lives and hormonal adolescent bodies, they'd done so out from under the thumb of their strict father.

When he called from Miami to speak with his daughter, Anita said Michelle was out, which she often was when he'd called in the past. He still thought of Michelle as a twelve-year-old. He wasn't there. He didn't know the teenage version. And he certainly didn't know what Anita had been through, what she was going through now. As soon as Michelle came home, Anita would tell him all about what had happened. Any day now.

As the weeks multiplied, Anita tried to convince Doug to tell his dad the news, such was her dread of her ex-husband's temper, his wrath, his disdain, but her son declined. Anita would have to handle this one on her own. Eventually, after a month, she could avoid it no longer.

It was as bad as she'd expected. Doug Sr.'s temper exploded. How could she allow this to happen, he raged. "He called me everything," Anita later shared. "He thought of Michelle as his little girl, but he didn't understand what was going on." She already felt weighted down with guilt and regret. She already blamed herself.

For the first week after Michelle went missing, Larry Lee called Anita every day. He said he was concerned for her and wanted to see if there were any developments. About a month after Michelle's disappearance, Larry Lee's truck was vandalized. The windshield was cracked and the passenger side of the body was crumpled down its entire length. Anita never heard directly from him again.

The day after this incident, a mysterious note appeared on Anita's front door:

> MICHELLE IS WITH US. SHE IS OURS FOREVER. YOU'VE COME TOO CLOSE. YOU COME THIS CLOSE AGAIN AND WE'LL MAKE HER SUFFER MORE. DANTE OF HELL. BLOOD OF THE VIRGIN. FULL MOON. THE VIRGIN CROSS FROM RED TO BLACK. BAD MEN TONIGHT. DEATH SOON TO B.K., B.G., T.C., J.M, C.F., B.F. AND OLD BROWN CAR.

The note included two indecipherable drawings, possibly made with blood. The initials were those of friends and associates who had, in one way or another, assisted in the search for Michelle. The same note was also left on the car of John "Sunshine" Madden, an acquaintance of the Anderson family who had helped look for Michelle. Madden had come to the Anderson home frequently during the early days of the search, often providing rides for Chas. Madden also drove an old brown car.

In 1980s American culture, a collective phenomenon occurred that has been dubbed, in retrospect, the "satanic panic." Many people believed Satanists were lurking in disguise amongst ordinary citizens, waiting to convert vulnerable souls to the service of the Devil. Several stories made headlines. It was a wave of societal hysteria that came and went, but between its beginning and end, ignited the imaginations of many.

Anita believed that the letter was a hoax and the writer was just playing off of this "satanic" hysteria. It didn't take long for her to suspect that the letter writer was actually Larry

Lee—or someone in his circle—looking for a way to scare Anita off or switch her focus. No one laid claim to the assault on Larry Lee's truck. But if Larry Lee was the writer, Anita thought, perhaps he believed that some of those on the list were involved. Perhaps he knew who was involved. Whatever the case, she made a copy of the "satanic" letter and turned the original over to Detective McNair.

In March, two months after Michelle had gone missing, Anita begged to get a small article about her daughter's disappearance published in the *Knoxville News Sentinel*. She'd tried earlier and been turned down; a *runaway* wasn't news. Finally, Anita saw an article about another missing teen and pointed it out to someone at the paper. *What's the deal?* They acquiesced, and followed through with a poorly and hastily assembled article with no byline. The information reported in the story reflected Larry Lee's account of what transpired that night, as given to Detective McNair. The article did not name Larry Lee Smith, nor did it challenge or question his story. It reflected the confusion and lack of direction in the non-investigation of a "runaway" who had now been missing for more than sixty days.

Chas came to the Anderson home almost every day. At first he was welcomed as an active part of the family support and search efforts. Many people showed him sympathy. After all, he was Michelle's boyfriend and had been friends with her brother for years.

One night, while he and the Anderson family sat at the dining room table, he suddenly collapsed into a heap and began sobbing uncontrollably. When Anita tried to console him, he ran to the bathroom hiding his face with his hands. She followed him, and through streaming tears he admitted his shame and guilt. He told her he felt responsible for being drunk that night and allowing Larry Lee to take him home first. He apologized and said that he felt the family blamed him. Anita assured him that was not the case. But in reality, they weren't sure.

As weeks passed and no real answers or clues emerged, people began speculating behind Chas's back, whispering accusations. *He was there, wasn't he? Did he just allow Larry Lee to drive off with his girlfriend? He must know something. They were fighting; did he get rough with her? Did he get sexual with her against her will? That one night when he just started crying, didn't it seem a little too intense, like maybe he was really crying about what he knew, what he'd done? Were he and Larry Lee partners in crime? Did Larry Lee have something on Chas; is that why parts of their stories seemed so much alike?*

During the period of searching and waiting, Doug remained stoic, floating on the periphery, keeping his shock, his grief, and his opinions largely to himself. When it came to his friend Chas, he just wasn't sure he bought into the idea that Chas was guilty—although he did wonder. Just the fact that Chas was there, drinking at Larry Lee's instead of taking Michelle home—and all the other things that went on— made Doug somewhat suspicious. And then there were the latest rumors, just beginning to emerge, concerning Chas's new girlfriend. Chas was already dating someone else, and people had witnessed him being abusive to her when he was drinking. Doug knew Chas had a bad temper, but believed he would never hurt Michelle, his friend's little sister...

"Chas reacted as almost everyone else did to the situation," Doug later recalled. "He cried openly in front of people, as if he were as worried as everyone else who was around at the time. Nothing appeared odd to me about Chas's behavior. Of course, with the initial shock of

Michelle's disappearance, I didn't know what to think or do about anything. All roads led to Larry Lee Smith."

In the months after Michelle's disappearance, Anita felt that she not only lost Michelle, but Doug, too. He was just eighteen, his sister was missing, and he needed his mother. But the loss of and search for Michelle became all consuming. Doug became more withdrawn. Though he kept his thoughts and feelings inside, his grandmother caught him crying in his room a couple of times.

"I have never told anyone this before," Doug confided much later to a friend. "The last time I would ever see Michelle was when she and Chas—and I can't remember who else was there—were leaving. I'd been drinking and pleaded with her not to go. I don't remember what she said. We argued back and forth, but I will never forget the last words that came out of my mouth before they left. I remember screaming: 'If you leave, I hope you never come back!' I went back into the house and slept. I will always be haunted by those words I can never take back. The next morning, welcome to hell."

The tawny complexions of both Doug and Michelle were plucked from their shared paternal genes. Doug was his father's namesake and a dead ringer. He'd also inherited his father's particular talent; he could draw and paint. When Doug Sr. and Anita met, he was an artist, a painter primarily of seascapes, portraits and wildlife. In the summer, when the kids were younger, the whole family would travel to art shows with him, sometimes for a month at a time.

Doug Sr. was thirty-nine and Anita twenty-one when they married. A petite and pretty brunette, Anita was a third-generation East Tennessean. Black-eyed, swarthy Doug Sr. had been born in New York and raised primarily in Miami. They'd met in Gatlinburg, the glitzy, neon-lit, tourist town cradled in the Smokies, twenty-five minutes outside Knoxville. Then they'd lived in Atlanta and Columbus, Ohio, before moving the family back to Anita's hometown, not long before they called it quits. Doug Sr. could be hard, spewing heat like the stack of a steam engine.

After the split, he'd settled back in Miami for good. The kids talked to him regularly on the phone, and Doug Jr. spent some months in Miami with his father when he was just turning eighteen, but Doug Sr. didn't return to Knoxville. He and Michelle, his dark-haired princess, communicated only by phone. She never visited him in Florida. When Anita finally informed him that Michelle was missing, he felt as desperate and devastated as the rest of the family. He railed at the torturous mystery of it all: the unasked and unanswered questions, the awful imaginings.

Michelle was still missing in April when Doug Sr. finally paid a visit to Knoxville. By then he'd backed off on blaming Anita and had begun to blame himself. "I'm *going* to get some answers," he assured his ex-wife, hands pushed deep into his hip pockets, grim worry upon his face. Doug Sr. questioned the kids who'd been with Michelle the night she disappeared. He also met with Detective McNair at the KPD. After completing these interviews, he went home to his son and ex-wife and said, "I want to talk with this Larry Lee Smith."

Knoxville south of the river seems like a different city altogether, with its hilly, winding roads. On the third day of Doug Sr.'s visit, he, Anita and Doug Jr. drove across the Gay Street Bridge and wound their way the few blocks east to narrow Fern Avenue, where Larry Lee's mother lived. The Smith residence, a small, two-tone-green, one-story rectangular box built on a basement, was tucked into a narrow, sloping lot in a neighborhood dotted with similar homes on similar lots. On its front side, only the main floor and small basement windows faced the street.

Doug Sr. pulled up near the compact house to have a look. When Doug Jr. stepped out of the car to see if he could recognize the truck in the driveway, he was startled by a man who appeared suddenly from behind, wielding a wrench above his head and ordering them to leave. This man, tall and broad, with tan skin and black hair, was Larry Lee's older brother, Brad, who lived next door to their mother. Doug Sr. explained who he was and said that he wanted to talk with Larry Lee.

Brad remained tense but slowly lowered the wrench. "My *mother* would probably like to talk to you," he replied. Doug Sr. negotiated a time for the meeting. Brad told him to return at eleven o'clock the next morning, and said he'd make sure Ruby and Larry Lee were there.

But after they got back to Anita's, Larry Lee called the Anderson house with the stipulation that Doug Sr. come alone. Anita was too emotional, Larry Lee said, although Anita denied that she'd ever been "emotional" with him. In Larry Lee's apartment the day after Michelle disappeared, listening to him tell his version of what had transpired the night before, Anita had been too overwhelmed and confused to know what to think and what to do. She hadn't so much as raised her voice.

Doug Sr. accused Larry Lee of doing something to Michelle, to which Ruby got on the phone and sarcastically replied: "They haven't found a body, *have they?*" Larry Lee wasn't done, however. He seemed nervous, frightened of Michelle's angry father. He blurted out that Michelle had actually run away because she was pregnant by Anita's friend, Len. Larry Lee hadn't told this to the police (if he had, Detective McNair never mentioned it), nor Anita, nor anyone else, for that matter.

After the heated exchange, Anita encouraged Doug Sr. to go ahead and meet with Larry Lee and Ruby, but he was angry, upset, afraid he might become violent. The meeting never took place.

At the end of the week, Doug Sr. departed from Knoxville even sadder than when he'd arrived. He thought that he'd be able to get to the bottom of things, to find answers that his mild-mannered, ex-wife had not. But he'd hit the same roadblocks Anita had. None of the kids had any answers. Of course, all of them thought it was highly unlikely that Michelle had run away, but the KPD was still pursuing the case as if she had. Doug Sr. was also beginning to realize that he might never see his beautiful daughter again.

As shocking and dubious as Larry Lee's allegation about Len was, and as unlikely as it was to be true, Anita was going to follow up on it. It could not go unanswered. She'd been so shocked by Larry Lee's claim that she tried to question him further, but he wasn't talking. Anita wrote him a letter inquiring about his accusation. He refused to answer, redirecting her to speak with his attorney.

This was the first Anita heard of Larry Lee having an attorney. She later learned that Larry Lee got an attorney through Ruby's connections; she worked as a housekeeper for a prominent political family in Knoxville. A few calls and arrangements could be made, a Smith family member later explained, and sometimes they were.

Anita questioned Len. He denied Larry Lee's claim. *Could Michelle have actually said such a thing to Larry Lee?* Anita wondered. No friends of Michelle placed any stock in what seemed like nonsense to them. It was just one more ridiculous distraction from the seemingly unobtainable truth.

But in her efforts to follow up, Anita was able to talk with a lawyer who had previously represented members of Larry Lee's family. The attorney was surprisingly candid. The family of Ruby Smith, he confided to Anita, could put on nice clothes and speak the language of Southern manners, sort of, but they were some rough folk. And it was from this attorney that Anita learned the most shocking information of all: "Larry Lee Smith," he said, "served time in a Florida prison for the kidnapping and rape of a young teenage girl there, in 1981 or '82."

Another crime? Larry Lee Smith had served time for rape? That was not what Anita had been told by Detective McNair. What if he didn't know? Anita called him with the news. McNair said he would check into it, get those records. But even with the passing on of this new information, nothing changed in the case. No one at the KPD sent for any records from Florida or followed up on this lead.

Five months had passed since Michelle's disappearance. Gradually, the search crowd thinned. Sightings continued to trickle in, however, and Anita held tenaciously onto hope. She would follow every false lead, every false sighting, every morsel of hope until the possibility of hope was gone, without a doubt. Anita's guilt, her remorse, began competing fiercely with her fear, her grief, her deep and growing despair. A racing stream of thoughts brought on a tightness in her chest like a fist pressing on her heart and lungs, smothering her. *I am to blame. If only I'd been here, she wouldn't have been able to leave. If only…*

In June, while on the way home from the family's Smoky Mountain cabin in Townsend, Tennessee, Anita's mother, Marie, stopped at an antique store in Sevierville and met a man named Vance who ran a small ministry that helped locate missing children and runaway teenagers. This prompted her to share the tragic story of her missing granddaughter.

Vance could help out, he said; he wouldn't charge a thing.

"I'll talk to my daughter." Marie said. "Can you write down your phone number?"

5. <u>THE INTERVIEWS</u>

It was a hot and humid June afternoon, six months since Michelle had gone missing. Vance and his two person crew set up the folding lawn chairs and camera tripod under the white, wood-paneled carport of Anita's red brick, Tacoma Trail home—just off the kitchen. The quiet street and large lawn provided some privacy for the interviewing. Occasionally a lawn mower could be heard rattling and roaring nearby.

Anita's gracious mother, Marie, her silver hair styled in a short bob, sat next to the kitchen door within easy reach of refreshments for the group. A plate of chocolate chip cookies rested on a table nearby.

Gathered for this interview were Michelle's best girl friend, Marci; Michelle's best guy friend, Todd; his younger sister, Ashley; and Doug and a few of his friends. Chas did not show. No one from the KPD had interviewed any of these kids, and it remained doubtful that they ever would—at least not while Michelle was still missing.

Vance's agenda was to complete an exhaustive profile of the missing teen, Michelle, the *runaway*—to document any known associations and patterns of behavior. He claimed it would assist in tracking and finding her. The motivation for *videotaping* the interviews wasn't completely clear to Anita, but perhaps it was easier than taking notes; she wasn't going to challenge a helping hand.

The interviews began with Anita, smoke swirling and wafting upward in hazy columns from the cigarette held between the first two fingers of her right hand, her left hand occasionally shooing the dancing vapors away. In her mellow manner, she answered questions and provided yet another account of the night Michelle vanished, and the days, weeks and months that followed—an exhausting list of false leads and fruitless chases. In between cigarettes, Anita sipped coffee and nibbled cookies. She read the "satanic" note that had been pinned to her front door the day after Larry Lee's truck was reported vandalized.

Anita described what Michelle looked like, who she hung out with, how she dressed, and so on. Michelle always wore a certain necklace, Anita said, never took it off. It was a 14 karat gold crab pendant, the zodiac sign for Cancer, a gift sent by her dad.

The next interview was Ashley, younger sister of Michelle's friend Todd. Ashley had a freckled, pixie-face and frizzy-curly, red-blonde hair. She wasn't a best friend of Michelle, she explained; they just partied together. Yet Ashley had information.

Ashley insisted that she'd received a call from Michelle at five-thirty the Saturday evening following the night Michelle had disappeared. When Ashley answered the phone, the female caller identified herself as "Michelle" and asked to speak to Todd. He was in the shower, Ashley told her, and Michelle said she would call back. She never did.

"You ready to give up all that red hair to stick by that story?" Vance teased.

"I *know* it was her. I know her voice and she said it was her," Ashley argued, a small furrow in her brow. Vance encouraged her to add any final thoughts she might have, anything she thought was important.

"I'd like to think Michelle is alive," she said, "but sometimes I think she's dead, 'cause ain't nobody found her." She paused, as if thinking this last line over. "Which also makes me hopeful. They haven't found a body."

When Ashley's handsome brother, Todd, sat before the camera, his blond hair pulled back in a ponytail, he confirmed that he and Michelle were good friends. In fact, it was Todd's opinion that he and Michelle were *best* friends. He'd been at Michelle's house earlier in the evening of the night she vanished; his girlfriend had wanted to visit. He said he believed his sister about that Saturday evening call from Michelle, but when questioned on specific details, his recollection was different from his sister's. The times were off by hours, and he wasn't in the shower in his account; he wasn't even in the house.

"Do you think she was pregnant?" Vance asked, making reference to the allegation made by Larry Lee. Anita had told Vance about Larry Lee's accusation, and although no one was giving any credence to this story, Vance had brought it up a number of times.

"To my knowledge," Todd replied thoughtfully, "Michelle never did *any*thing with *any*one." Then he added, grinning slyly, "I mean, I kissed her once or twice."

"Todd, have you heard from Michelle?"

"No."

"You've never seen her?"

"Not since the night of the party."

"Do you think it was the drinking?"

"Could've been."

"Do you know who Jesus is?"

Todd nodded in the affirmative.

"Do you think she's in Knoxville?"

Todd threw his head back, then drew a deep breath and exhaled. "I don't know what to think about this whole situation."

Next up was seventeen-year-old Marci. Although Marci was two years older than Michelle, the best friends had a number of things in common: both girls were exceedingly cute with personalities described by most as sweet; both had blown off school, hooking classes together, but had been working to reverse that pattern (Michelle had brought her grades up and had been commended by the principal); both had troubles with their dads and rebelled against their moms; and both could hold their liquor. Marci would admit this last detail to Vance. But despite their sometimes wild and devious ways, Marci and Michelle came across to others as innocent and demure. It was part of their contradiction, part of their mischievous teenage charm.

On camera, Marci appeared as a fresh-scrubbed beauty in her blue tank top, with deep-set eyes and wide cheekbones. As she stared into the lens, Marci spoke with an air of quiet maturity in a velvety soft drawl. Her sandy-brown, wavy hair was parted and pulled back.

"My name's Marci," she began, a mildly sad look on her face, "and I was Michelle's best friend."

"You still *are*, aren't you?" Vance said.

"I *still* am. Wish she was here." Marci slid into a nervous grin.

"You want to wave to her in case she sees this?"

"Hi," said Marci, waving awkwardly to the camera.

During the interview Marci provided yet another accounting of the evening Michelle went missing—how

Michelle said she'd be right back when she left with the group; how she had called back to the house twice that night saying she was on her way, but never returned. Vance asked about Michelle's menstrual periods and about Len, referring again to Larry Lee's allegation that Michelle had run away because she was pregnant.

Marci didn't give *any* credence to *that* rumor, she said emphatically. In fact, as far as Marci knew, Michelle was still a virgin. Marci admitted that she and Michelle partied frequently, but that night made her rethink a lot of things. Since Michelle's disappearance, Marci had stopped drinking altogether.

And Marci also didn't believe Larry Lee's account of that night. Michelle wasn't dropped off at the corner of Cherry and Jefferson, near Chas's house, as he'd claimed. She believed that the fate of Michelle rested in the hands of Larry Lee, and all the false leads, which had come to nothing, wouldn't change that. "I'd like to think she's out there somewhere, but I don't think Michelle ran away."

The next day, Chas sat before the camera. Doug and his friends had rounded him up that morning and brought him over. Chas's large, dark eyes, stared into the lens. His long, rock-star-like curly hair was tucked under a gray and burgundy baseball cap worn with a matching gray T-shirt.

"Tell us who you are," Vance said.

"I'm Chas. I was Michelle's boyfriend when she turned up missing," he answered in a flat voice, followed by a nervous smile exposing a mouth of crowded teeth. Chas believed that the man interviewing him was a police detective. He unconsciously ran the fingertips of his right hand across his upper lip. "What do you want me to say now? What happened that night?"

Chas appeared somewhat ill-at-ease, frequently averting

his eyes from Vance when answering an open-ended question, one that required more than a yes-or-no answer. At Vance's prompting, Chas explained how he'd met Michelle and how long he'd known her.

"Were you good friends?" Vance asked.

"Yes, we were," Chas confirmed, eyes focused directly on Vance.

"How would you describe Michelle?"

His eyes shifted to the left. He stroked the beginnings of barely visible chin hairs. "She was a really nice person, outgoing. She liked to party a lot. She was fun to be with. Other than that, I don't know what to say." His focus shifted back to Vance.

With prompting, Chas went on to describe the party at Michelle's house and the continued partying at Becka's friend's place afterward. He recounted how he, Michelle and Becka then left with Larry Lee in his truck, going with him to his apartment.

"Larry Lee was trying to make passes at Becka," Chas explained, eyes flitting, fingers stroking his chin. "To make advances—get somewhere with her. But after a little while, Becka wanted to go home. She was asking him to take her home, and he finally agreed to. That was about two o'clock or two-thirty in the morning." He and Michelle had ridden along, but returned to Larry Lee's apartment because he said he had champagne to finish.

"Was Michelle sleeping then?"

"No, she wasn't."

"Was there any point that you and Michelle got into an argument?"

"Yes, there was. That was toward the end. She'd fallen asleep, passed out, whatever you want to call it, and Larry Lee carried her up the stairs. He thought we were going to do something, so..." He paused and turned his head and his eyes toward the side yard again.

Instead of waiting for a response, Vance jumped in: "What do you mean? Go somewhere? *Party?*"

"Umm..." Chas hesitated.

"Hit the sack!?" Vance added, in a tone that seemed inappropriately jovial.

A grin spread across Chas's face. "Uhh..." His eyes shot toward nothing then back again to Vance. "Hit the sack," Chas chose from the options offered by Vance.

"You and Michelle?"

"Yes."

"One kind-of-a-personal-question," Vance said with a chuckle. Chas nibbled his finger as he listened. "You don't have to answer. It doesn't really make a difference. Was Michelle a virgin?"

Now looking directly at Vance, Chas replied in his flat tone, "I *believe* she was. She said she was."

"Okay," Vance said. "Just wondering. Please continue. What happened next?"

"After Larry Lee carried Michelle upstairs, I was sitting there on the side of the bed, and she started calling for 'Mike' or somebody, and we started yelling." Chas looked away again, rubbing his knuckles slowly back and forth across his upper lip.

"You wanted to know who *Mike* was, *huh?!*"

"Yes," Chas answered.

"A little *jealousy*, was there?" Vance teased.

"Yes, there was." Chas grinned widely now.

He went on to give the account of Michelle rushing out of the apartment, his running after her, Larry Lee insisting upon driving them home, and his sitting in the bed of the truck until he was dropped off first at the end of his street.

"Were you pretty stoned? Did you crash when you got home?" Vance asked.

"No, I sat up and got something to eat."

"How long were you up?"

"Probably forty-five minutes."

"Had you sobered up by then?"

"Yes, I had."

"What time did he drop you off?"

"That was around four a.m."

"Who all was there at that time?"

"My grandfather and grandmother."

"Brother?"

"No, he was in Houston, Texas."

This last comment stood out to Anita. As she recalled, someone in her family had spotted Chas's brother Bobby just days after Michelle's disappearance. And according to her recollection, Chas had told them that Bobby was still up when he got home that night and had eaten something with him. If Chas was telling different versions, he didn't seem to be able to recall which one he'd told to whom.

"Did you feel safe leaving Michelle with Larry?" Vance probed. Chas paused, eyes scanning the yard. Before he answered, Vance continued. "Or were you just so pissed about the other incident?"

"I was just so pissed about the other incident."

"Was she pretty well—"

"Yes, she was messed up," Chas confirmed, cutting in.

"Was she passed out up front?"

"No, she wasn't."

"Was she sitting next to him or the window?"

"The window."

"What do you believe happened to Michelle? Did she ever mention running away to you?"

"No, she did not. The whole time I was dating her, I never heard her say that."

"If Michelle ran away, who do you think she would contact first?"

"I think she would call Marci."

Chas went on to say that if Michelle was out there he wished she would contact someone "to relieve a lot of people's consciences and make a lot of people feel more at ease to know that she was okay."

"Do you ever pray for her?" Vance asked.

"Yes, I do."

"Do you believe in Jesus?"

"Yes, I do."

"Why'd you stop coming around here?" Vance asked, indicating the Anderson home. "Too many bad feelings?"

"Too many bad feelings, and I thought people were getting tired of me being around. I was here day in and day out."

"How long after Michelle disappeared did you start dating your new girlfriend?"

Chas cast his eyes up as he calculated in his head. "About three-and-a-half months."

In the end, Vance's efforts didn't come to much. He gave Anita a copy of the videotape and showed Michelle's picture around. A few people claimed to have seen her, but these sightings turned out to be false. Anita and her parents accompanied Vance to a place or two, but it was all for naught.

"He pretended to investigate," Anita later said of the production and the outcome, "but it was useless. I don't know why he bothered. I was willing to give him a chance, grasping at *anything* or *anyone* who might help us."

In the ensuing months, any fantasy Anita still held that Michelle had run away was fading. On October 1, 1987, days short of the ten-month anniversary of her daughter's disappearance, Anita sat down and wrote a letter to no one in particular and everyone in general who might have occasion to read it. She wanted the newspaper to publish it; she wanted the Knox County District Attorney, Ed Dossett, to read it; she wanted someone to hear her and help her—Please!

Dear _____,

My daughter, Michelle Denise Anderson, age 16, [Michelle had a birthday over the summer] has been missing since January 10, 1987. We have heard hundreds of rumors since then, however to my knowledge, no one has heard a word from her. The local authorities believe that she is a runaway. We do not believe this. The circumstances under which she disappeared are unusual: She attended a party on the night of January 9 where she and two friends accepted a ride from a man, Larry Smith, 26 years old, who was a stranger to all of them.... [She went on to describe the events after the party and Larry Lee reportedly dropping Michelle off alone.]

...Larry Smith would not submit to a polygraph and the police have questioned him only once. I later found out through his family lawyer that he was in prison in Florida for raping a fourteen year old girl, and his parole wasn't up until January of this year... I am convinced that my daughter would be home if it had not been for this man. Why is the criminal protected?

I have been unable to obtain a warrant for contributing to the delinquency of a minor [for buying and supplying alcohol] and the police will not ever question this man again, despite his record of rape. I hope that he is innocent and that Michelle is just afraid to come home. But he could be guilty of a crime even worse than rape. My family and I are nearly crazy from worry with absolutely no answers. Michelle has appeared on television nationwide through the "Missing Children Help Center." Even on that report they said to "expect foul play." If Larry Smith had not been involved, I might be able to accept that Michelle did run away, but she had no reason to do so, and she had nothing with her except her purse. I am writing to you out of desperation; I don't know what to do next or where to turn.

Sincerely,
Anita H. Anderson

6. <u>CAPTIVE BRIDE</u>

It was the holiday season, 1987—the first for the family without Michelle. She'd now been missing for nearly a year and no one was any closer to solving the mystery of her disappearance. Anita was struggling to get through, willing the days of celebration to pass by quickly. She'd gone out to an office Christmas party on a Friday evening, and her mother, Marie, had stopped by the house to pick up a cake pan when the aqua-blue wall phone began ringing.

"Hello?" Marie answered.

"Who is this?" a strange sounding female caller asked on the other end.

"Who are you looking for?" a surprised Marie replied, trying to decide the best way to respond to this odd caller.

"I found this number on the picture of a dark-haired girl. It was on my coffee table. Is my husband messing around with her?"

"Umm... I don't know. Can you tell me your name and describe this picture?"

As Marie chatted with the suspicious woman, who identified herself as Celia, she tried to put her at ease and comprehend the meaning of her call. She eventually realized that the "picture" was the flyer about Michelle.

Celia sometimes suffered from spells of misapprehension and occasional occurrences of unreasonable paranoia. Thus the unusual manner in which this call began. Marie assured Celia that no one there knew her husband and explained that her daughter, Anita, had distributed many flyers of her missing daughter. It was Anita's phone number on the flyer.

As Celia calmed, the two women chatted. Marie told Celia all about Michelle's disappearance, about her last being seen late one Friday night the previous January, riding in the truck of a man named Larry Lee Smith.

"I know who he is!" Celia exclaimed suddenly. "He's the ex-husband of my friend Sara. Sara Smith!"

Celia was Sara's friend and former neighbor. Marie was stunned by the caller's fortuitous connection to Larry Lee. She listened with great interest, taking down Celia's information and phone number. When Anita arrived home, Marie was waiting to deliver the news.

Anita called Celia the next day. Celia told her she'd already spoken to Sara, who had agreed to meet with her. A couple days later, Anita and her boyfriend, Ted, followed the directions they'd been given to Celia's house. She lived in an older Knoxville neighborhood where the avenues are named after well-known American cities: Milwaukee, Orlando, Chicago, and so forth.

"Yes. Well, okay," Celia said stiffly as she answered the knock at her front door. "We'll go meet Sara now." Celia wore her golden-brown hair long and uneven. She had recently begun to believe that she might be a witch, pulling dark and complicated messages from the Bible verses she compulsively read. Sara had tried to convince her friend otherwise, but the voices in Celia's head held increasingly greater sway over any on the outside. Still, her heart was kind and her intent was good. She climbed into the car with Anita and Ted. "Turn right at the end of the next block," she instructed.

Sara opened the door to her second floor apartment. She was a striking woman of twenty-four, slim, medium height, with dark, silky hair that she wore long and straight. "Hi. Come on in. I've got coffee, coke or beer," she offered with a warm smile in a throaty-yet-feminine voice. As her guests took a seat, Sara lit a cigarette and asked, "What has Larry Lee done now?"

Anita filled Sara in on the circumstances of Michelle's disappearance, her own encounter with Larry Lee the day after and what had transpired (or not) in the nearly twelve months since. Sara focused intently on Anita as she talked. The weight of Anita's story seemed to bear down upon her.

When Anita finished, Sara inhaled deeply, allowing some moments of silence to pass before responding. "I wish I could give you some good news... but he is a *bad* man. He raped me, tortured me, nearly killed me. I'm *terrified* of him. And his mother won't believe any of it. She protects him every step of the way."

The odds had been heavily stacked against Sara from the moment she was conceived inside the womb of her drug-addicted mother. She was the seventh and final child of a woman who had given up babies four and five for adoption. If Sara had been one of those siblings, she might have had a chance.

As it was, she was first molested as a child by an uncle who'd also molested her mother. The ongoing rapes by her uncle were followed by those of her brothers, cousins, and stepfathers. This became Sara's normal, accompanied by neglect, yelling and regular beatings. For the longest time, she didn't know that life wasn't this way everywhere. She still startled at the sound of a zipper or woke with a start if she heard it in a dream. The smell of cigar smoke could trigger panic.

Sara had loved school, loved learning, although she struggled. It was hard being the "poor kid," a label she keenly felt. Her clothes were hand-me-down; her hair was a mess. Dressing and grooming her youngest child was far down on the priority list of Sara's mother, preoccupied as she was with other things. By age nine, Sara was helping her locate veins to inject pain killers, narcotics that added far more pain to the family than they ever removed. By age twelve, Sara's mother was finding veins for her. Then her mother began coaxing her attractive young daughter to trade sex with her male friends for a fix.

At age fourteen, Sara, by then a raven-haired beauty, decided she'd had enough. She ran away, hitchhiking as far as Tucson, Arizona, where she met a guy who befriended her, allowing her to stay with him and his mother in their trailer for a while. Then they bought her a bus ticket home. She called her mother. Yes, she could come home. No, she wasn't in trouble. But as soon as Sara returned, she was picked up and placed in juvenile detention for three weeks for running away and missing school. That would teach her.

Before long the routine of Sara's dismal life resumed. The year was 1979, and she was now fifteen. At a park in South Knoxville she met a small-time dope dealer named Larry Lee Smith, who sold her some pot and eventually asked her out to the movies. He was eighteen and kind of cute: brown, bushy curls, round blue eyes, a sort of turned-up nose and a wide, seemingly friendly mouth.

Sara accepted his offer, and a romance began. Two months later she was pregnant with their child. For Sara, this development brought hope. Her mother immediately kicked her out, which seemed more than ironic to Sara because her mother had never cared where she was or what she did. She didn't want another kid to raise, Sara surmised. But Larry Lee loved her and wanted to marry her. Sara would be free of her past at last. Everything was going to be fine.

Larry Lee had a private basement room in his mother's house; the basement had its own entrance from the back. Larry Lee was into photography and had a dark room down there. They began their life together, a life that seemed okay to her at first. He was attentive, generous, *normal*, at least as close to normal as she'd ever known. She thought she loved him.

Larry Lee's mother, Ruby, however, was a woman given to fits of screaming about nearly anything. At first, Ruby tolerated the young woman in her basement. She was carrying the baby of her baby, after all. But as Larry Lee's attitude toward his teen bride changed, so did Ruby's.

Around the seventh month of Sara's pregnancy, cracks began to appear in the façade of Larry Lee's *normalcy*. Sara had invited Cindy, an old school friend, over to the house to hang out. The three of them rode in Larry Lee's car to the Pizza Hut on Chapman Highway to grab a bite before returning to the basement room. There Larry Lee offered Cindy a Quaalude, something Sara didn't think was such a good idea. But her adolescent husband was cooking up one of his plans, plans that Sara had yet to become aware of. Cindy took him up on the offer.

It had been a humid East Tennessee day and Sara was feeling sweaty. She announced that she was going upstairs to take a quick shower. She'd be right back, she said, and climbed the stairs to the first-floor bathroom. Sara cranked the music up loud and hummed with the radio as she worked up a lather over her pregnant teenage body. Rinsing away the last of the soap, she turned the shower off, stepped out and reached for the towel. Then she became very still. Sara thought she heard something, loud voices, like someone was yelling. She turned the volume down and made out muffled screaming.

Wet and half naked, Sara bolted down the stairs and followed the sounds to the basement bedroom. There she found Larry Lee on top of Cindy, wrestling her down, forcing himself on her. Sara climbed on top of her grappling husband and attempted to pry him off. Cindy struggled free and got away, accusing Sara of having set her up. Shocked and hysterical, she grabbed her clothes, haphazardly pulling them on and bolting out the door.

Sara was baffled and mortified. "What were you thinking!?" she yelled. Larry Lee brushed her off, insisted that Cindy wanted it but changed her mind. Larry Lee's demons were making their appearance. This was the attempted rape that he would later confess to the prison psychiatrist in Florida. It was the first real hint for Sara of what lay ahead.

Instead of defending himself, Larry Lee hurled accusations at Sara, accusing her of messing around with his big brother, Brad. Sara denied his charges, but he became increasingly cruel to her. Not long after the attempted rape, while Sara was still pregnant, Larry Lee punched her in the abdomen, a beginning to the future beatings she would endure.

In the summer of 1980, their son, Joseph "Joey" Ray Smith, was born—"Joseph" after the middle name of Sara's father, whom she'd met only a few years before, and "Ray" for the middle name of Larry Lee's father, who'd been gone from his life for nearly as long as he could remember. It was a couple of weeks later that Larry Lee revealed the full nature of his darker side.

Sara liked to drink. Alcohol warmed her body and numbed her wounded psyche. But this drink Larry Lee made for her seemed different. She suddenly felt dizzy, disoriented, and then nothing. As she slowly came to, wrapped in a thick haze, she heard strange, distant sounds—drilling of some kind. As the fog slowly lifted, she realized that Larry Lee had drilled holes in the corner bedposts, through which he'd inserted large hooks. Sara was on her stomach, a dog collar around her neck, arms chained to either post, a gag in her mouth. The sexual torture was about to begin. Sara still had stitches from having given birth to a nearly ten-pound baby two weeks earlier. This didn't concern Larry Lee. He sodomized her while she was chained in this prone position. And when he was done, he beat her on the back of her head.

She had better keep her mouth shut, he warned her, or he'd harm the baby, cut him up in little pieces. "Don't think I won't do it," Larry Lee threatened as he unchained one of Sara's arms. Then he got in his car and left. It took a while for Sara to get her other hand free and crawl up the stairs. She was bleeding and needed help.

"What happened to you?" Ruby demanded, sounding annoyed, the baby in her arms.

"Your son did this to me!" Sara cried.

Ruby would hear none of it. Sara was lying, she said.

When Larry Lee returned he chained Sara again, for two weeks this time. He beat her randomly, without provocation, using his fists, coat hangers, broom sticks and, on at least one occasion, a skillet. He was teaching her, Larry Lee explained. He wanted her to beg. And beg she did. She did anything he said. *That was the plan:* Larry Lee confided to her that he'd always had a fantasy about keeping a sex slave. Soon, he had her performing sexual favors for his friends. He plied her with alcohol and drugs and then threatened to chain her up again if she didn't comply. And he taunted her with the things he would do—or said he had done—to baby Joey, who she'd rarely seen since the torture began.

Then Larry Lee expanded his base. He worked as a night auditor at the Holiday Inn where his mother, Ruby, worked as a waitress, one of three jobs she held simultaneously. He had keys to all the rooms. If a guy came in wanting a girl, Larry Lee pimped out the services of his captive bride. Then he forced her to dance in a topless bar, where he'd position himself at a table on the side, collecting her earnings.

Ruby had very little use for this wounded, often intoxicated, woman-child that her baby boy had brought into her home. Sara and Larry Lee eventually moved into a little apartment, and Sara enrolled in high school, as required by local law. Ruby kept the baby, allowed Sara to see him once a week. At this point, Sara was completely under their control. She played by their rules, so well that one night, while both Ruby and Larry Lee worked, they let her watch Joey by herself. This was her chance. As soon as they left, she took a cab to her mother's house.

"You've got to help me," Sara pleaded, ultimately and surprisingly convincing her mother to allow her to move back home. The threat of harm to the baby had been Larry Lee's hold on Sara. Now control of the baby was her way out.

While Joey stayed with Sara's mother, Sara continued going to school. A week after her escape, Larry Lee entered the high school and approached Sara in the hallway. He reached for her hand and twisted her wrist as he pushed it into his pocket. "Say anything, and I'll break it," he whispered in a menacing tone. Then he led her out of the building, put her into his car and drove to the apartment they'd shared. "To this day," Sara would muse years later, "I wish I'd let him break it."

Her extreme fear had motivated her calculated escape. Now, face-to-face with her captor, her fear left her feeling defenseless. Sara just wanted the torture to stop. It would, but not before Larry Lee delivered one final, futile, near-lethal wallop.

Once inside the apartment, he knocked her out with a cast-iron skillet. When she came to, he was astride her, repeatedly punching her in the chest and abdomen. "Get the baby," he told her. If she didn't, Larry Lee said he would go after Joey Ray himself. But Sara knew this was unlikely. Her brother and stepfather lived at her mother's house, and she knew Larry Lee would never confront them. He tried to avoid those confrontations. He found male fists frightening.

"You can forget it," she said through her tears. "My mother won't let you have him. Just kill me, *please*." Then something happened that amazed Sara: Larry Lee shed a tear.

"Go get the baby and come back!" he demanded, and then he released her. She called a cab, stumbled into her mother's house and collapsed. She had broken ribs and a bruised body, but she would never go back, and Larry Lee would not kidnap her again.

Sara was now free to fight the demons in her head, the nightmares of trauma and torture from the eleven months she had spent with her rapist husband, a psycho she'd married to escape from an abusive childhood. Now her abusive mother was her deliverance, all things being relative. It was early 1981, and Sara was just turning sixteen. Five months later, Larry Lee would be living in Clearwater, Florida.

Ruby loved her grandson, Joey. Almost to a fault, thought Sara. She'd watched Ruby's protection of Larry Lee and her inability to hold him accountable for anything. She didn't want that pattern repeated on Joey. But Ruby believed Sara was inadequate to care for her grandson's needs. She began a custody battle that would last four years. Ruby had resources that Sara did not. And Ruby had visitation.

Sara also loved Joey, and she wanted to get this parenting thing right. But in time, she returned to the work she knew best and paid most. Sara was young and sexy. Men paid to see her dance and take off her clothes. It's what Sara thought she was worth, and it was almost all she'd ever known.

It also paid the bills and supported the habit she used to cope with her trauma and the haunting dark side of the way in which she made her living. She plied her demons with alcohol and drugs. She ran through a series of unsavory boyfriends—she wouldn't have known how to attract any other kind—but she exited the relationships herself, she claimed, if the guys so much as acted like they might get rough.

Ruby made reports against her to child welfare officials who, in turn, monitored Sara closely. She kept it relatively together for a while but blew it big time one day when Joey was four. Sara had given birth six months earlier to a daughter, and her boyfriend was another troubled soul. Sara was feeling overwhelmed by everything and angry with Joey for an incident. In the heat of the moment, she resorted to the belt. The marks were still visible that weekend when he visited Ruby. Sara would lose custody shortly afterward.

She wasn't really sure how she felt about this. Sara hated the connections she believed Ruby had as a result of her employer and felt powerless to win against them. On the other hand, this parenting thing was a real challenge. The only parenting Sara had experienced was full of pain and neglect. She didn't know how to value herself or validate her children. The whipping incident with Joey had left her feeling shaken, defeated and ashamed. Maybe Joey was better off with Ruby.

Not long after losing Joey, she decided to give up on the parenting thing altogether. To raise her daughter in her incestuous family seemed like a questionable proposition. And Sara's growing want and need of mood-altering substances to dull her mental pain was another impediment to adequately caring for her offspring. When her daughter was six months old, Sara placed her with an adoptive family and would not meet her again until after she turned eighteen. At Ruby's, she had visitation with Joey. Sara never had any more children.

Sara told Anita that she knew Larry Lee had served time in Florida for rape the year after she left him, but she didn't know the details. She had little contact with the family. She did know that Larry Lee had returned to Knoxville sometime the previous year. He'd brought a girl with him, Maryanne, but she was gone now.

After hearing Sara's story, Anita involuntarily leaned forward in her seat. Tears spilled from her eyes and trickled down her cheeks. She pulled some tissues from her purse to absorb the flow. When Sara saw this, she too began to cry. For a few moments, no one spoke.

Finally, Ted thanked Sara, and she and Anita exchanged phone numbers. After dropping Celia off, Ted drove Anita home. They sat in shock. After an extended silence, he made them each a stiff drink.

During the past year, Anita had coped by following leads and persistently pursuing snippets of publicity about her missing daughter, meeting with only marginal success. Still, this had been her focus, her lifeline, her hope against hope that all these leads meant something, meant that Michelle was still out there somewhere. But as she reflected on Sara's story, the horrible things she'd endured at the hands of Larry Lee, all the remaining hope she held regarding Michelle's fate washed away.

7. <u>WALKING THE DOGS</u>

Late in 1988, almost two years after Michelle's disappearance, Joseph P. DeVuono, Special Agent with the FBI, Knoxville Field Office, had business in the West Towne Mall branch of Charter Federal Savings Bank, where Anita's cousin, Susan, was employed. Susan was much younger than Anita, only five years older than Michelle. She'd been close to the family since their return to Knoxville. In her cordial way, the bubbly, blonde Susan made small talk with Joe—as he insisted he be called—and she asked about his job with the Bureau. He was a warm, approachable kind of guy, Susan observed. He had dark, friendly eyes. She decided to take a chance.

Susan told him about her cousin's daughter, Michelle, a sweet and lovely girl who was fifteen years old when she went missing. Susan explained that the last person known to be with Michelle the night she vanished had a criminal record for kidnapping and rape. The story pulled at the compassionate young agent. On his next visit to the bank, Susan was waiting with a scrapbook of clippings and pictures of Michelle. He found the whole case so disturbing, he said he would find some information on the Knoxville Police Department's investigation. But there was nothing to find.

The more Agent DeVuono learned about the circumstances of Michelle's disappearance, the less he understood why the KPD had continued to treat the case as a runaway. It seemed so obvious to him that there was more to it. And you don't treat a disappearance as a runaway just because a lot of kids run away, he thought. The fact that Larry Lee had a criminal record for sexual assault and was with her the night of her disappearance was enough to open the case as a potential kidnapping.

Agent DeVuono approached his boss with just that request. But the KPD case was two years old; his boss was reluctant. As a rookie agent, DeVuono wasn't sure he could muster enough credibility to convince his superior to let him give it a try. Eventually, he talked him into it.

"You've got thirty days to come up with something," his boss said.

DeVuono's involvement and interest in the case brought comfort and some hope to Michelle's devastated family. They were so hungry for someone's concern, understanding, attention to what they'd gone through in their own investigation. Joe DeVuono was the FBI, and he got it. Finally!

Agent DeVuono touched base with KPD Detective McNair, who proposed the theory that Michelle was still alive. He repeated Larry Lee's story that Michelle ran away because she was pregnant. He suggested that Agent DeVuono check out medical and women's clinics. The new agent doubted this strategy, but respectfully followed McNair's lead.

Agent DeVuono knew that photo identification could be unreliable, but he needed to begin somewhere, and he had only thirty days. He showed Michelle's picture to staff at local clinics and immediately got a hit. One of the staff said they recognized her, and that she'd been there just a few days earlier. This supposed sighting got the special agent's blood pumping due to a specific detail offered up by the witness. Michelle had a mole that wasn't very visible in pictures, but this witness had accurately described it.

Holy mackerel! This is fantastic, thought DeVuono. He was so excited that he almost shared the news with Anita, but then decided to hold back until he'd actually found Michelle. He started looking at patient names and sign-in logs, but couldn't find a match. He followed up on one lead, visited a girl in a trailer, but she wasn't Michelle.

It was the end of a work week. Agent DeVuono's plan was to resume his search on Monday. Over the weekend, however, two weeks after the FBI had officially opened their case on Michelle's disappearance, a new, course-changing development occurred.

It was a wet Sunday afternoon, January 22, 1989. After a low of twenty-one degrees overnight, the afternoon temperatures had climbed into the mid-fifties, melting snow from earlier in the day and turning the precipitation into a light rain. At five o'clock, just as the sun was setting on this Super Bowl Sunday, twenty-year-old Jason James was walking his dogs through the damp woods near the Alloway community in Cumberland County, 70 miles west of Knoxville.

He was climbing a hillside up from a small stream near a clearing for some power lines when he saw a white object protruding from the dense carpet of leaves. He thought it looked like a piece of Styrofoam. The canines ran ahead and sniffed the ground, their probing noses exposing the object more clearly. Jason caught up with them and squatted for a closer look, then bolted quickly back to a standing position. It wasn't Styrofoam—it was a human skull.

He called his dogs and ran back to his house, where he immediately phoned Cumberland County Sheriff Dale Elmore in Crossville, the county seat. Elmore and his men, Investigators Benton Threet and Avery York, met Jason and accompanied him to the discovery site. Beneath emerging stars and a nearly full moon, flashlight beams illuminated more human bones and remains. The officers returned to their station and called the Tennessee Bureau of Investigation.

The next morning, outside the sheriff's office in Crossville, Sheriff Elmore and his investigators met with TBI Agent Jim Moore and Tennessee State Forensic Anthropologist Dr. Bill Bass and his team. For almost twenty years Dr. William Bass had been a professor of forensic anthropology at the University of Tennessee, Knoxville (UT), the flagship campus of the state university system. He was head of the Department of Anthropology there and was also the founder of the UT's Forensic Anthropology Center, dubbed the "Body Farm." Accompanying Dr. Bass that morning were Dr. Alison Galloway, Assistant Professor of Forensic Anthropology at UT, and Murray Marks, UT graduate student.

They formed a car, truck and cruiser caravan, drove as close as they could to the recovery site and walked the remaining distance into the remote woods. Newspaper and television crews had learned of the gruesome discovery and already arrived to cover the investigation.

One of Susan's coworkers called to tell her a body had been found near Crossville. Susan called Agent DeVuono. "I was hoping you hadn't heard that," he said, concerned about Susan's level of stress (she was five months pregnant). He volunteered to call Anita. After getting his call, Anita turned on the local news and watched the investigation unfold on TV.

Dr. Bass and his team assessed the scene. The skeleton was

Dr. Bass, the forensic team and officers walking uphill from the stream to the site of the remains in the woods.

scattered, but mostly complete, lying on and under layers of leaves. Dr. Bass quickly determined that the body had been placed on top of the ground, not buried. Fall had come and gone twice since the unknown victim had been hidden in the woods, and two layers of leaves had collected upon the

Red flags were placed by Dr. Bass and his expert team at the location of each and every forensic find in the excavation of the remains.

The blue jeans of the victim had all but disintegrated by the time her body was discovered. The bones of the pelvic girdle were still contained within the semi-intact hip section of the size 5 Levis. The zipper was closed and no underwear were found with the remains.

remains. Abandoned wasp nests inside the skull and the jeans indicated the body had been fully decomposed by the previous spring. So it had lain there at least a year without flesh.

Although the skeleton was found to be almost complete—ninety-eight percent, it was later determined—it was spread out over a twenty-foot diameter, suggesting that small animals had rooted over and chewed on the body after it had been deposited. A pair of decayed, size five Levis were still zipped, the label readable inside, but the victim had on no underwear. A yellow and white striped sweatshirt lay

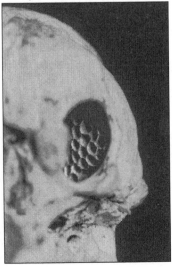

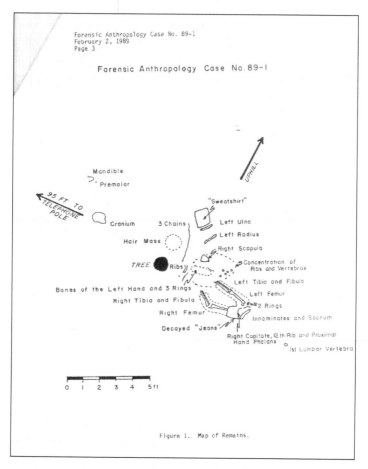

Forensic Anthropology Case No. 89-1
February 2, 1989
Page 3

Forensic Anthropology Case No. 89-1

Figure 1. Map of Remains.

nearby. The team carefully collected and cataloged the remains. They placed red, rectangle-shaped flags at the site of each find.

Based on information obtained from dental maturation, long-bone growth and growth-plate fusion, Dr. Bass determined that the victim was between the ages of fourteen and sixteen. Noting characteristics of the cranium and the pubic bones, he determined that the skeleton belonged to a female and that her body had been in the woods for two years. Characteristics of the head and face determined that she was

Caucasian; other features indicated that she was between 5' and 5'3" tall.

An abundance of jewelry was found among the remains: four silver rings, three chains and four pendants. One pendant held a small gold crab.

Media coverage began immediately. Articles emanated from the *Crossville Chronicle, the Knoxville News-Sentinel, the Knoxville Journal* and the *Chattanooga Times.* "Skeleton of young woman found," they announced; then "Nationwide search launched to learn victim's identity." A southeast regional teletype went out to law enforcement agencies followed by a nationwide alert requesting help in identifying the remains. Messages began coming in from around the country. A spokesperson for the television show *America's Most Wanted* called inquiring as to whether a known fugitive could be linked to the victim, and if so, the producers requested to be notified; they would be interested in filming an episode.

On Tuesday more details of the case were featured on the Knoxville evening news. Susan was watching. There was Dr. Bass holding the skull, examining it and discussing his forensic findings with a reporter. A vial of formaldehyde containing the victim's hair was held up for display. The image of the dark curl suspended in liquid burned a memory in Susan's mind that she would never be able to forget. And then the reporter described the jewelry, including the crab pendant.

Susan called Anita.

Tears spilled down Anita's cheeks, soaking into her sweater as she reached for a box of tissues. Looking back, she had always known how this would end. That first night after Michelle had disappeared, after the chase with Larry Lee Smith when Anita had come home consumed by panic and fear, her mother's intuition had told her the outcome.

"I just knew at that point that Michelle was dead," she later confided. "I *felt* it." But it was a feeling that Anita had pushed down as far as she could for as long as she could. Two whole years. But she knew for certain now. Before Dr. Bass could confirm an identity, she knew that the female who had spent the last two years alone with the sounds of the forest on that remote Cumberland County hillside was Michelle.

When Agent DeVuono and KPD Homicide Investigator Randy York arrived at Anita's house to give her an update, they saw that she already knew. "Her heart was broken," observed York, who had just been assigned to the case. "I felt so bad for her."

Twenty-nine teeth of the victim were retrieved from the site. On Wednesday, January 25th, dental bitewing radiographs were produced from the remains by Dr. R. Douglas Beals, Michelle's dentist and uncle, and Dr. Bass and his staff. These were compared with ones taken of Michelle's teeth three years earlier in her uncle's office.

Both men determined that they had found a match. Jane Doe No. 89-01 was now positively identified as Michelle Denise Anderson, date of birth 6/24/71; last seen 1/10/87; remains found 1/22/89. Agent DeVuono was present in Dr. Bass's lab when he made the announcement. Dr. Bass held up the skull in triumph. Another forensic case solved. Agent DeVuono felt crestfallen.

On Thursday, January 26, 1989, the *Knoxville News Sentinel* ran a story with the headline "Remains identified as Knoxville girl," byline Maria Cornelius, staff writer. It briefly recounted the discovery of the remains the previous Sunday, gave a description of Michelle and the party she attended, and then repeated Larry Lee's account of what had transpired that night (though it did not name Larry Lee; to date, no news coverage had mentioned him by name). This account was attributed to a Tennessee Bureau of Investigation report. The TBI, however, had never investigated Michelle's disappearance. The report was simply the preliminary missing-person report compiled by Detective McNair two years earlier and then passed along to the TBI when her remains were found.

In the same article, Anita was quoted as saying that she had some relief in finally knowing her daughter's fate, to at least know something. Soon after, she was interviewed by Channel 10 News. The reporter asked what she'd like to say to the person who killed her daughter, what she wanted. "I would like to kill him," Anita replied. When she later saw the piece, she was so shocked that she didn't do any more interviews. She hadn't been shocked because she'd said those words; she'd been shocked because deep down, she knew she meant them.

For the next few days, the papers covered any new details. The cause of death had not been determined, but the papers did name who would be investigating the case: Detective Jerry McNair and Homicide Investigator Randy York. "McNair was assigned to the case two years ago when Michelle was reported missing," his supervisor, Lt. Charles Coleman told the press. "The police are starting new. We were just notified, and a two-year-old complaint takes time."

After two years, there had been no real investigation by the KPD into Michelle's disappearance. The investigative file contained statements taken from Anita and Larry Lee Smith, the original copy of the "satanic" letter left on Anita's door, and a simple preliminary report stating that Michele was a missing person. So when Lt. Coleman told the reporter that the investigation into Michelle's disappearance and death was "starting new," he told a partial truth. In fact, it was just *starting*. The press were now ringing Anita's phone and knocking on her door, but she was advised by the police to avoid saying much while the "new investigation" was ongoing.

On February 2, 1989, the final report on Case No. 89-01 was issued by the UT Forensic Anthropology Center. Dr. Bass was unable to determine the exact cause of death, although he could rule out stabbing or a gunshot wound as evidenced by the skeleton. While most of the skeleton had been recovered, a number of small bones were missing, including the hyoid, the fragile curved bone in the throat that is usually broken during strangulation. Without it, the forensic team lost potentially valuable evidence. With the murder unsolved, Dr. Bass was hesitant to release the bones back to the family, who wanted healing and closure and believed that the physical remains of Michelle needed to be given a proper burial. Anita called him with that request.

"You want the *bones?*" he asked, a tone of surprise registering in his voice, or at least that's the way Anita heard it. It was the response of a forensic anthropologist concerned about evidence in an unsolved case. Anita, however, was a grieving, heartbroken mother. Dr. Bass's Forensic Case 89-01 was all she had left of her baby. They weren't speaking the same language.

Dr. Bass convinced Anita to allow him one more day to photograph the bones for any future reference. He then released them to Rose Mortuary. The funeral service was set for Friday, March 3, 1989. Anita's heartbroken father bought a lovely casket and he alone went to the mortuary to view his granddaughter's remains.

In a *Knoxville Journal* article headlined: "Teen's burial Friday; death still a mystery," Dr. Bass expressed concern to reporter Chuck Griffin when asked about the situation:

"If you don't think of everything that's going to come along, you've buried your evidence."

Although Dr. Bass could not determine the exact cause of death, he could express his professional opinion: there were signs of foul play. He noted that no underclothing, shoes or socks were found on or with the victim. It appeared that Michelle had been dressed hurriedly and deposited in the woods minus those items. "She wasn't walking in Cumberland County barefoot," Bass was quoted as saying. He theorized that Michelle had been killed at another location and driven there. As to the timing: "She was killed the day she disappeared or the day after."

Michelle's remains revealed the secret of how long she had lain in those woods, but not how she had died. As her soft tissues decomposed, so did any damning evidence left by her killer. "Death still a mystery," proclaimed another newspaper headline. The Tennessee Bureau of Investigation turned over Michelle's clothing remnants and related "debris" to officials at the Knoxville Police Department, who forwarded the evidence to the FBI lab in Quantico, Virginia, for analysis.

In a letter dated April 7, 1989, Knoxville's Chief of Police, Phil E. Keith, recorded the following evidence as being forwarded to the FBI lab:

A. Pubic Hair
B. Head Hair
C. Cloth fragment and debris from bones
D. Debris from clothing (1)
E. Debris from clothing (2)
F. Blue jeans from victim
G. Hooded pullover sweat shirt from victim

Chief Keith requested that the following be determined from this physical evidence: the sex, age and race of the victim from the hair samples, whether any semen was detected in the blue jeans hip and crotch remnant and whether any evidence of knife or gunshot wounds could be detected in the sweatshirt and bluejean remnants.

Deoxyribonucleic acid (DNA) testing was still years away from the level and sophistication that would eventually become routine. In 1989, the blue jeans fragment was never tested for DNA, an issue that would become central to efforts to solve the case in the future.

Just after sending the evidence for analysis, KPD Chief Keith also sent the "satanic" letter to see if anything could be learned from the handwriting or the two drawings possibly made with blood.

On June 6, 1989, sixty days after the evidence collected from the recovery site had been sent for analysis, KPD Chief Keith received the FBI lab report. Test results on the possible blood samples found on the "satanic" letter were determined to be inconclusive. However, a written recommendation regarding the *storage* of this "blood sample" was made by the FBI lab and returned with the lab results. It requested that the "remaining blood stain be cut out, placed in an envelope and returned to the Knoxville Police Department with instructions to *freeze* for future comparison purposes [DNA]."

The report also noted that six latent fingerprints were found on this letter and its accompanying envelope. Photographs of the prints were available through the lab "for any future comparisons you may request." The report also included an analysis of the handwriting on the note and suggestions for comparing any handwriting samples to it in the future.

The semi-intact blue jeans hip section and the deteriorated sweatshirt tested negative for gunpowder residue. No blood was found on any of the items. The blue jeans were determined to be "unsuitable for examination" in the effort to test for the presence of semen.

All submitted specimens were noted as having been returned to the KPD by registered mail for future reference: the evidence scrapings, debris and hair samples, now stored in three pillboxes, two ziplock bags and one slide.

Yet when the *future* arrived, no one at the KPD (or the TBI) knew what had become of this expertly collected, analyzed and catalogued evidence.

It could not be found.

8. <u>ATLANTA BOOGIE</u>

Following the official announcement that the remains of a teenage girl found on a wooded Cumberland County hillside were those of Michelle Anderson, Anita was again instructed to report downtown to the Knoxville Police headquarters. There she briefly encountered Detective McNair. He greeted her in passing but made little eye contact. McNair, it turned out, would no longer be assigned to the case. Instead, Anita met with Homicide Investigator Randy York.

Federal jurisdiction in kidnapping cases requires that the victim be transported across state lines. The remains of Anita's hazel-eyed daughter were found within the state of Tennessee, but in a different county (a rural county, at that) from where she went missing, so the Tennessee Bureau of Investigation had jurisdiction. The FBI closed its kidnapping case and opened a Domestic Police Assistance case in its place. Crossville-based TBI Agent Jim Moore requested a man on the ground in Knoxville to carry out the local interviews and investigation, although the case remained officially the TBI's. York was selected to carry out the local investigation.

For nearly two decades the handsome, dark-haired investigator had been part of the KPD rotating six-man homicide team. He looked long and hard at the KPD record on the disappearance of Michelle Anderson, which he'd just inherited. Then he looked again. There was no mention that Michelle's disappearance was suspicious, or that the last person seen with the missing fifteen-year-old was a convicted kidnapper and rapist of a similarly-aged girl in Florida.

What York saw most clearly was what was missing, what had not been done. No investigative interviews, no evidence, nothing. He cringed. Jerry McNair was a nice guy and a close friend. There were all those false sightings, York tried to reason to himself. Maybe they threw McNair off from investigating further, although not a one of them had ever been substantiated.

"Within days of her disappearance, somebody should have been looking at this case hot and heavy, interviewing everyone at that party with Michelle," York would later note, hesitant to speak critically of his former friend and colleague, or those that supervised McNair's work. "Certainly, after a few days... I hate to say it. I thought a lot of Jerry, but he just wasn't a barn-burner." And no one over McNair at the KPD, apparently, seemed to have noticed a problem with his handling of the case.

So the investigation into Michelle's disappearance actually *began* with the finding of her remains. York, who carried a tape recorder, finally amassed a long-overdue investigative file. "I talked to kids for days," he recalled. "I had a book."

By interviewing Anita, Chas and the other adolescents, York tried to reconstruct what had occurred the night Michelle disappeared. He couldn't rule out Chas as a suspect because of Larry Lee's claim that he'd dropped Michelle off near Chas's house in the late hours of the night she disappeared. Chas denied that Michelle had ever come to his grandparents' house that night. "I shared a bedroom with my grandfather," he claimed. "If someone had come to the door to speak with me, my grandfather would have known."

York's money was still on Larry Lee. He learned of Larry Lee's criminal history, interviewed his estranged wife, Sara, and heard about the horrific abuse she claimed to have experienced at the hands of the suspect. York began tailing Larry Lee closely. "He's got a worm in his head," York later noted. "He's a *bad* guy."

York received quiet assistance from FBI Special Agents Joe DeVuono and Grey Steed. DeVuono focused primarily on investigating the kidnapping and murder, while Steed provided advice about investigative techniques and supervised the collecting of information to be used by the Behavioral Science Unit (BSU) at the FBI Academy in Quantico, Virginia. They were working on a psychological profile of the suspect.

On Tuesday, February 7, 1989, a week and two days after Michelle's remains were discovered, DeVuono and an FBI colleague showed up at the Wendy's restaurant on Chapman Highway in South Knoxville where Larry Lee was then employed. They showed identification, introduced themselves and asked to speak with him privately. They informed him that they were there investigating the disappearance and murder of Michelle Anderson.

Larry Lee said he'd already talked to the police, told them everything he knew. Agent DeVuono informed Larry Lee that the FBI was offering him the opportunity to take a polygraph examination in order to remove himself as a suspect in the case. Larry Lee said he wanted to call his lawyer, and walked to the back of the restaurant. After remaining gone for a few minutes, he returned and announced that his attorney was in court.

Agent DeVuono then advised Larry Lee that he'd already spoken to the attorney in question, who'd claimed that he did not represent Larry Lee at this time. Was there another attorney he wished to call?

Larry Lee's eyes shifted nervously as he tried to think of another way out. He knew his rights, he told them. Furthermore, he didn't believe in the polygraph. Yet Larry Lee reluctantly agreed to accompany the agents to the local FBI field office in a bureau vehicle. "Do they know if someone stabbed or shot her?" Larry Lee asked during the ride.

Dealing directly with violent criminals wasn't normally a part of Agent DeVuono's investigative domain. Dealing with a character like Larry Lee was a new and unpleasant experience for the young agent, whose senses were on alert. "I felt as if I were in the presence of pure evil," he later said. "A psychopath with no remorse."

In the reception room of the FBI field office in downtown Knoxville, Larry Lee was nervous. While sitting with another agent, he made conversation and tried to deflect focus away from his being a suspect to him being a victim. He told the accompanying agent that two weeks before Michelle's remains were found, his yard had been littered with garbage and threatening notes—although he couldn't recall what messages they'd contained.

"Didn't your truck get trashed shortly after the girl went missing?" the agent asked. Larry Lee nodded, then told him that the day after Michelle disappeared a Knoxville police detective [McNair] had searched his Western Heights apartment and found nothing. He asked to make another phone call, to a different lawyer. Permission was given. Larry Lee called his mother instead. After a few minutes of mumbling into the phone, he twisted his head away from the receiver and toward the agent. "Am I under arrest?" he asked.

"No. As we said before, you're not under arrest."

Larry Lee repeated this information into the phone, after which he informed the agent that he was no longer willing to take a polygraph examination or speak with the FBI agents. He was taking his mother's advice; he was leaving.

Agent DeVuono and his colleague were obliged to accommodate Larry Lee by offering to drive him back to his place of employment. "No. Take me to my new lawyer's office," Larry Lee said as he directed them to the corner of Gay Street and Summit Hill Drive. Ruby had come through for her deviant son one more time. As they reached the intersection, Larry Lee turned to the agents. "You would think by now you would have caught the guy who did it... or the girl," he said, grinning. Then he climbed out of the car and walked inside the building.

Like York, Agent DeVuono had little doubt in his mind about the guilt of Larry Lee, but he also hadn't ruled out Chas as an accomplice. Tragedy had followed Chas since Michelle's disappearance. Less than a year after she'd gone missing, he had a falling out with his brother, Bobby, who accused Chas of being a drunk like their father. Bobby, who was gay, was seeing a young man named Melvin. One night he asked Chas to party with them, but Chas refused. He never saw his brother again. Bobby and Melvin got into an argument over taking a road trip to Mississippi—Melvin wanted to go and Bobby didn't—so Melvin killed him, dumped his body, and drove down to Mississippi in Bobby's truck. In an eerie coincidence, Bobby's body was found alongside a road near Crossville, not far from where Michelle's remains were found. It was a double whammy that year for Chas. First Michelle, then Bobby. And he wasn't there either time to help.

* * *

In early April 1989, more than a couple months after Michelle's remains had been discovered, Chas answered a knock at the door of his grandparents' house. When he stepped out onto the wide, gray planks of the front porch, he met Joe DeVuono and a colleague. They identified themselves as special agents of the FBI investigating Michelle Anderson's disappearance and death.

"We'd like to talk to you," DeVuono told him.

"No problem," Chas said, but then he explained that he'd promised his pregnant fiancé, Venus, that he would accompany her to the doctor. Agent DeVuono said this wasn't a problem and asked Chas to stop by their field office. He then told Chas the address, phone number and directions. What he didn't tell Chas was that he was being watched. A short time after the agents left, a dark hatchback picked Chas up. No car fitting that description was seen at the alleged doctor's office at the appointed hour, and Chas did not show for his interview at the FBI field office that afternoon.

A few days later the agents stopped by Chas's house again, this time coaxing him into their car and driving him to their office to administer the polygraph exam. Chas ran through the whole story: who he was, who he was with, what he and Michelle did that night, what he did after she didn't come home. At one point during the questioning, the polygraph showed evidence of deception and the examiner told Chas he was either lying or hiding something. Chas, who already seemed near breaking, began sobbing intensely. Then, almost as quickly as he had broken down, he pulled himself back together.

To the agents, it was like he had thrown a switch, turned off the feed to his emotions and his tears, snap, just like that. "That's all I know," Chas told them, also closing down any further communication. By then he'd had two years to compartmentalize and block out his involvement, reasoned DeVuono, whose instincts told him that Chas had more knowledge than he was admitting. He may not have been directly involved in Michelle's death, but he knew something.

York stepped up his surveillance of Larry Lee. He observed that Larry Lee had a pattern: after leaving a local club or bar, he'd prowl around in his car at night. "Everywhere he went, I—or someone from KPD—was there, and I made sure he knew I was there," York recalled. "I'd find out what people he'd had contact with, and I'd go interview them. His lawyer filed on me, claiming harassment."

In the meantime, the FBI agents became close with Sara Smith. She was terrified of her estranged husband, but really wanted to be of assistance in the case. She had no doubt that Larry Lee was capable of harming Michelle and believed that he had. She gave the agents information that helped the FBI Lab in Quantico establish a profile of the suspect. She also agreed to call Larry Lee on the phone and record their conversation. After chatting with him a little, she casually mentioned that she'd heard about the murdered girl, Michelle, and that he was a suspect. The agents hoped he'd offer up some incriminating details, but Larry Lee didn't reveal anything they could use. The call may have only made him more suspicious.

KPD officers were tailing Larry Lee one night when they observed him coming to the aid of a girl whose car had run into flooding up in the Fountain City neighborhood in North Knoxville. It appeared to them that Larry Lee was trying to get this girl into his car. They couldn't let that happen, so they rolled in on him, intervened in the situation, asked if they could be of assistance. Larry Lee backed off, but he knew he'd been followed.

It was a short time later that Larry Lee, in the words of Investigator Randy York, *boogied*. He fled Tennessee and headed southeast to Atlanta, Georgia. Everyone involved in the investigation felt some satisfaction that they had contributed to his flight, although there had been no arrest in the case.

But a family member of Larry Lee claimed that another event had also motivated his decision to boogie: the brake line on his truck had been cut. He had reportedly discovered this as he drove down Fern Avenue and was unable to stop before crashing into a house at the bottom of the hill. Larry Lee left town just after that incident and headed for the home of his aunt, Ruby's sister, just outside Atlanta.

Part Three
Georgia Justice

9. <u>FRIDAY THE THIRTEENTH</u>

For eighteen-year-old Amanda Sanders, Friday, October 13, 1989, had begun as a near-perfect day in her home town of Stone Mountain, Georgia. The blonde-haired, blue-eyed beauty had spent the morning with her best friend, Leslie, at Stone Mountain Park, where they'd posed for a photographer Amanda had met at the doctor's office where she worked as a receptionist. The weather had been wonderfully cooperative with a high of nearly eighty degrees. The girls struck poses by a stream and in front of Stone Mountain, a dome of solid quartz and granite featuring a bas-relief sculpture of Confederate heroes Stonewall Jackson, Robert E. Lee and Jefferson Davis sitting astride their horses. The carving is the size of three football fields, the largest of its kind in the world. At its base, the girls did cartwheels and cheerleading jumps while hamming it up for the camera. "These are going to be great!" Amanda had exclaimed.

Now it was late afternoon and Amanda stood in the parking lot of the Stonemont Shopping Plaza, staring under the open hood of her sporty looking 1986 gold Mercury Topaz. She'd bought the car with her own money after graduating high school the previous June. She was still making payments on it. And it wouldn't start.

To make matters worse, she was right outside Stone Mountain Billiards, an alcohol-free, teenage pool hall where her boyfriend worked, and they'd just had a fight. After having such a blast with Leslie at the park, she'd been looking forward to spending the evening with Steve. When she found out he'd already made other plans—plans that involved drinking at a frat party with his older brother—she'd sulked out to her car without saying goodbye. She didn't want to go back in and ask him for help.

But she couldn't just stand there staring at her engine, either. She'd only lifted the hood because that seemed like what you were supposed to do. She didn't know what she was looking for. Finally, she sucked up her pride and went back inside the pool hall. Steve said he couldn't leave the premises while customers were inside and he was the only one working. Amanda called a girlfriend to come get her, but the girlfriend wasn't home.

Feeling totally dejected, Amanda wandered back outside to her car. As she stared at the lifeless engine, she suddenly became overwhelmed and began to cry. She'd recently moved out of her parents' home and was sharing an apartment with a friend. She worried that now she might be facing costly car repairs, repairs she couldn't afford. And she didn't want to ask her parents for money. As the only daughter in a family with four sons, she knew they'd give it to her. Her parents adored her. The pictures she'd taken that morning were going to be a Christmas gift to them to add to the large photo collection of her that they displayed at the top of the stairs—dubbed the "shrine of Amanda" by her teasing and protective brothers. But she was just learning to be on her own, and she didn't want to ask for their help.

Just then, a bushy-haired guy with a day's growth of beard exited Eddie's Trick Shop, a novelty store of costumes and accessories located next door to the pool hall. He'd been shopping for a Halloween mask for his son back in Knoxville. He paused and stared at the attractive, young woman crying alone in the parking lot. He tucked his red shirt into the brown pants of his Krystal restaurant uniform and stood there for a few moments surveying the scene. Then he strode in Amanda's direction.

"Can I help?" Larry Lee asked as he approached Amanda from behind.

"Oh!" she exclaimed, startled, wiping her eyes, not aware that anyone was near. She turned to look at the young man who was not much taller than her. "My car won't start. I think maybe it's my clutch. My boyfriend works inside, but he can't come out because he's the only one on duty."

"Maybe you need a new boyfriend," Larry Lee joked. His thick fingers stroked his unkempt mustache. "I used to work at a parts store. Let me take a look."

Amanda felt guarded against this stranger, but she was also worried about her car and grateful for his assistance. At his request, she handed him her keys. Larry Lee squeezed behind the steering wheel and made several fruitless attempts to turn over the engine. Suddenly, it roared to life. Amanda cast her eyes toward the sky and let out a sigh of relief; her seeming good Samaritan broke into a wide, ripple-lipped grin.

"Let's take it around the block, make sure it's running okay," Larry Lee suggested. He leaned over and unlocked the passenger door for Amanda. "Make sure it's not the clutch."

Inside the pool hall Steve had called to a few of the guys to walk outside and take a look at Amanda's car, but just as they exited the building, they observed the man in the red and brown uniform approaching the Topaz. At a distance, they took him to be some kind of auto mechanic. A few moments later, when they heard the car engine roar to life and then saw the man open the door for Amanda to climb in, they assumed he'd taken care of the problem. "Some guy got it started," one of the boys informed Steve as the group shuffled back inside.

Amanda was torn by Larry Lee's suggestion, but unsure how to resist. *He was being helpful, wasn't he? This is okay, right?* Besides, he was in the driver's seat, the car was running, and he was ready to move out. She couldn't let him take it without her. It was her car; she *had* to be in it. And in the few seconds it took for those thoughts to flash like Christmas lights in her bewildered mind, she found herself in the car with Larry Lee, pulling onto busy Memorial Drive.

"So, what were you crying about?" Larry Lee asked, glancing between the road and winsome Amanda.

"Nothing. My boyfriend and I had an argument. He wants to go to a frat party with his brother, but they'll have alcohol there, and I don't like him to drink. Nothing really."

"Do these seats recline?"

Amanda paused, wondering why this guy was asking such a thing. "Partially," she finally answered. "They don't go all the way down. The lever is by the side of the seat." Amanda turned her head to look out her window. Larry Lee was making her uneasy.

It was rush hour on a Friday afternoon. "There's too much traffic here," Larry Lee complained. He said he wasn't familiar with the roads in this town. He needed a low traffic area in a business zone to "test" the car.

"The only road I know that circles back to the billiards is Village Square Drive," Amanda said, directing him to a less crowded thoroughfare that was also dotted with shopping centers and apartment complexes.

Larry Lee navigated the Topaz behind strip malls and around dumpsters. Suddenly he pulled the car to a stop behind a row of businesses and cut the engine. Amanda nervously and instinctively opened her car door. "Sounds like it's maladjusted," Larry Lee announced loudly, quickly diagnosing the car's problem just as some teenagers came walking by. He fired up the engine and shifted the car into gear. Amanda barely had time to shut her door before Larry Lee pulled away.

"Can you take me back now? Amanda asked. "Please."

"Yeah," Larry Lee said. "Sure."

He crossed the street into yet another shopping area. In back of a Kroger grocery store, he swung the Topaz behind a dumpster sitting perpendicular to the building and cut the engine. Larry Lee turned toward Amanda, stared at her as he slid his right arm up the back of the passenger seat. Then he struck, whipping his arm over the seat and wrapping it firmly and tightly around Amanda's neck. With his left hand, he unzipped the pants of his Krystal restaurant uniform.

"You're hurting me!" Amanda cried out as she gasped for breath. Her hands instinctively wrapped around her captor's wrist and arm and she dug her nails into his skin.

"Shut *up* or I *will* hurt you!" he barked back. "Unzip your pants!"

"No!" she shrieked.

Larry Lee tightened his grip on her throat and pressed the heel of his left hand against her forehead. Amanda couldn't speak. She couldn't breathe. Pure terror consumed her as tears spilled down her cheeks. "See how easy it is?" her captor hissed, a crazed look in his eyes. "I can break your neck in three seconds, and I *will* if you don't do what I say." His chokehold loosened just enough that Amanda could suck in a few quick breaths. She reluctantly tugged down the zipper of the shorts she'd worn during the photo shoot. As Larry Lee's hand tightened around her neck again, he forced her head down toward his lap.

Yet Amanda wasn't going down without a fight. In her heightened state she'd already surmised that he didn't have a weapon, aside from his hands and brute strength. *And so what if he did?* If her choices were submit or die, die might be winning out. She believed this man was going to kill her, so she decided she had no choice but to fight. And maybe, if she could find a way to escape, she could get someone's attention. It was still daylight in downtown Stone Mountain.

As Larry Lee pushed her head closer to his exposed genitalia, Amanda tried to wedge her hands in front of her face. She managed another quick breath and let out a soul-piercing scream. Larry Lee's grip slipped momentarily and she began kicking, flailing, fighting this pudgy bastard who'd approached her as a wolf in sheep's clothing.

"Shut up!" Larry Lee barked, recovering his grip, tightening, trying to maintain control of what was, for him, a rapidly deteriorating situation, a daylight abduction going terribly wrong.

Unable to breathe, Amanda stilled her kicking, but kept her feet pressed against the window. "Put your feet down," he ordered, "before someone sees you!" She slid her feet down by the arm rest, pushing the toes of her shoes just under the door handle. She stayed still and quiet.

Larry Lee started the car again but kept Amanda's head in a lock-grip over his lap. He drove out of the shopping area and onto a semi-residential side street. He didn't seem to know where he was or where he was going. He just steered the car with his left hand while the right one leapt back and forth between the gear shift and Amanda's bruised neck. He even coerced her into helping him shift gears from her awkward angle by maintaining his squeeze on her throat.

Barely able to breathe, Amanda remained still. As they drove, Larry Lee loosened his hold. When Amanda felt his grip had loosened enough for her to break free, she pushed her toes against the door handle and kicked the door open with her feet. Her legs dangled down onto the street, dragging her favorite shoes over the blacktop before they were ripped free.

"Shut that door!" Larry Lee snapped and swerved the car toward a light pole, threatening to slam the door into it if she didn't do as he said. When Amanda refused to comply, he reached across her and pulled the door shut himself. Then Larry Lee repositioned his right hand, pressing in even harder against his victim's throat.

No longer able to breathe, Amanda lost consciousness. Her body went suddenly limp.

After only a few seconds, Amanda slowly regained her cognitive powers, but remained completely still. She could hear Larry Lee mumbling to himself, "I just wanted five minutes… I didn't want to hurt her… I just wanted five minutes… I didn't want to hurt her."

He turned onto busy Rockbridge Street and began slowing for a red light when suddenly and unexpectedly Amanda bolted up, arms flailing, legs kicking, voice screaming in his face. Her sudden retaliation didn't free her from the car, but it caught the attention of a driver in front of them, a man in a vintage Dodge truck.

At first glance in his rearview mirror, Michael Decker, associate professor at the Atlanta College of Art, thought he saw two young people in a "sports car" sitting very close, so close that it appeared the girl might be sitting on the guy's lap. He turned his attention back to his four-year-old daughter, who sat in the passenger seat beside him. But something made him glance in the mirror again. And that second look revealed a different and altogether unnerving scene: the girl was screaming and slapping her hand against the front windshield.

Decker realized she was trying to get someone's attention.

He twisted around for a clearer look out his rear window and saw that the driver had a chokehold on the girl's neck. She was screaming for help. "He's going to kill me!" Decker thought he heard her yell.

The traffic light turned green. The cars in line in front of the professor began to move forward. He glanced at his daughter, then back at the mirror, and shifted his truck into park. He threw open his door and stepped outside to confront the other driver.

The other driver just stared back at him, wide-eyed, panicked. He looked to see if he could swing around the approaching Decker, but that lane was blocked by heavy oncoming traffic. So he veered the gold Topaz around the professor's truck on the passenger side, careened over the curb and across a residential lawn before fleeing down another street.

Michael Decker knew something seriously amiss was afoot. He had to act. He jumped back into his truck, secured his daughter's seat belt, and gave chase.

Larry Lee's eyes darted back and forth between the curvy road he was speeding along and the rearview mirror where he could see Decker's truck racing to keep up. He released his grip on Amanda.

"Do you know who's following us?" Larry Lee said, clearly panicked. Amanda rolled down the window, taking advantage of her regained freedom to suck the cooling air into her wounded windpipe. "I don't know *who* that is," she gasped. "Take me back *now,* or I'm going to jump out of the car!"

"I *am* taking you back," Larry Lee yelled. "But I can't if we're being followed!"

As they reached the rear entrance to Stone Mont Plaza, Decker saw that the area was devoid of other vehicles and pulled back. With his daughter beside him, he couldn't risk a direct confrontation here. He swung around to the front of the plaza and stopped in front of the first business he came to: Stone Mountain Billiards. He had no way of knowing that the kidnapping and assault he'd just witnessed had begun at this very spot. He quickly unbelted his daughter, lifted her off the seat and raced inside.

"Someone needs to call the police!" he yelled as he burst through the door. He told the manager—Steve, Amanda's boyfriend—about the assault he had just witnessed. He described the young blonde-haired girl in a gold Topaz and said they were, at that very moment, approaching the plaza from the other side.

"That's my girlfriend's car!" Steve yelled. He rushed into the office to make the call. From a window he saw Amanda's car being maneuvered toward the side entrance of the parking lot.

"The truck's gone," Amanda said. Larry Lee slowed down but passed through a stop sign and into Stonemont Plaza. Amanda reached over and pressed a button on the car's steering column, bringing the car to a lurching halt. While Larry Lee was momentarily dazed, she grabbed the keys, flung her self out of the vehicle, and raced toward the pool hall. At the same time, Larry Lee threw open the driver's door and bolted for his black AMC Pacer.

Just as Amanda reached the pool hall entrance, several teenagers came bursting out, armed with pool sticks. Larry Lee could see the worked-up faces racing toward him across the parking lot. He threw up his hands to cover his face and yelled into the air, "I didn't touch her! I didn't touch her! I don't know what she's talking about." Then he jumped into his car, fired it up and threw it into reverse.

He was backing up as the guys with pool sticks began beating on the slanted rear of the hatchback. Larry Lee slammed the car into gear and gunned out of Stone Mont Plaza. Steve watched from the office window and jotted down the Pacer's tag number on a box of Marlboro Lights just as the telephone rang. It was the police calling back; they were on their way.

As Larry Lee fled the scene, the guys with the pool sticks hurried back into the billiard hall to check on Amanda. Operating on pure adrenalin, she'd made it into the game room before collapsing on the floor. She was hysterical, crying, in shock. Steve, Decker, and the pool hall's teen patrons couldn't believe her war-torn condition: shoes missing, pants unzipped, shirt askew, hair tussled, face red and makeup smeared. Her swollen neck bore blood-red stripes from the near-fatal choking. Forty-five minutes had passed since Amanda's kidnapper had coaxed her into taking her car for that "test drive."

Steve had his arms around her. "Oh, baby," he said, stunned. Not sure what else to say or do, he got her a Coke.

Amanda took down several large gulps and then yelled, "He tried to rape me!" Then she threw up on the floor.

At five-forty-five p.m. the DeKalb County Police arrived at Stone Mountain Billiards. Officer Philip Cresti took the initial report, and the police forensic squad went to work.

They photographed Amanda, the red marks and bruising around her neck, and took tissue samples from beneath her nails. Then they lifted the assailant's prints from her car.

Two of the teens volunteered to look for Amanda's missing shoes and found one in the middle of the street near the intersection of Hambrick and Village Square Road. They turned the badly scraped and torn shoe over to Amanda. The police then collected it along with the cigarette box that had the Pacer's tag number written on it.

Detective Gwen Horne with the DeKalb Police Youth and Sex Crimes Division arrived to interview Amanda, her boyfriend, Decker, and two teenage witnesses. Based on their description of the suspect and the events, Case Detective Horne issued a BOLO—an official *Be On the Look-Out*—to metro area police precincts and a teletype with the same information to sheriffs' departments and other law enforcement agencies.

The alert described a white male between the ages of twenty-eight and thirty-five, approximate height five feet eight inches, weighing 175 to 195 pounds with collar-length, reddish-brown, bushy hair and a mustache. He was noted to be a possible suspect in a reported kidnapping and sexual assault. The Krystal uniform the suspect had been wearing was also in the report, as well as a description of the dark-colored, two-door '76 AMC Pacer with the tag number SKM 213.

Later on the evening of Friday the 13th, Amanda was called down to the DeKalb Police Station to view a photo lineup. Detective Horne had located a picture of the owner of the AMC Pacer. That image was mixed in with five other similar ones.

"Take your time. Tell me if you recognize any of these men," the detective instructed her.

Amanda studied the photos for only a few minutes. None

of them were of Larry Lee. "No, I don't recognize any of these," she told the detective in a mildly disappointed tone. "He isn't here."

Early on the morning of Saturday, October 14th, 1989, before daylight, Deputy Sheriff Michael Stapp was on patrol for the Rockdale County Sheriff's Department in Conyers, Georgia. Semi-rural Rockdale County, part of the greater metropolitan area of Atlanta, shares a border with the counties of Fulton to the west, Gwinnett to the north, and DeKalb to the east. Stapp's department had received an alert from the DeKalb County Police to be on the lookout for a black '76 Pacer with Georgia tags driven by a white male fitting Larry Lee's description.

Officer Stapp spotted such a car exiting the Majik Market on West Avenue in Conyers just before five o'clock in the morning. The black Pacer turned in the direction opposite that of the passing patrolman, but Officer Stapp made a U-turn and pulled up behind the car while it was stopped at a traffic light.

Deputy Stapp checked the BOLO; the tag number identified was a match to the black Pacer in front of him. He switched on his patrol lights. A panicked Larry Lee sped through the red light and up onto Interstate-20.

Officer Stapp radioed for backup and followed the black Pacer onto the interstate, siren wailing, his cruiser lights pulsating electric red and blue against the predawn sky. At this point, Larry Lee must have known he couldn't escape. He turned off at the next exit, and pulled into a Kroger parking lot. Two flashing cruisers pinned him in, but he didn't resist. When the officers got him back to the Rockdale County jail, a DeKalb County officer was dispatched to pick up their man.

Amanda and some of the other witnesses were asked to

return to the DeKalb County Police headquarters, to the Criminal Investigation Division, where they were shown a new photo lineup. This set of images included Larry Lee's recently taken mug shot.

One by one the witnesses, including Amanda, fingered the photo of Larry Lee. Some identified him as the messy-haired man who had driven off with Amanda. Others had seen him when he arrived back at Stone Mountain Billiards approximately forty-five minutes later, racing toward the Pacer as Amanda stumbled toward the pool hall disheveled and distressed. Either way, they all confirmed it: he was the guy.

Larry Lee was brought from his holding cell in the DeKalb County jail to the interview room for questioning. On duty to conduct the interview was Detective L. M. Moore of the DeKalb County Youth and Sex Crimes Division.

Pulling out a chair opposite Larry Lee at the rubber-topped table, the plain-clothed detective extended her hand, locked his gaze briefly and introduced herself: "Hello, Mr. Smith. I'm Detective Moore."

10. <u>MATTERS OF THE COURT</u>

On January 9, 1990, nearly a year after Larry Lee's flight to Georgia, FBI Special Agents Joe DeVuono and Grey Steed met at the Knoxville Police Department with KPD Investigator Randy York and his superior, Lieutenant Charles Coleman. Since Larry Lee's departure, no real progress on Michelle's case had been made. The purpose of the meeting was to review an investigative strategy proposed by the FBI's Behavioral Science Unit in Quantico, which had completed a psychological profile of the suspect. Lt. Coleman was hesitant to commit the department to the rigorousness of the proposed plan, however, and the group explored a compromise: the FBI would provide assistance in the parts of the plan that the KPD felt were beyond their means.

Following that meeting, the supervising FBI Special Agent in Charge, William E. Baugh, Jr., issued an internal memo reviewing and outlining the proposed and revised investigative strategies. He expressed concern that "unless the FBI continues to play a role in this investigation, a rare opportunity to resolve this homicide will pass."

York's first move was to attract some attention in the

local press. The case had received little coverage since the first weeks after Michelle's body had been discovered. And now, a year later, the story was all but forgotten. York wanted to keep it fresh on people's minds, so he contacted *Knoxville News Sentinel* reporter Jim Balloch and asked him to write a new piece. He wanted it be a "one-year-later" type story to remind the public that the case was unsolved and the killer still out there. It couldn't name Larry Lee directly—his lawyer was already threatening York and the KPD with harassment—but it could certainly hint at his involvement.

Balloch turned the story into a frontpage feature. It was the longest newspaper piece written to date about the disappearance and death of Michelle. It included a large, somber image of Anita standing in front of a mantle covered with framed photos of her murdered daughter.

Even though Balloch did not name Larry Lee Smith, the article was the first mention in print that his version of events was suspect: "It is clear the investigators do not believe everything they were told by some of the people who were last seen with Michelle," Balloch wrote. He then quoted York: "We are now looking into the possibility that she was never let out of that truck on Cherry Street, which is what we were originally told."

York hoped that either Larry Lee or Chas would see the article, panic, and start pointing a finger at the other. At the very least, they'd sweat knowing the investigation was still moving forward. Unfortunately, Larry Lee wouldn't see the article. At least not immediately. When it ran in Knoxville, he was incarcerated in a Georgia jail, awaiting trial for the kidnapping and assault of Amanda Sanders.

Three weeks prior to the investigative team's meeting at the KPD, four nail-filled pipe bombs had been mailed through the USPS to several locations across the Southeast. One killed a judge in Birmingham, another an attorney in Savannah, Georgia. The other two packages were intercepted—one at the federal courthouse in Atlanta and the other in the Jacksonville office of the NAACP—and disarmed. The FBI labeled the case VANPAC. Joe DeVuono was among the agents sent to Atlanta to assist in the investigation. He arrived the last week of January 1990.

Agent DeVuono knew that Larry Lee had gone to the Atlanta area. During his downtime, he set out to track Larry Lee's activities in the region. He followed his trail of employment and spoke with former supervisors and coworkers. At a landscaping job Larry Lee held from late March through early August of 1989, he'd claimed an injury to his back—although the manager suspected the condition was exaggerated—and filed for workers' compensation. He hadn't shown up for months while he was being treated by a chiropractor. After that, he'd returned to the fast-food industry, to which he was more accustomed. He obtained two jobs, one at a Krystal and the other at a Wendy's.

According to his former coworkers, Larry Lee had been transient for a period of time, sleeping out of his vehicle, first the small truck in which he'd traveled from Knoxville, then an older model AMC Pacer that he'd borrowed from a friend. It had originally been yellow before someone spray painted it black. After that, he began sharing an apartment in Lawrenceville with a coworker, Monica Houston and her husband, Joseph—the owners of the Pacer—and their two daughters, ages nine and twelve. Apparently, there had been some concerns about Larry Lee being left alone with the girls. Some accusations were made, but none of the coworkers knew anything specific.

It was from one of these former coworkers that Agent

DeVuono learned of another arrest. On May 20, 1989, a young school girl named Caroline Leigh Bronti, selling fundraising items door-to-door with her friend, had knocked at the door of the shared Lawrenceville apartment. Larry Lee answered.

"Come in," Larry Lee coaxed the young girl.

"No, thank you," Caroline anxiously replied. Larry Lee continued to try and lure the girl into the apartment, but when his efforts failed, he grabbed her by the arm and pulled her inside. Caroline's friend raced away and quickly summoned help. Larry Lee was arrested and charged with misdemeanor assault. He eventually struck a deal and pleaded guilty to the lessor misdemeanor charge of simple battery. He served sixty days in jail and received an additional ten months of probation.

Larry Lee was constantly propositioning female customers, his former coworkers told DeVuono; the man was vulgar around women. And he had a regular habit of telling lies. A coworker laughed about one lie in particular: Larry Lee claimed he had a "memory impairment" that allowed him to recall only six months into the past.

His supervisor at Krystal said that Larry Lee had abruptly stopped working at the restaurant sometime in October. He had not been seen nor heard from since.

No one Agent DeVuono interviewed knew that Larry Lee Smith was, as they spoke, sitting in a jail cell in adjoining DeKalb County. Agent DeVuono needed to return to Knoxville and would not learn of that development for several months.

It was Tuesday morning, April 3, 1990, and Agents DeVuono and Steed and Investigator York attended a meeting at Knoxville's City-County building with Knox County

Attorney General Ed Dossett. The purpose of this gathering was to reach an agreement between the local and federal authorities as to what type of immunity and/or protection could be offered to Chas for his cooperation in providing evidence against Larry Lee, if he could or would do that. (The investigating officers still suspected that Chas knew more than he was telling.) Through his attorney, Chas had agreed to undergo hypnosis, and the FBI agents were attempting to negotiate payment for this procedure through the attorney general's office. Ed Dossett endorsed this plan.

Following this meeting, York, Steed and DeVuono filed out of the second-floor office and into the atrium hallway. As they made their way down the wide, cutaway stairs, they passed attorney Rupert Keener, who'd had occasion to represent members of the Smith family in the past, including Larry Lee.

"Investigator York," the attorney said with a nod of his head as he clutched a thick leather briefcase.

"Hello there, Rupert," York said in his friendly East Tennessee drawl. He introduced Agents DeVuono and Steed and alluded vaguely to the meeting they'd just left. "You know, Larry Smith was the last person with Michelle Anderson the night she disappeared. We're tryin' to see if we can't get some help and some answers," York said. "He was in the Atlanta area. Not sure where he's gotten to now."

"Well, I heard he's been arrested over there again. Charged with assaulting another girl," Keener said. "He's in jail in Decatur. Been there for some months."

"You don't say?" York replied, catching the narrowed eyes of both DeVuono and Steed. "Thank you for that update, Rupert. We'll look into it."

The attorney nodded again to the three men, who continued their descent to the first-floor lobby. "Geez,

I'm glad we ran into ol' Rupert," York mused as the three made their way down the glass-lined corridor and exited the building into the morning chill.

"At least we know where Smith is," Steed observed as he reached for his lapels and pulled them together in an effort to block out the unseasonal cold front that had moved in the day before.

"I'll get right on this," DeVuono said. He was somewhat dazed by the attorney's news—news his recent research hadn't uncovered. The first thing he did upon arrival back at his desk was to put in a call to Georgia.

"DeKalb County Police Department. How may I direct your call?"

"This is Special Agent Joe DeVuono with the FBI office in Knoxville, Tennessee. I want to speak to the officer handling the case against a Larry Lee Smith, who I understand is currently incarcerated over there."

"Detective L. M. Moore," a female voice responded after three rings.

Agent DeVuono introduced himself and explained the purpose of his call. Detective Moore confirmed that Larry Lee Smith had been arrested in DeKalb County, back in mid-October. He'd been picked up for the kidnapping and attempted sexual assault of an eighteen-year-old in broad daylight in the town of Stone Mountain. He'd remained in jail ever since. She agreed to fax over a copy of her case report.

The news that Larry Lee had struck yet again troubled Agent DeVuono. The trial was scheduled to begin in less than two weeks, although Detective Moore informed DeVuono that a plea deal may be in the works. Assistant District Attorney Elizabeth MacNamara was prosecuting; the detective gave the agent MacNamara's phone number.

Just seconds after hanging up, DeVuono dialed MacNamara's office and got ahold of her. He outlined the disappearance and murder of fifteen-year-old Michelle Anderson in Knoxville. He even enlightened the prosecutor about Larry Lee's 1981 rape conviction in Florida. Agent DeVuono said he would fax over documents to support the specifics.

In turn, Elizabeth MacNamara apprised DeVuono of the strength of the state's evidence against Larry Lee in the Amanda Sanders matter. She believed that they had a solid case with the accused facing fifty years for his crimes—assault, kidnapping and attempted sodomy. But to prevent Amanda from having to testify, she'd offered Larry Lee a deal of twenty years in exchange for a guilty plea.

Agent DeVuono and Investigator York faxed their documents on the criminal and psychological history of Larry Lee. After reviewing them, MacNamara placed a call back to DeVuono. She informed him that she'd reconsidered her position. Larry Lee posed too much of a threat. Based on DeVuono and York's work, she withdrew her offer of twenty years for a guilty plea; MacNamara wanted to go to trial, and she would push for the maximum sentence.

11. <u>STATE OF GEORGIA VS. LARRY LEE SMITH</u>

On the morning of Monday, April 16, 1990, rays of spring sunlight filtered through the blossoming dogwood branches and onto the lawn of the historically ornate DeKalb County Courthouse. The Superior Court trial of the State of Georgia vs. Larry Lee Smith (case #90CR1858) was just getting underway, Judge Curtis V. Tillman Jr. presiding.

Larry Lee had been arraigned on a four count indictment: (1) aggravated assault with intent to rape, (2) aggravated assault with intent to rob, (3) kidnapping, and (4) criminal attempt to commit aggravated sodomy. He pleaded "not guilty." Elizabeth MacNamara, who graduated Phi Beta Kappa from the Emory University Law School, was prosecuting for the state.

Defending the accused was W. Keith Davidson, who ran his small, private practice out of nearby Snellville. Larry Lee had hired him, but no doubt Ruby paid his fees. Davidson had also represented Larry Lee on his assault charges in the Caroline Bronti case. He would later claim that his client pleaded guilty in that case only because he needed to focus on the trial at hand.

Seated in the gallery directly behind the defense table were two of the most important people in Larry Lee's life: his mother, Ruby, and his sister, Nancy, who had always been like a second mother to her baby brother. After a panel of twelve jurors and an alternate had been selected, a pretrial motion was considered: the defense didn't want local news cameras in the courtroom.

W. Keith Davidson, who looked to be in his thirties with blond hair and a thick, muscular build, entered a motion for the television cameras to be removed. He called twenty-nine-year-old Larry Lee to the witness stand to present evidence justifying this request. The defendant had groomed himself for the trial. He wore a gray suit paired with a bold yellow tie and his hair was now cut short and parted on the side. Gone was the unruly mustache that had dominated his upper lip on the day of the assault the previous October.

Larry Lee took a seat on the wooden witness chair and confirmed to his attorney that he planned to testify in his own defense, which was why he was worried about the cameras. His primary concern was for his personal safety. "While I've been in DeKalb County jail, somebody has found out approximately what my charges are and my life has been in jeopardy. I have had to be moved several times, and I am in fear that if my face appears on cameras or on TV, that my life will be in jeopardy."

Larry Lee's other area of concern was that, underneath it all, he was simply a shy kinda guy. "I get nervous in front of cameras," he admitted. "I believe that I would be so selfconscious of that camera that I would not be able to testify properly."

A brief debate followed among the attorneys and the judge.

The newsman representing the television station reported that Larry Lee's image had already been recorded. Cameras are allowed in courtrooms, Judge Tillman concluded; his hands were tied. The television cameras remained.

After instructions were given to the sworn-in jurors, the trial got underway. "I think we are ready for opening statements," Judge Tillman declared. "You may proceed."

Both the prosecution and the defense presented their opening remarks to the jury, telling the panel of twelve-plus-one what the substance of their respective cases would be, what the jurors could expect to see and hear presented by each side during the trial, and who would be called to testify. Then the state began presenting its argument for the conviction of Larry Lee Smith of the crimes with which he'd been charged. In all, the state would call ten witnesses and submit thirty-eight pieces of evidence.

Tall, attractive, auburn-haired Elizabeth MacNamara rose from her seat and called Amanda Sanders, the principal and first of the state's witnesses, to take the stand. After being sworn in, the petite and pretty teenager eased nervously onto the shiny witness chair. "State your name for the record," MacNamara instructed.

"Amanda Diane Sanders," she responded, but her answer was spoken too softly to be clearly understood.

"Adjust that microphone just a little bit and lean forward and talk into it, please," the judge directed.

Amanda repeated her name, this time louder, then answered questions about her age (eighteen), where she lived, where she worked, what kind of car she drove and then finally the events of that day—the day she was kidnapped and assaulted by the defendant. Amanda testified about having a disagreement with her boyfriend, Steve, then walking out to her car, only to find that once it started, it stalled and wouldn't start again. She went back into the game room before returning to her car.

"What happened when you came back to your car?" MacNamara asked.

"This man approached me."

"Amanda, look around the courtroom and see if you could point out to the jury the man that stopped and wanted to help you on October the 13th."

She glanced at the defendant, then away again as quickly as her eyes would avert. The sight of her assailant brought on a flurry of physical sensations: pounding heart, clinched stomach, quickened breath. For a brief flash of a moment Amanda thought she might faint; she gripped the rail of the witness stand. "He's sitting over there. That's him. The one with the yellow tie and gray suit."

Larry Lee twisted around and exchanged looks with his mother and sister. Facing the front again, he wore a crooked grin and shook his head from side to side.

Prompted by MacNamara, Amanda went on to describe the ordeal of the assault.

"Why did you get in the car?"

"Why?" Amanda repeated, a little thrown by the angle of the question.

"Why did you get in the car, Amanda?"

She searched for the words to explain. "I don't know. It's just that it was my car... and he was in it. He was going to help me."

MacNamara pointed to State's Exhibit #12, a map of the area. Amanda stepped down and used a pointer to trace for the jurors the route her abductor had traveled, marking significant buildings and locations with an X. When she had completed this task, the court recessed for lunch.

* * *

When court resumed, defense attorney Davidson rose to begin his cross-examination. He paused and stroked his wide, square jaw as if contemplating his strategy. When he finally began, he zeroed in on Amanda's reported conflict with her boyfriend on the day of the alleged assault.

"When Larry Lee came up to you, you mentioned that your boyfriend was working in the store, didn't you? Do you remember him saying that you ought to get yourself a new boyfriend? Do you remember that? You testified that you got in the vehicle voluntarily."

From there Davidson did his best to portray a different scenario than the one advanced by the state. When Larry Lee reached his hand behind Amanda's seat, the second time he'd stopped her car, wasn't he perhaps just "flirting" with her? When he "grabbed" her by the neck, how was her head turned? Hadn't Larry Lee, in fact, brought Amanda back to the billiards parlor? Couldn't the whole interaction have been an incident of flirtation blown out of proportion?

"Did he say you were pretty?" Davidson asked.

"Not that I recall, no."

"The conversation never strayed into what y'all had planned for that evening?"

"No!"

When Davidson was done, MacNamara stood for redirect; she had a thing or two she wanted to clarify. "Amanda, when he first grabbed you by the neck, was he holding you anywhere else?"

"By the hair."

Then MacNamara had Amanda come down from the stand to demonstrate for the jurors just how Larry Lee had grabbed and held her. "You pretend that I am you and show the jury how it was that he was holding you."

Amanda complied.

"You didn't interpret his grabbing you by the throat and pulling your head down as his just making a pass at you, did you?"

"No, he was hurting me!"

"You have no doubt in your mind that he wasn't just asking you to go out on a date?"

"No, I knew he wasn't. That's not how somebody goes about asking somebody out on a date!"

Next up to testify for the state was Professor Michael Decker. He described what he had witnessed on that Friday—a young girl being choked by a young man in a car that pulled up behind him at a traffic light. He identified the "young man" as Larry Lee. The defense had no questions for Mr. Decker.

MacNamara then called Steven "Steve" John Redmond, Amanda's handsome, dark-haired boyfriend. He also identified Larry Lee as the stranger who'd offered assistance to his girlfriend and subsequently returned her to the billiards parlor in a terrible state. Steve recalled the events of that tumultuous day. He confirmed that he'd been the one to write the defendant's tag number on the box of Marlboro Lights and that he'd put in the call to the DeKalb County Police Department. The defense had no questions for Steve.

Donny Harbin, the young man who had retrieved Amanda's badly scuffed shoe from the roadway, was next on the witness stand. He'd been among those that spilled out of the billiards parlor, pool sticks in hand, as Larry Lee raced toward his car.

"Do you see anyone in the courtroom that you saw on October the 13th?" MacNamara asked.

"Yes, ma'am. That dude right there in the yellow tie." The

defense had no questions for Donny.

DeKalb Police Officer Philip Cresti, who first responded to the call that evening, testified next, followed by Rockdale Sheriff's Deputy Michael Stapp, the officer who spotted and arrested Larry Lee in the pre-dawn hours on the day after the assault. Davidson did have a question for Deputy Stapp. He asked if Larry Lee had run through an actual red light—or was it merely a caution light?

"No, it's a red light there," the deputy replied with certainty. Davidson then established that Larry Lee had cooperated once Deputy Stapp pursued him onto the highway. Yes, the deputy confirmed, the defendant had surrendered without further resistance.

The seventh witness called by the state was Detective L. M. Moore, an eight-year veteran of the DeKalb County Police Department and the lead detective on Amanda's case. She testified that on the evening of Saturday, October 14th, she had interviewed Larry Lee at Central Headquarters in the Criminal Investigation Division. She'd Mirandized him using the department's Miranda Rights form.

"And did the defendant agree to make a statement?" MacNamara asked.

"Yes, he did." She went on to testify that Larry Lee's statement—actually written down by Detective Moore at his request—was given freely without the use of threat, intimidation or coercion.

"If the defendant *wanted* to write that statement, could he have done it?" MacNamara asked.

"Yes," the detective answered, further stating that after it was written, she'd read it back to him, and he had neither posed questions nor made corrections before signing it.

At this point, MacNamara presented States Exhibit #40, Larry Lee's police statement, dictated at eight o'clock Saturday evening, October 14th, and written down by Detective Moore:

> I request that Detective L. M. Moore write this statement for me; It was around 5:30 to 6:00 PM yesterday evening 10-13-89, when I came out of Eddie's Trick Shop, located on Memorial Drive. I saw this Amanda Sanders crying. Something was wrong with her car. I asked her if I could help. She said she thought she had dropped the clutch. I told her I would take a look. I got in and started the car. I told her let's take it around the block to see what's wrong. I pulled over twice because of the noises I heard in it. This is when I started thinking I could take this car and go home. I was thinking of my home Tennessee. Her car had a full tank of gas and I was thinking of some way I could get her out of the car somewhere, so she would have to walk, before she called the police. I began thinking about going on the interstate. I told her to lay down on the seat, and she started fighting. I grabbed her by the neck, and put her down in my lap. My pants were buttoned, and I started the car back up and took off. She told me to take her back to the billiard place. I told her that I would. She started screaming and I didn't want to hurt her. I told her the only thing that I was going to do is rob her. I took her back, and jumped out of the car and ran. I got into my car and drove off. I got scared and I couldn't take anything that wasn't mine.

In his cross examination, Davidson had weighty questions to ask. How long had Detective Moore spoken with the defendant in the interview room before beginning to write his statement? About ten minutes, she replied. As Larry Lee talked, she wrote.

Davidson seemed skeptical. "Do y'all have tape recorders?"

"Yes, we do."

"Did you tape this conversation?"

"No, I did not."

The defense attorney challenged the idea that Larry Lee

launched into a long narrative that resulted in the signed statement. With no tape recorder or police or court recorder documenting the interview, Davidson cast aspersions upon the authenticity of the detective's version.

"Did you investigate the psychological background of Amanda Sanders?

"No, I didn't."

"Thank you."

The state's final witness would not be available until the next day. She was being flown in from out of state even as the court decided whether to allow her to testify. Calling this witness had been a late-in-the-game decision for the prosecution and one that met with considerable resistance from the defense. MacNamara wanted to introduce a witness from a "similar transaction."

As a general rule, proof of independent crimes is inadmissible against a defendant at trial, which is why Larry Lee's recent conviction for the assault of Caroline Leigh Bronti was not introduced during his current trial. But Rule 403B of the Federal Rules of Evidence—a code of law enacted in 1975 to increase uniformity and fairness of evidence admissible in the U. S. federal court system—allows for admission of "similar transaction" testimony, testimony from a prior offense that is similar to the current offense. Although states retain the authority to determine their own evidence codes, most are based, at least in part, on the Federal Rules of Evidence. Even so, it's seldom black and white: while Georgia employs a more liberal policy in allowing similar prior convictions for sexual misconduct into trial evidence, Tennessee exercises a more restrictive and cautious approach. Ultimately, Larry Lee Smith would be impacted by both.

In authorizing the state to present evidence of a similar

prior offense, the Court must weigh against permitting unfair prejudice, confusing the issues, misleading the jury, or wasting time and causing delay. To qualify as admissible, this "similar transaction" evidence must meet certain criteria: it can't be used to establish character, but it can be used to establish proof of motive, opportunity, intent, preparation, plan, knowledge, identity, or absence of mistake or accident. In other words, it establishes a *pattern*.

Davidson objected to MacNamara's move to introduce evidence of this "similar transaction," because it would certainly hurt Larry Lee's case. MacNamara had reached out to Katherine McWilliams, Larry Lee's kidnapping and rape victim in 1981. While the lawyers quibbled over the admissibility of her testimony, Katherine was on a flight from Florida.

Davidson acknowledged that he'd been served with notice of a "similar transaction," but only two weeks prior to the trial (when MacNamara had learned about it herself, from the phone call she'd had with Agent DeVuono). Davidson argued that since the state hadn't made it clear *pretrial* that they intended to call this witness, it was unfair to do so now.

Because there was still plenty of time remaining in the afternoon, Judge Tillman dismissed the jury so he could hear arguments and rule on the admissibility of the "similar transaction."

MacNamara presented him a summary of the 1981 Florida kidnapping and rape case that led to the arrest and conviction of Larry Lee. She argued for the admissibility of this evidence based upon the many similarities. She pointed out that the defendant's *pattern* was to assist young women in distress, especially when that meant the *opportunity* to offer a ride with the *intent* to get them alone in a vehicle, ideally his. As part of his *plan,* he used choking to disable his victims.

Judge Tillman was persuaded.

The next morning, April 17, 1990, Elizabeth MacNamara stood before the jury and announced that she would be calling the prosecution's final witness. She also informed the jury that she "would tender into evidence the information, change-of-plea and judgement in the case of State of Florida versus Larry Lee Smith."

For the record, defense attorney Davidson objected.

"Your Honor, we call Katherine McWilliams," MacNamara said.

An attractive, petite twenty-three-year-old was sworn in and took the stand. MacNamara began her direct questioning: "Would you state your name, please."

"Katherine McWilliams."

"Katherine, how old were you in 1981?"

"I was fourteen."

"On the evening of July the 11th of 1981, where were you?"

"I was on Clearwater Beach with a few friends from the New Port Richey neighborhood that I lived in." Katherine described her dilemma nine years earlier when she was in danger of missing her curfew and her subsequent acceptance of a ride from a stranger. She then described how this stranger had assaulted and raped her before delivering her back to her neighborhood.

"Do you see the man that you ran into in Florida back in 1981?"

"Yeah."

"Could you point him out for the jury, please?"

Katherine pointed to Larry Lee. She could easily recognize him, but she later admitted that she couldn't get over how much he had aged in just nine years. The weight, the prematurely graying hair; he already looks so old, she thought.

For Katherine, now an adult, being called to testify in the Amanda Sanders assault trial brought a kind of closure for her. She was a young teen when her own assault had occurred, and Larry Lee had dodged a trial by accepting a plea deal. This trial was the first time she'd been able to testify about her own ordeal.

"Katherine, have you discussed your testimony with anybody else in this case other than telling me your story?" MacNamara asked.

"No, I haven't."

The witness was instructed to step down.

STATE'S EXHIBIT NUMBER 21

Photocopy of Dekalb County, Georgia, mugshot of Larry Lee Smith, entered as evidence in the trial for the 1989 assault on Amanda Sanders.

12. <u>OKAY. THEN WHAT HAPPENED?</u>

The State of Georgia rested its case in the trial of Larry Lee Smith, and the defense began theirs. Larry Lee was their only witness. The defense argument was primarily twofold: first, Larry Lee was just helping this damsel-in-distress, good guy that he was; and second, his misleading police statement was given under duress.

The poor girl, Amanda, had been crying about her car and her boyfriend wouldn't help, so the defendant stopped to lend a hand, although he claimed he wasn't much of a mechanic. Still, he helped—against his better judgement, because ever since he made that mistake, that *error in judgement* in Florida where he kidnapped and raped Katherine McWilliams, Larry Lee had been fighting an uphill battle against prejudgment.

On the stand Larry Lee admitted that it was his idea that he and Amanda take the car for a test drive. But he insisted it was Amanda who directed them down side streets away from heavy traffic. When prompted to explain why he had pulled behind buildings and shut off Amanda's car *twice*, Larry Lee explained: "I heard some kind of noise, and I thought, well maybe the brakes or something, you know, were going to give her some problems, so I pulled into one shopping center and I opened my door and she opened hers. I turned off the car and I just shook the car a little bit with my foot to see if I could hear any noise and I didn't hear anything. But all this time—"

"What do you mean, shook it with your foot?" Davidson interrupted.

"Well, you know, like I kind of stepped out. I was halfway out and holding onto the steering wheel and just seeing if I could move it a little bit."

"I see."

"And then she shut her door and I shut mine, and I started up the car and drove across the street into the parking lot on the other side. All this time, though, we were talking about her boyfriend, how he shouldn't drink, and I was telling her about how I had quit drinking because of bad experiences, you know. I just tried keeping the conversation going, because I didn't know... I really didn't know her that well.

"And we pulled over behind another shopping center and I stopped and I said, did you hear any noises? And she said no, and then I... I just kind of flirted with her. And I put my hand over on the back of her seat, and she panicked. I mean, it was like... okay, one minute she was real nice and talkative and the next thing I know, she's like, *What are you doing? What are you doing?* You know, and started pushing on me and hitting on me. So I grabbed her. I said, 'Whoa, whoa, whoa... Let me take you back to where we were and let me get my car and leave.'"

"*Okay.* Then what happened?"

"I started up the car and started moving and she tried jumping out of the car and I grabbed her by the throat. I said, 'Look, I'm not going to rob you or anything. I just want to get back to where my car is.' And she started beating on me and everything. That's when we stopped at this red light and this guy started getting out of this truck when she was beating on me, and I thought *my God,* I was scared. I thought I was going to be beat up on."

Larry Lee went on to describe driving frantically back to the parking lot where the borrowed Pacer was waiting and then being chased by guys swinging pool sticks as he made his getaway. He had befriended this girl with car trouble and look what it got him.

The defense strategy for the "similar transaction" case—the abduction and rape of Katherine McWilliams in Florida—would be different. Larry Lee couldn't deny that crime; he'd pleaded guilty to it back in 1982. Instead, he admitted to everything, but claimed that he had been passed out drunk in his truck by the beach and could barely drive. It was just a foolish, drunken mistake that filled him with remorse, guilt and shame. He had learned his lesson, he told the jury. He sure was sorry.

"Okay. Now, let's go back to something," Davidson said. "You heard Katherine McWilliams testify?"

"Yes, sir, I did."

"Now, that was what, about ten years ago?"

"About nine, sir. Yes, sir."

"All right. You pleaded guilty down there. How's that affecting some of the things that are going on now? What difference has that made to your life?"

"That has affected my life to where every time I get around a female, I'm scared that they're going to overreact and because of my record, every time I turned around, somebody's throwing it up at me. And I just run from situations where I shouldn't. I overreact to them and..."

"Was that part of your panic situation on October 13th?"

"Yes, it was. It's always on my mind. I haven't forgot what I did. I had no right to do what I did, and I know that."

"Larry, on the day, October 13th, you were in the car with Amanda. When she told you she wanted to go back, did you immediately take her back?"

"Yes, I did. I *wanted* to go back."

"Okay. Did you ever intend to rob her?"

"No."

"Did you ever intend to rape her?"

"No."

"Did you ever try to forcibly cause her to sodomize you?"

"No."

"When you went over to help her, was it your intention to harm her in any way?

"No, it was not."

"Thank you."

Elizabeth MacNamara rose from behind the waxed wooden table and strolled in slow, calculated steps to the front. She'd been waiting for this, her chance to cross-examine Larry Lee Smith. She held the defendant's gaze for a few seconds, then began.

"Mr. Smith, if it wasn't your intention to rob Amanda Sanders, why did you tell the police that it was?

"Because I was saying whatever they wanted to hear because I really was hoping to get a lesser charge."

"So you're now denying that was your statement?"

"I'm saying it was part of my statement. That is not all of my statement. That is only the way it was put down, and I did not reread it. I was just scared."

MacNamara cut to the chase. "You were scared because you knew you tried to rape someone."

"No, ma'am."

"What were you doing in Rockdale County at five o'clock in the morning on October the 14th? You're not from this area originally. Where are you from?"

"Tennessee."

"You seem to like to help girls in trouble," MacNamara said. "You helped Katherine McWilliams back in 1981, didn't you?"

"No, I did not."

"Well, you gave her a ride home. Wasn't that why you stopped and helped her, she was in trouble? You stopped and helped Katherine McWilliams just like you helped Amanda Sanders."

"No, ma'am. What I did to Katherine McWilliams was wrong. I did what I did, and I never should have done that and I know that, and I paid for it a hundred times over."

"So you're just a victim of circumstances here?" MacNamara chided. "You made one mistake back in 1981 and you're never going to live it down?"

Davidson stood. "Your Honor, I'm going to object to this type of question. It's just a smart aleck comment."

The judge sustained the objection and instructed MacNamara to be less argumentative.

"Thank you, Your Honor," she responded, then resumed questioning the defendant. "You don't disagree that you got into the car with her and that it was your idea to test drive the car?"

"No, I do not."

"Once you got the car cranked, why didn't you just leave?"

"I don't know. I've been asking myself that for the last six months."

"You thought Amanda Sanders was kind of cute, didn't you?"

"Well, yes. I agree with you. I'm not going to deny that."

"And it's your testimony that you put your arm around her and that's when she panicked?"

"Yes, ma'am. That's when everything just started flying. That is when she panicked, and when she panicked, I panicked."

"You panicked so much that you grabbed her around the neck."

"I grabbed her around the neck after she was trying to jump out of the car, and we were going pretty fast and I didn't want to see her jump out and get hurt."

"You didn't grab her around the throat in the Kroger parking lot?"

"No, ma'am."

"You didn't ask her to unzip her pants?"

"No, I did not."

"Her pants were unzipped when she got to the billiards."

"I don't know about that. I wasn't there at the billiards."

MacNamara paused, letting silence settle over the room. "So, if Amanda Sanders has testified that you stopped the car, put your arm around her and grabbed her around the throat, grabbed her by the forehead and told her to unzip her pants or you would break her neck, she's lying?"

"Yes, she is."

"Can you think of any possible reason why she would lie about that? She doesn't know about your prior record."

Larry Lee said he didn't know why Amanda would be saying these things, except perhaps to make her boyfriend jealous. Maybe she didn't think it would go this far, he speculated. She probably didn't realize anyone had taken down his tag number. He claimed that when the police wrote down in his statement that he said he was thinking of getting Amanda out of her car to steal it, what he really said was: *What was he supposed to do when she began attacking him, put her out of her own car?* But they got it all wrong.

Larry Lee said the whole mess was just one big misunderstanding. And the sodomy thing, how could that be possible with a fat guy like him? Yes, he pushed her head down, hitting his leg with her face, but only because she was hitting him and he was trying to protect himself. He had the seat pushed all the way up, so between him and the steering wheel, where was her head going to be? And as far as his pants being unzipped, he had an explanation for that apparent misunderstanding, too.

"And your pants *weren't* unzipped?" MacNamara asked.

"No, they were not."

"She's lying about that, *too?*"

"No. I tell you what I figure it is. Okay. I was wearing my Krystal uniform, which is brown Krystal pants and a red Krystal shirt. Okay. The pants zipper is closed, but it sticks out because I had to let the pants out at one place. Maybe that's what she thought. She saw the zipper, but she did not see it unzipped because I know for a fact that I had a safety pin holding those pants up, because the zipper is broke. My mom has tried to fix that zipper before and she's right here and she could tell you that."

Ruby sat behind her son's place at the defense table, her expression serious, her features sharp. Her eyes surveyed the courtroom as everyone's gaze shifted her way.

MacNamara's questioning led back to the police statement that Larry Lee continued to dispute, even though he acknowledged that he had willingly signed it. It had been "condensed," he said, and things had been taken out of context, had been misconstrued. He was scared, that was all. One of the detectives had yelled at him, threatened him with never seeing daylight again.

"But you were here when Detective Moore testified,"

MacNamara said, "and she said that she read you your rights, that you gave her your statement. It took about ten minutes, and when you finished giving her your statement, she reduced that statement to writing. You heard her testify to that?"

"She wrote it because she wanted to, number one," Larry Lee shot back. "I can write. I can read. I love to read and I'm capable of writing my own statements. If she had wanted me to write that statement, I'm sure that I could have. I mean... I didn't go through high school, but I do have a GED and I was making arrangements to attempt to go over here to Georgia Tech, which is in Gwinnett County, to take up landscaping."

"So, when the statement says, 'I requested Detective L. M. Moore to write this statement for me,' that's wrong, too?"

"She said, 'I'm going to write this for you.' And I just let it go the way she wanted it to go. That is exactly what I did."

"So this is Detective Moore's statement. This isn't your statement."

"That is half my statement *twisted*."

"Let's figure out which half is yours." MacNamara walked him through it point by point, asking at each one, *Now is that your line or is that Detective Moore's?* In the end, Larry Lee owned most of the statements as his. But he continued to complain that the condensing had omitted pertinent details. He denied that he said anything about a full tank of gas or robbing Amanda.

"And you admit that you gave Katherine McWilliams a lift in 1981 and you took her and raped her?"

Davidson objected, "It's been asked and answered, Your Honor."

"Sustained," Judge Tillman replied.

"But you had no intention whatsoever of doing the same thing to Amanda Sanders?"

"No, I did not."

"I have nothing further," MacNamara concluded.

"We have no further questions, Your Honor, and we rest," Davidson added.

As Larry Lee returned to his seat, he pressed his wide mouth into a smile for his mother and sister.

13. <u>LADIES & GENTLEMEN</u>

On the third day of Larry Lee Smith's trial, Elizabeth MacNamara and W. Keith Davidson presented their closing arguments. The jury was led into the courtroom and given instructions by the judge. In the indictment, the defendant was charged with four separate offenses; the Court provided the jurors with a legal definition and explanation of each one.

In her summation, MacNamara referenced the charges and the evidence presented against Larry Lee Smith, then focused on the case and testimony of Katherine McWilliams. It was powerful corroboration for the prosecution—the story of the *similar transaction*. "Katherine came here to testify to show you what Larry Lee Smith *intended* to do. The judge instructed you that you could consider her testimony for purposes of determining *intent*.

"Look at the similarities between these two crimes. You've got two teenage girls: Amanda Sanders, barely five feet tall, ninety-eight pounds; Katherine McWilliams weighed less than a hundred pounds in 1981 when she was fourteen-years-old. Both of them were adolescent girls in trouble. Amanda's car had broken down, her boyfriend was unable to come and help her. Katherine was about to violate her curfew. She needed a ride home and the boys she was with weren't going to take her home.

"Along comes Larry Lee Smith more than willing to help a young girl in distress. He gets them both into a car, takes them to some secluded spot. In Katherine's case, he managed to complete the rape. She fought back but she wasn't in the enviable position Amanda Sanders was in. She was in a spot that was so secluded there was no one to help her. There was no Michael Decker there for Katherine McWilliams. She was in an apartment. She was alone.

"And what did the defendant do? He grabbed both victims by the neck to the extent that there were marks on Katherine's neck and there were visible marks on Amanda's neck. That's common scheme, ladies and gentleman. That's a pattern of behavior.

"In both instances he had the victim fondle his genitals prior to the rape. Amanda Sanders—after he told her to unzip her pants, after he threatened to break her neck—he forces her head into his lap with his pants unzipped. Katherine McWilliams was forced to fondle his genitals before he raped her. They're consistent, ladies and gentleman. They're the same kind of act.

"He forced both girls to stay low in the car. Katherine was forced to get down in the car with her hands over her face. Amanda, he kept her head down the whole time they were driving and he says that he didn't know where he was going.

"And then he returns both girls home unharmed, I'm sure Mr. Davidson will argue. Unharmed, except for the fact they were assaulted and Katherine was raped.

"This man looks for opportunities, ladies and gentlemen.

He probably doesn't *stalk* these women. He doesn't *plan* all these things out in advance. If you ever wondered about that stranger that your mother warned you about, then look across the courtroom, because there he is.

"There's the man, Larry Lee Smith. That's the man you've been warning your daughters about and warning your children about, that you yourself have been warned about all these years. That's the man: the man that gets young girls into cars."

W. Keith Davidson paced in front of the jury box. Turning to face the twelve men and women, he thanked them for their time and attention and provided a brief lecture on the nature of reasonable doubt. The prosecution, he reminded them, had the burden of proving Larry Lee Smith's guilt *beyond* a reasonable doubt. Then he launched into an attack on the state's case.

Davidson did his best to frame the facts presented and events described as reflective of Larry Lee's innocence rather than his guilt. Davidson accused the police of "filtering" and condensing the police interview into a one-page statement.

Amanda wasn't a *victim*, he claimed. She was just "flirtin' around" and got cold feet. She'd become all *panicky;* and when she panicked, he panicked—what with his history and all. Amanda thought about what her momma and daddy had told her about getting in the car with strangers and here she was. The girl needed a plan: "Rape!" she yelled. Poor Larry Lee; this guy couldn't catch a break.

And like his client testified, Davidson did not deny that Larry Lee kidnapped and raped young Katherine McWilliams nine years earlier. Instead, he acknowledged it, but told the jurors that Larry Lee was now a *different* man, a changed one who had learned "from his stupid, stupid acts" of those earlier years.

Davidson reminded the jurors that Larry Lee *did not* assault Amanda as he had Katherine. He had matured. It was all a misunderstanding. Flirtation gone wrong. A *misunderstanding.*

Next Davidson ran through the individual charges for the jurors: assault, aggravated assault, kidnapping and sodomy. Larry Lee didn't *assault* Amanda, he'd just tried to control the hysterical girl and defend himself against her wild attack. Fat ol' Larry Lee against little ol' Amanda? *Come on!* If he wanted to sexually assault her, he *could* have.

Kidnapping? Larry Lee was just a fool—what with the previous charges and all—to have offered the test drive. But *kidnapping?* No way! He turned back toward the billiards hall, didn't he?

And then there was the sodomy issue. Mere acts of preparation do not prove an attempt to commit a crime, Davidson pointed out. Even if Larry Lee *had* unzipped his pants and tried to force Amanda's head down, no *sodomy* occurred; Amanda had confirmed this on the stand. She had kicked, screamed, scratched and gone unconscious, but she had not, in any way, come in contact with the penis of Larry Lee Smith. She had been very clear about that. No contact equals no sodomy, Davidson concluded, skirting around the fact that the charge was *attempted* sodomy.

As his argument wound to a close, Davidson punctuated his words with large, emphatic gestures. He argued that none of the charges were true. They were erroneous, overkill, blown all out of proportion. Amanda had run into the billiards hall claiming Larry Lee "tried to rape" her—she didn't say he kidnapped her or robbed her or sodomized her! "In South Atlanta, that's simple battery. Here with a little white girl in Stone Mountain, that's aggravated assault!"

* * *

The jury completed their deliberations and returned to the courtroom. "Ladies and gentlemen of the jury, have you arrived at a verdict?" inquired Judge Tillman.

"Yes, we have, Your Honor," the foreperson responded. The jury found Larry Lee Smith *guilty* on three of the four charges: two assault charges (one with robbery) and kidnapping. He was found *not guilty* of the attempted sodomy charge. Davidson's strategy had gotten him at least that much.

MacNamara was disappointed. She had been hoping for a sentence of at least fifty years. In fact, she'd felt pretty confident about it. But of those projected fifty, the attempted sodomy represented thirty. Without it, the best she could hope for was twenty-two.

She argued for the maximum sentence: twenty years for the kidnapping and a year each for the two battery charges, to run consecutively, twenty-two years. She reminded the Court of the defendant's 1981 conviction for rape and then referred to Larry Lee's conviction just months earlier in Gwinnett County for battery against the young Caroline Leigh Bronti. This last part was new information for the Court.

Although Larry Lee's assault on Caroline Bronti was consistent with his proclivity to entrap young women, it had not been deemed a "similar transaction" and therefore had not been admissible during the trial. But MacNamara could introduce this information during sentencing.

"Here in Georgia he has kidnapped a very young girl and held her for a period of time," MacNamara read from the police report. "The jury found him guilty of simple battery. He had 'offensive contact with her.' And we feel that based on his record and based on the evidence that you've heard in this case, that a sentence of twenty-two years would be appropriate and we ask you to so sentence."

The surprised judge turned to Davidson. "Counselor,

were you representing the defendant when he was found guilty in Gwinnett County?"

"Yes, I was, Your Honor."

"Who is Caroline Leigh Bronti, please?" the judge demanded.

"Your Honor, if I could see that," Davidson requested as he reached for the court document submitted by the prosecution. His eyes scanned the record. Davidson had represented Larry Lee in the case, but he never saw nor met the victim. Judge Tillman gave Larry Lee an opportunity to comment on the circumstances of that case, but he declined.

"Your Honor, we stipulated to the police report in that case," Davidson said, "and didn't... we didn't do any real investigation in that case because this case was pending. In other words, it was not a finding of guilty, it was actually a plea."

He argued that the two assault charges in the Amanda Sanders case should be merged, emphasizing the lack of long-term bodily harm to the victim and the relatively short time she was held in Larry Lee's captivity.

After consideration, Judge Curtis V. Tillman of the Superior Court of DeKalb County, Georgia, sentenced Larry Lee Smith to twenty years in prison, the sentences for the assault charges to be served concurrently. Larry Lee was returned to the DeKalb jail to await transfer to a state prison, a process that could take a couple of months. Eight years had passed since Larry Lee was sentenced to prison in Florida for the assault and rape of Katherine McWilliams. Now he was returning to prison, this time in Georgia, and it was for a much longer sentence.

Back in Knoxville, news of Larry Lee's conviction and sentence was greeted with feelings of both relief and frustration. Investigator York and Agents DeVuono and Steed were still hoping to charge him with Michelle's murder.

14. <u>LIES & LENIENCY</u>

Just after Larry Lee Smith had been sentenced to twenty years, but before he was transferred to a Georgia state prison, the FBI field office in Knoxville submitted a written request to the District Attorney's Office in Stone Mountain asking for permission to interview Larry Lee in the DeKalb County jail.

Written by William E. Baugh Jr., Special Agent in Charge of Knoxville's field office, the letter briefly touched on the gravity of the Michelle Anderson case and concluded: "It is still the belief of all investigators involved that Larry Lee Smith either solely or with the assistance of Chas Frost [Michelle's boyfriend] was involved in her disappearance/murder. It is anticipated that agents Grey Steed and Joe DeVuono of the Knoxville Office, along with KPD Homicide Investigator York, will attempt to interview Larry Lee Smith in the future.... Thank you again for your assistance in this matter and congratulations on your recent conviction of Smith."

On a sunny, eighty-degree spring Friday, May 4, 1990, Steed, DeVuono and York were in an FBI sedan on their way to Decatur, Georgia, to interview the recently convicted inmate. They arrived at the DeKalb County jail at one o'clock in the afternoon. When Larry Lee was brought into the interview room, he immediately recognized Agent DeVuono. "I wish to see my attorney," Larry Lee demanded. Steed took the lead, assuring him that he could terminate the interview at any point he desired.

Larry Lee agreed to stay long enough to listen to the purpose of their visit. Yet when the special agents produced an FBI form entitled "Interrogation; Advice of Rights," which advised him of his rights and contained a "Waiver of Rights" to sign below that, Larry Lee threatened to leave the room if he was asked to sign it. He'd learned from that mistake in the Amanda Sanders matter. Larry Lee told them that he understood his rights, including the right to terminate the interview, but he wasn't signing anything.

Steed informed Larry Lee that the FBI and the KPD had reason to believe Chas was also involved in Michelle's disappearance. They wanted to explore what potential testimony Larry Lee could provide in this matter. Because the feds were interested in helping the KPD solve the crime, if Larry Lee cooperated, perhaps he could get federal time, or a sentence that ran concurrent with the Georgia time.

The idea that these suited special agents of the FBI were visiting him in the Georgia jail, seeking his testimony and making him an offer, must have intrigued Larry Lee, because he stayed in the interview for four hours. He considered their offer and agreed to the following: *If his role and/or knowledge of Michelle's murder constituted a federal crime, any sentence given would not exceed twenty years, would run concurrent with his current sentence and would be served in a federal prison with the recommendation that he receive some type of psychiatric counseling; if his role and/or knowledge of Michelle's murder did not constitute a federal crime, but his evidence and/or testimony was helpful in obtaining prosecution for the party or parties involved, the federal government would make the Georgia Parole Board aware of his assistance.*

If the FBI and the KPD could do that for him, Larry Lee informed them, then he claimed he "would produce irrefutable evidence of the time, date, place and method of Michelle Anderson's death." In addition, his evidence would implicate other parties involved in the matter. Although Larry Lee never offered any names, he claimed that up to three other individuals were involved, and that Michelle's death was part of a "satanic" ritual, although he, himself, had limited involvement.

When pressed by the agents as to whether Chas was involved in Michelle's death, Larry Lee responded: "Chas's problem is the same as my problem in that Chas knows the details of how her death came about and who was involved." While Larry Lee avoided offering any specifics about his alleged evidence, he made numerous statements about what an excellent photographer he was and that he knew how to use a telephoto lens. He implied that photographs existed at his mother's house. Photographs that could be of assistance in the Michelle Anderson case.

At the end of the afternoon-long meeting, Steed, DeVuono and York knew that Larry Lee wasn't being honest about his involvement. But as long as the possibility remained that more than one person was involved in or had knowledge of Michelle's death, they reasoned that Larry Lee might still be a source of useful information. They played along for now.

On May 14, 1990, nine days after visiting the DeKalb County jail, Agent Steed signed off on an official letter to Larry Lee:

Dear Larry,

I have recently had the opportunity to sit down with both the state and federal prosecutors to discuss with them the Michelle Anderson investigation. As I indicated repeatedly to you, it is difficult to obtain matters that you seek without a more specific proffer [indication of evidence] of your potential testimony....

Larry, I truly believe you have information that would help bring this matter to an end and would assist Michelle's mother in putting this matter behind her. If your role is as limited as you claim, it is my belief that it is in your best interest to work with us in resolving this matter. I look forward to hearing from you.

Agent Steed never received a reply.

Larry Lee probably suspected that the FBI and KPD were grasping at straws. If they had physical evidence, they would have charged him already. What he didn't know, was that the FBI had implemented a strategy to persuade either Larry Lee or Chas to implicate the other in exchange for some kind of leniency or advantage. Steed, DeVuono and York always shared the belief that Larry Lee was responsible for the disappearance and death of Michelle Anderson. But they also believed it highly possible that Chas had some complicity in the crime, or at least in events leading up to the crime (no one really knew what had happened upstairs in Larry Lee's bedroom that night). They had been in talks with Chas's attorney about an immunity deal just before they learned of Larry Lee's trial.

After visiting Larry Lee in prison, the agents opened another dialogue with Chas's attorney. They still offered immunity for his client if he would admit guilt and testify against Larry Lee. But now they could put more pressure on him. They made sure Chas was aware that Larry Lee had made statements indicating that Chas had complete knowledge of Michelle's murder. Although reportedly shaken by this information, Chas continued to deny any further knowledge or involvement. He did cooperate by providing samples of his hair, fingerprints and blood.

Next, the team put together an elaborate cat-and-mouse strategy that involved Larry Lee's estranged wife, Sara, and Chas meeting at Knoxville's McGhee Tyson Airport. Each of them was sent in wearing a wire with the belief that they were there to entrap the other. To raise the stakes, the agents informed their informants that the airport was chosen because the metal detectors would assure that the other person was unarmed. Sara was instructed to bluff Chas with alleged information from Larry Lee, revealing that he intended to implicate Chas if Larry Lee was ever confronted with Michelle's disappearance. She told Chas that Larry Lee was cooperating with authorities in exchange for leniency.

The plan failed. Chas continued to deny any further knowledge. Maybe he was clever—no doubt he was afraid—and maybe he just didn't know more than he'd already told, at least about the *death* of Michelle. But the Knoxville officers wanted resolution to their case and continued to seek his cooperation through his lawyer, who bought into the benefit of his client cooperating with the authorities in exchange for immunity. He encouraged Chas to comply.

For a while the team moved forward with the plan to hypnotize Chas. They contacted a psychiatrist in Nashville who was skilled in the technique. Chas had agreed to go through with it, although his attorney raised the question of the admissibility of a confession given under hypnosis. The answer to that question was initially dodged, and then the plan fell through altogether. The issue of payment of the five-hundred-dollar fee was the final insurmountable barrier. That responsibility would have fallen to the KPD, or perhaps the TBI, and neither wanted to pay it.

In June 1990, Chas's attorney composed a letter to Agent DeVuono. In it, he referenced talking to Chas "one more time" about the offer of immunity. The attorney indicated that he had discussed with his client the threat of Larry Lee's possible cooperation, implicating Chas as having been "present and having knowledge of Michelle's death." But Chas continued to maintain that what he had told the authorities was all he knew.

"Chas remained unmoved and unpersuaded," the attorney wrote, "and I have reached the opinion that Chas is consciously telling us the truth. I have been wrong before, though, and I certainly do not claim any magical powers. I did make my best effort to persuade Chas to cooperate and to provide additional information. He insists, however, that he has already done that. If you wish to talk further, do not hesitate to call me."

Matters with Chas never progressed past this point. And Larry Lee never offered any evidence that implicated Chas, or leads related to his tale of witnessing Michelle's murder in a "satanic" ritual.

Upon Larry Lee's transfer from the DeKalb County jail, he became an inmate of Hays State Prison, Georgia Department of Corrections. As a matter of setting up the new prisoner's file, the parole office in DeKalb County sent a letter to the FBI field office in Knoxville requesting criminal background information on the new inmate. DeVuono responded with a complete history of Larry Lee's known crimes.

Steed, DeVuono and York had made every effort to pick up the cold trail of evidence and solve Michelle's murder; it just wasn't going to be. In March 1991, Special Agent Joseph P. DeVuono completed a final report on the FBI investigation into the disappearance and murder of Michelle Anderson, and the FBI closed its case.

In the offices of the Tennessee Bureau of Investigation and the Knoxville Police Department, the case would remain open, but inactive. In time, forgotten to all but a few. Investigative records and stored evidence would be passed over, misplaced, and eventually lost.

BOOK TWO

Part One
Picking Up a Cold Trail

1. <u>NO REASON TO RUN AWAY</u>

When Michelle Anderson first went missing in January 1987, social worker Sasha Reynolds and her family lived in the same North Knoxville neighborhood as Michelle's family. Sasha had never met the olive-skinned fifteen-year-old, although her son Seth knew her from school and had once confided to his mother that he thought she was pretty. Michelle was in his gym class.

Then sometime after that talk, maybe weeks or months—Sasha couldn't remember anymore—he had walked up the hill from Fulton High School, across the wide porch of their craftsman bungalow, and given her the disturbing news. "Remember the girl in my class that I told you about, Michelle Anderson? She's missing."

Seth had his mother's full attention as he probed the opened refrigerator for a suitable snack. Sasha had given up meat; what he wouldn't give for a thick burger right now. "She didn't come home last weekend," he continued. "The kids said some weird guy gave her and some others a ride home. Michelle was the last one to be dropped off, but she never got there."

Over the next few weeks flyers with Michelle's picture appeared at the local grocery store and in other neighborhood and outlying venues. It bothered Sasha to see them. Michelle's photograph depicted a smiling teen with dark, wavy hair feathered back. Her large, lively eyes focused slightly upward in the direction of the photographer. A soft light washed across her face and down the front of her wide-striped blouse, bouncing off the luster in her hair. Michelle wore a small gold pendant that rested perfectly in the hollow of her neck, exposed between the open lapels of a stand-up collar. In her ears were gold loops the diameter of pennies.

What happened to her? Sasha found it hard to put the case out of her mind. Neighborhood kids were buzzing with rumors that the guy who'd given Michelle a ride home had done something to her, even though the investigating officer reported that she probably ran away. "Where, exactly, does Michelle's family live?" Sasha finally asked Seth one day, and then she looked up the phone number.

She didn't know Michelle's mother, Anita. And she didn't want to cause her more stress, but Sasha had a question to ask. She entered the numbers on the touch-tone keypad of the canary-yellow wall phone and made the call. As the phone rang, she unconsciously wound her fingers through the looping cord, and tried to imagine the pain that Anita must be going through.

"Hello?" Anita's voice was soft on the other end.

"Hello," Sasha began. "This call may seem a little strange, but I wanted to ask about your daughter. My name is Sasha Reynolds and I live in the neighborhood. I've seen the flyers with your daughter's picture. My son and daughter go to Fulton. My son has a class with Michelle." Sasha was feeling nervous as she went on to describe the rumors she'd heard from the neighborhood kids. Then she asked Anita outright:

"Do you think your daughter ran away?"

"No," Anita replied quickly in a still-soft voice. "Michelle had no reason to run away."

Anita explained that she didn't like that the police detective assigned to the investigation, Jerry McNair, was handling it as a runaway case; she'd told him as much.

Sasha Reynolds knew Detective Jerry McNair. They'd shared a couple of cases when she was investigating child abuse and neglect for the Tennessee Department of Human Services (DHS). She put in a call to her former colleague.

"Hi, Jerry. Sasha Reynolds here."

"Yeah. You doin' okay?" he responded in his low-key way. He was nearing the end of his career at the KPD, moving closer to his state retirement age, something he talked about a lot.

"I'm good. Listen. I want to ask you about a case I hear you have, the girl that's missing in North Knoxville. Michelle Anderson."

"Yeah."

Sasha told him what the neighborhood kids were saying about the guy who'd supposedly given Michelle a ride home. There was a beat of quiet. Then McNair confirmed that he'd heard those stories.

"Michelle's family and friends don't think she ran away," Sasha continued. "And Michelle never got to the boyfriend's house."

"He says he dropped her off. What am I supposed to do?"

Sasha's abdomen clinched when she heard those familiar words. With Detective McNair, the investigation often started and stopped with that statement. In her experience with him, his easygoing, docile demeanor translated to a general lack of initiative. If a case didn't split itself wide open before him, he shrugged his shoulders. *What am I supposed to do?*

* * *

Sasha had shared her first case with McNair a few years earlier, a referral from the University of Tennessee Hospital concerning a two-year-old girl admitted with internal trauma and bleeding. The toddler had allegedly passed out while riding her Big Wheel on the sidewalk outside her parents' public-housing apartment. Her condition was critical; it was unknown whether she would pull through.

When Sasha interviewed the girl's parents, they made a good first impression. Money was clearly in short supply for this biracial couple residing in the city's newest public-housing complex, but they were very different than the people Sasha usually worked with from this area. Both were exceedingly soft-spoken and mild-mannered. Their house was orderly and the three attractive children—a ringlet-headed daughter of three, a second daughter aged two (the one in the hospital) and an infant son—were always nicely dressed and well groomed. The family attended church on Sundays and each parent reported that the other was good with the kids. It was just a mystery how this two-year-old ended up in the ICU from a Big Wheel accident. Only it couldn't be. "Someone injured that child—period, dot," a friend of Sasha's told her.

When the two-year-old was reported to have suddenly collapsed on her Big Wheel, she and her siblings had been at home with their father. The mystery was the nature and extent of the child's injuries, internal injuries unlikely to have been produced by a fall from the seat of a Big Wheel just inches off the ground. Everyone agreed that the explanation for her condition made no sense, but the father was sticking with his story. The mother stood by him, too, but she also seemed confused and scared, afraid she'd lose her children.

While the two-year-old began to recover, the question as to what really happened to her remained unanswered.

Detective McNair had the parents' statements and took no further action on the matter. He didn't see what else he could do—*like continue to question or pressure them to produce a story that made sense,* Sasha wanted to scream at him. She felt frustrated and in a quandary. This case appeared to be going nowhere.

On her own, Sasha determined to root out a resolution. She stepped up her visits to the home and tried to time her visits so that she would have an opportunity to talk with the father alone.

On one of these visits, while talking casually with him, using self-disclosure to build rapport, she mentioned how stressed out she remembered being at times when her kids were young. "I would lose it sometimes," she confided. He nodded in agreement. "Do you ever lose it?" she asked him. He nodded in agreement again. "Did you lose it that day?" Again, he nodded in the affirmative. And then Sasha got the story, the true story.

The father had become upset with the two-year-old daughter. While sitting on the floor in front of the sofa, he swung his arm outward toward the little girl, caught her in the abdomen with his forearm and slammed her back into the sofa's front trim-board. The force of the impact produced the hidden injuries. Even though the little girl stopped crying and went out to get on her Big Wheel, she suffered severe internal bleeding and soon passed out.

The father told Sasha that he was relieved on some level to have gotten that off his chest. He allowed Sasha to drive him to the KPD to give a new statement to Detective McNair. The child had nearly died, the father got time, and McNair got credit for solving the case.

When the stars lined up for Sasha to share a second case

with the detective, she tried to alter that course before it began. She'd received a report that two teenage sisters were being housed at the local runaway shelter, having escaped from their parents' temporary home, a two-room motel suite. They were alleging sexual abuse at the hands of both parents.

She went to the shelter to interview the sisters. As their story unfolded, revealing a level of family dysfunction and sexual abuse that was shocking, even to someone who investigated abuse for a living, Sasha contemplated the gravity of the case. The girls were giving clear and consistent details, coming off as very credible, and saying they would be willing to follow through with prosecution.

Sasha stopped mid-interview and excused herself. She had to call the assistant district attorney who coordinated the investigative teams. After she informed him about the nature of the case, she asked what detective would be assigned. The assistant DA put her on hold, then picked back up, and said, "Detective McNair."

Sasha had a good track record; she'd handled her clients well, conducted competent interviews, collected essential facts, wrote better-than-average reports and testified effectively in court. At this point in her career, she'd earned both credibility and influence among her colleagues, so she thought it was reasonable to say, "Please don't assign McNair to this case." She knew she was pushing the boundaries here—social workers didn't normally make such requests—but what surprised her was the sense of urgency in her voice.

"*Why?*"

"Because he will blow it," she answered.

"I'll call you back," the assistant DA replied. But when he did, his answer was blunt: "You've got him."

Sasha returned to the next room and completed the interview.

The girls' parents were informed that their daughters were being taken into temporary custody by DHS and would not be returning home at present. At some point, the parents were instructed to report to the police station for questioning. Sasha wanted to be there. In no other case had she participated in this portion of the investigation; it was not within her duties. But this case was different: she didn't trust McNair's work.

The detective agreed to allow Sasha to question the parents with him. They split them up and took turns with each one. The couple had traveled the country in a motor home, hauling their family secrets from state park to state park, below the radar of local officials. The father was tough and seasoned, the mother his codependent co-conspirator. They were professionals at lying and evasion. They weren't giving an inch, especially not to a passive, teddy-bear cop and a social worker.

But Sasha knew they were scared.

After hours of questioning, she and McNair regrouped and compared notes. She tried to convince him that there was probable cause with the girls' statements and their willingness to testify. But McNair just answered her with his trademark shrug of the shoulders. He didn't see where he could go from here.

"Don't let them leave," Sasha urged. "Call a judge. Get an arrest warrant." She'd seen it done many times.

"I can't do that," he responded.

"YES. YOU *CAN!*"

But he didn't. Sasha watched as the parents, probably amazed by the opportunity they'd just been given, slid out of the police station into the night. Before daylight, they'd slipped silently out of the state. At least they'd left their daughters behind.

Within a few days, Sasha got a call from the assistant DA.

"Would you like to tell me, I told you so?" he offered.

"I told you so," she responded.

Three years later the parents were arrested on a routine traffic stop in Florida. By then they had several outstanding arrest warrants. They were extradited back to Tennessee where they stood trial. The daughters testified as they had always said they would, and the parents were sentenced to prison.

So to Sasha, Detective McNair's lack of interest in the matter of Michelle Anderson was all too familiar. She felt bad for Anita, knowing that the police had already given up on her little girl. But circumstances in Sasha's own life pulled her away from the story, and from Knoxville. She accepted a job offer in Alabama to coordinate a family program in a residential treatment center. It was in Alabama that she met her husband, Bert. Her work and her hectic personal life took over, and Michelle's disappearance drifted to the distant recesses of her mind. She was no longer in touch with the Knoxville community. She didn't know what had transpired in the case after she moved. She never heard about the discovery of Michelle's body or the joint investigation by the FBI, TBI, and KPD. She had never even heard the name Larry Lee Smith.

Things changed on a lazy winter afternoon in the mid-1990s—nearly a decade since Michelle had gone missing. Sasha and Bert were watching a TV show that profiled police cases that had used forensic science to identify bodies and solve crimes. The narrator began talking about a case involving the skeletal remains of an adolescent female found in the mountains of East Tennessee. That got Sasha's attention. She'd lived there for twelve years.

Then forensic anthropologist Dr. William Bass appeared on-screen, discussing his findings. For Sasha, watching this scene unfold before her was a bit surreal; she had minored in cultural anthropology at the University of Tennessee, Knoxville, when Dr. Bass was head of the anthropology department there. He'd admitted her to the graduate program. In 1981 she'd studied under his late wife, nutritional anthropologist Dr. Mary Ann Bass.

A picture of Michelle Anderson flashed on the screen. And there it was, confirmation of what Sasha had always suspected. Michelle had been murdered. The narrator ended the segment by noting that the crime remained unsolved.

While the show didn't cause Sasha to spring into action, it did plant a bug in her brain. Even though she was busy working as a program director for adolescents in foster care, running a part-time therapy practice and writing and editing for a local publication Bert had started, she began to entertain the idea that she might learn a little more about the unsolved case of Michelle's murder, maybe even do a little digging on her own. Whenever those thoughts cropped up, she quickly dismissed them. Too much time had passed, she told herself. She couldn't even remember the name of Michelle's mother, and no one she knew did either.

Detective McNair had, himself, passed away about six years after Michelle's remains were found. He'd run over a nest of ground bees while mowing his lawn in late spring and was attacked by a swarm of the aggressive insects. He died from anaphylactic shock a short time later.

Still, Michelle's case stayed with Sasha. And as the years ticked by, it began to haunt her.

On a Saturday in late September 2007, Sasha and Bert stopped in the local Ace Hardware store in Guntersville, Alabama, a town on the Tennessee River named for a trader who'd settled among the Cherokee there back in 1785.

The couple were in need of supplies to work on the small, mountaintop cottage they'd purchased nearby.

On the way back to their car, Sasha spotted the local weekly newspaper in its rack. She deposited two quarters and scanned the small-town community headlines. She wasn't expecting what she saw: "Authors to speak on latest 'Body Farm' book." The next day, Sunday, Dr. William Bass was scheduled to speak about his book, *Beyond the Body Farm*, at the Guntersville Senior Citizen's Center.

In the decades since Sasha had been a student at the University of Tennessee, Dr. Bass had become even more renowned in forensic circles, mostly through the research that he and his colleagues and students did at "the Body Farm" on the edge of the UT campus in Knoxville.

Then Sasha learned that his book was coauthored with Jon Jefferson, a Guntersville native! The two men had collaborated under the pen name Jefferson Bass and had also published a series of popular body farm mystery-thrillers.

Really? Dr. Bass here? Tomorrow? Sasha was stunned. This was her chance. She would approach Dr. Bass after his talk and see if he would discuss the cold case of Michelle Anderson.

2. <u>NOW I JUST WAKE UP SAD</u>

Sasha leaned forward and nervously placed her copy of *Beyond the Body Farm* in front of Dr. Bass. She'd found his talk fascinating, but she'd also been distracted by the anticipation of this moment. She remembered the very day— over twenty-five years before—that she sat opposite him as he admitted her into the graduate program in anthropology, but she hadn't studied under him—forensic anthropology wasn't her concentration—so Sasha didn't expect him to remember her all these years later. Dr. Bass gave her a friendly smile, but a look of recognition did not register on his face.

Conscious of the long line of people waiting patiently to get their books signed, but determined not to miss this opportunity, Sasha launched into a rapid-fire speech, informing Dr. Bass who she was, that she had studied under his late wife, that she needed to speak with him about an old unsolved murder case from outside Knoxville—the Michelle Anderson case—on which he had been the forensic investigator years earlier.

Dr. Bass stared at Sasha with a kind but slightly bewildered look. After a few seconds, he flipped her book open to the back, jotted down his phone number, and pushed it toward her.

As Sasha walked away, avoiding the angry glares from those still waiting in the long line, she tingled with excitement.

"Hello?" answered the friendly voice on the other end.

"Hello, Dr. Bass. This is Sasha Reynolds. I spoke with you a few days ago about an old case of yours at your talk in Guntersville."

"*Yes. Yes.* How can I help you?"

Sasha explained her interest in the Michelle Anderson case and what she knew about his involvement, having seen the forensic show in which he had been featured. Dr. Bass still seemed unclear about which case she was referring to; it had been nearly twenty years since the remains had been discovered, and he'd researched a lot of cases in his career.

"Do you remember where the body was found?" he asked.

"I seem to recall that it was near Crossville," Sasha responded, relieved that she'd remembered that detail from the forensic TV show years earlier.

It began to come back to him. "Yes, I remember the case," he said. "Her uncle is a dentist here in town. He identified the body through her dental records. I've got the case files in my office. I also keep copies of the newspaper articles related to the cases. I'm retired now and don't go into the office everyday. But when I go in, I'll locate the forensic report and the newspaper articles and send you copies."

"Thank you so much!" Sasha replied, grateful and moved by Dr. Bass's generosity. After providing the professor emeritus with her mailing address, she reflected on the surprising and encouraging way in which events were suddenly unfolding, opening up opportunities, like a series of doors, for her to walk back into Michelle's case. There was so much she didn't yet know about what had transpired since Michelle went missing and Sasha had moved away, but she was determined to learn.

When Dr. Bass's promised package arrived, Sasha pored over every report, every article, every detail. She began connecting the dots and filling in the missing pieces, which only led to more dots and more missing pieces. Dr. Bass's files gave her specifics she could research and the newspaper articles provided a key name: Anita Anderson, Michelle's mother.

Armed with her newly-acquired knowledge of the case, Sasha felt confident reaching out to Anita. Now the task would be to locate her. *How would she respond? Would she think Sasha was some kook from the past, stirring painful memories?*

Sasha began her search online and soon got a hit: a probable address and phone number. On December 1, 2007, Sasha dialed the number. An answering machine picked up, and she left a message. A day later, she got a return call from Anita's long-time partner, Ted. He asked what Sasha wanted and what the call was about. He sounded cautious, defensive, but not unfriendly. She briefly explained her interest in the now twenty-year-old case of Anita's daughter. Ted seemed somewhat disappointed that Sasha was seeking information, not necessarily providing any.

"So, you don't have any information?" he asked.

"No. I don't."

After a pause, he said, "I guess I can have her call you."

Sasha wasn't sure that would happen. But it did happen. Anita called her the next day. She too was cautious. "Who are you again?"

Sasha repeated what she had told Ted the day before and also told Anita about calling her all those years ago, shortly after Michelle had gone missing. Anita faintly recalled that someone from the neighborhood had phoned to ask if Anita thought Michelle had run away. Sasha then explained her history with Detective McNair and Dr. Bass. Her contact stirred Anita's pain, but also brought her some sense of comfort—a strange person out of nowhere was interested in her daughter's cold case.

"You must surely imagine my shock to get a phone call like this after so many years," Anita said. "My son Doug and I have never been able to accept Michelle's death, and it is still very hard to talk about. Too painful." It was unfinished business for this quiet family, a scabbed-over wound festering below the surface of verbal and emotional expression.

Anita's communications were initially like this: guarded and polite. But as she and Sasha exchanged more calls over the next few weeks, she became more open.

"Life as I knew it ended on January 10, 1987," Anita confessed to Sasha one night over the phone. "We will never be the same." She admitted that she continued to see Michelle in her dreams nearly nightly, all these years later. In virtually the same dream, over and over, Michelle comes to her after having been away but won't tell her where she's been. As Michelle prepares to leave again, Anita panics, becomes fearful "of never seeing my baby again."

"In the early years, I used to wake up screaming," she tearfully explained to Sasha. "Now I just wake up sad."

It was a little surprising to Sasha that Anita let her in as easily as she did, needing whatever it was Sasha might be offering, grateful for the interest in her daughter's case and any possibility of resolution it might bring these decades later. Despite her quiet, low-key demeanor, Anita *needed* to talk. "I really hope that you and I can accomplish something," Anita told her. "You're the first intelligent person who has contacted me. The others were either 'psychics' or just plain weirdos."

It was from these conversations that Sasha first heard the name Larry Lee Smith. His name had not appeared in any of the reports or newspaper articles sent by Dr. Bass. Anita filled Sasha in on her strange meeting with Larry Lee and the lack of an initial investigation into his involvement in Michelle's disappearance. She also told Sasha about the possible involvement of Michelle's boyfriend, Chas, and the unsuccessful murder investigation into both Larry Lee and Chas after Michelle's remains were found. Sasha was glad to learn that Larry Lee had received a twenty-year sentence for the assault of Amanda Sanders in Georgia. A small consolation.

Halfway through Larry Lee's twenty-year sentence, he came up for parole. Anita was notified in writing by the Georgia Corrections and Parole Board Office of Victim Services in Atlanta. She, along with her sister, brother-in-law and cousin, attended hearings, wrote letters, and sent emails to make sure Larry Lee stayed behind bars. Their efforts paid off and the parole board upheld Larry Lee's sentence. Anita and her family continued their campaign every time Larry Lee came up for parole, but time was running out.

If Sasha was interested in Larry Lee, Anita told her, she could pull up his profile on the Georgia Department of Corrections website. Anita had kept tabs on him there for years.

Sasha went to the website, followed Anita's instructions, and there he was. She studied his round, pudgy face and his small, steel-blue eyes, accentuated by the blue collar on his Georgia prison garb. His now-short hair had turned almost entirely silver-white, with but a few fading hints remaining of the brown it had once been. He weighed two-hundred sixty pounds and was noted to have obtained a scar on his left forearm. Larry Lee was forty-six years old in 2007 and two years away from being released from Hays State Prison in Northwest Georgia.

When Sasha began digging back into the Michelle Anderson case, she'd thought of it as a curiosity, an unsolved riddle from her past. But now, having talked to Anita, having heard her anger and her pain, she realized there was so much more at stake. And with Larry Lee nearing the end of his sentence, time was of the essence.

The next time the two women talked, Sasha had just one question for Anita: "When can we meet?"

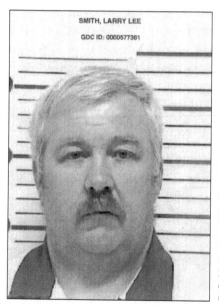

SMITH, LARRY LEE

GDC ID: 0000577361

"There he was, the first Sasha had ever laid eyes on him, the man who had driven off with Michelle. She studied his round, pudgy face and his small steel-blue eyes staring straight into the camera lens. Larry Lee was 46 years-old in 2007 and in the 18th year of his 20-year sentence in Georgia."

3. <u>ANITA AND DOUG</u>

Anita and Doug took a seat on the sofa in the Knoxville hotel room. Anita smoothed her long, off-white sweater over her olive-colored slacks. A petite woman, she sported short hair that fell in wispy waves around her face. She rested her tan purse upon her lap, smiling hesitantly, though she carried an air of heavy-hearted reserve about her.

Beside her, Doug wore a dark, button-up shirt under a crisply styled leather vest. His black, curly hair was long, parted precisely down the middle and pulled tightly back into a snug, neat ponytail. Sasha was glad Doug had joined his mother. Anita had told her that Doug was reticent to discuss Michelle—they all were—but that he was willing to sit down with Sasha if it could do some good.

They talked again about the circumstances of Michelle's disappearance and the ensuing investigations. They speculated about how events might have unfolded that tragic night, how things might have been handled differently. They also filled Sasha in on their lives since the investigation.

Anita's life had grown more placid with the passing years, although the unremitting grief of her daughter's unsolved murder hovered over her. She had met Ted in the year after Michelle disappeared. They were still together twenty years later, living not far from her elderly parents. She'd taken a job with a company that offered security and good benefits. She considered it her best job, but she was inching toward retirement, and she could feel it. That was okay with her.

It had been a number of years since her ex-husband, Doug Sr., had passed away. After the police returned Michelle's crab pendant, the one given to her by her father, which she'd worn every day, Anita herself had worn it every day. She took comfort that something of Michelle's was with her at all times. But recently Anita had come to fear that she might lose it. She couldn't explain the source of this fear, but just a few days before the interview, she'd removed the pendant. Better to keep it put away, she explained, where it was safe.

Doug's life was fairly quiet, too, like Doug himself. He stayed private, his personal circle tight and small. He worked and lived near his mom and helped her look after his grandparents. He mowed their lawn and trimmed their bushes in the same meticulous and precise way that he combed his hair and arranged his clothes. Anita described him as an artist, a perfectionist. He continued to write poetry and songs and to draw. He never married, although, Anita noted, "He would probably make a fine husband and father. Doug is a very good person with a lot of feelings."

Doug remained attentive but largely quiet. Yet when he did speak, his input was thoughtful and insightful. He seemed relieved to be getting these stories out in the open. As he and Anita explored his recollections, Sasha turned to him and asked: "Were you and Michelle close?" The innocent inquiry seemed to land with a thump in his chest. Doug followed it with ten seconds of silence. He tried to regain his composure, but then stood without a word and walked out the door.

Tears spilled down Anita's cheeks and she began to sob.

"I'm so sorry," Sasha whispered.

"I think I would have been okay if he hadn't done that," Anita said, her voice cracking. "He doesn't talk about this. I'm surprised he's talked this much today. He just told my cousin, Susan, that he's never really accepted or come to terms with Michelle's death."

When Anita indicated that she was ready to continue, Sasha asked, "Did you ever go to therapy?"

Through new tears Anita shook her head no. She'd thought about it, just never did.

"How did you cope? How did you grieve?"

"I guess at first by just doing everything I could to find out what happened. Later, I sometimes drank," she admitted. "You may have expected me to say God or church, but I was very angry with God. I really haven't coped very well. You can see how fresh the pain still is."

Aided by the power of nicotine to calm the nerves, Doug regained his composure and returned to the interview. "I'm not used to being asked questions about this," he said.

"You've held it inside for a long time," Sasha reflected.

He nodded in the affirmative. "Without Dad around, I think that I was protective of Michelle—sometimes overly, and evidently not enough." He explained that after Michelle went missing—and especially after her body was found—he had trouble discussing her with anyone, even Investigator York. He couldn't process it. He was in shock.

Sasha asked Doug about Chas, who'd been Doug's friend for four years before he began dating Michelle. Doug said he hadn't stayed in touch with Chas through the years, but knew he was still around. About a year earlier, Doug had run into him and learned that he'd fallen at work and was seriously hurt. But Doug didn't know anything else.

"Why do you suppose the investigators thought Chas might have been into satanic worship?" Sasha asked. Anita had alluded to this in a previous communication with Sasha.

Doug shrugged his shoulders. "People probably thought I was, too, but I wasn't."

"Why would people think that?"

"I joked about it a lot, you know, the heavy metal and everything, but I never took it seriously," Doug explained. "Never *knew* anyone who took it *seriously*. Chas had an inverted pentagram tattooed on his arm. To my knowledge, it represented nothing more than a band called Møtley Crüe. It was on their album covers and was very popular at the time. We all knew of the symbol's satanic association, but I don't think anyone took it seriously."

As they brought the interview to a close, Doug offered Sasha his email address, in case she had more questions for him. She appreciated this gesture of trust.

Anita suggested that Sasha contact KPD Investigator Randy York, but she could no longer tell Sasha how to reach him since he'd retired. She'd heard that he had another job, but couldn't remember the details. Eventually, after calling around, Sasha got a tip that led her to York's office voicemail, where he currently worked as a legal process server. She left a message.

A few days after Sasha's meeting with Anita and Doug, Anita followed up with an email:

> Thank you so very much for taking the time to meet with us. I didn't expect that reaction from Doug, but he's right, we never talk about it. It would be helpful, I am sure, to do so and get past the crying, which we thought we did a long time ago. But it is still hard. The holidays are always so hard for us because of the timing. I dread them

every year. Obviously she shouldn't have been out there. Obviously I should have been a better mother. The worst part is knowing that I could have prevented it. My grief is overshadowed only by my guilt.

4. <u>YORK</u>

Retired KPD Investigator Randy York was a punctual man. He still lived in the Knoxville area and arrived at Sasha's hotel room in the downtown Hampton Inn at exactly one o'clock in the afternoon, as planned. "I hated that we couldn't solve the case," he said as he settled onto the sofa. "Larry Lee Smith's one sick guy." Of medium height and build, the handsome York was dressed in khaki-colored slacks and a yellow button-down-collar shirt. His dark, neatly-trimmed hair had only a touch of gray; his overall appearance reflected the look of a man a decade or so younger than his actual years. "You know," he continued, "years before, I'd arrested his brother, Brad, on burglary charges. They were really rough people."

Sasha took the chair opposite York and again explained her interest in Michelle's case. They had spoken on the phone already, when Sasha had explained who she was and what she hoped to learn from him on her visit to Knoxville. York had been more than happy to sit down with her. In the hotel room, she updated him on Larry Lee's current inmate status, explaining that he had less than two years of his sentence left to serve. She also discussed her history of working with Detective McNair and her questions about his handling of Michelle's case.

York thought a lot of the late detective, he told her. McNair was his friend. York had been a pall-bearer at his funeral. Yet he recognized that the investigation into Michelle's disappearance had not developed as it could have. The "investigative file" he'd inherited from McNair had been virtually empty.

"Jerry drug his feet on this, *big time*," York lamented. "Within twenty-four hours, two-to-three people should have been interviewing the kids at that party and others. Certainly after a few days—at the least when she didn't return—someone should have been looking at this thing hot and heavy. Keep in mind, this wasn't really my case," he said. "I hate cleaning up somebody else's mess."

Although the case was never *officially* York's, no one did more work on it than he. When Michelle's remains were found in an adjacent county, the case officially transitioned from McNair and the KPD to the Tennessee Bureau of Investigation. The TBI got involved for two reasons: Michelle's remains were located in rural Cumberland County, outside the KPD's jurisdiction, and the TBI regularly helps rural counties with homicides.

"After her body was found," York continued, "a TBI agent from Crossville, Jim Moore, called and asked me if I'd do the follow-up here, interview her friends and all." York was moved and motivated by the case. He threw himself into it—with FBI Special Agents Grey Steed and Joe DeVuono coaching and assisting him along the way.

Back when York was interviewing the teenagers involved with the case, he'd run into the "satanic panic" full force when he was told that Chas and Doug were involved in devil worship. While he hadn't known what to make of Michelle's brother—the unreadable, withdrawn young man with long hair dressed all in black—he never fully bought into those stories. And as for the "satanic" note that had been left on Anita's door, York thought it was just another ruse by Larry Lee.

During the investigation, York talked to Ruby a number of times about her son, telling her that no young female was safe around him. "Ruby would get so mad," he recalled. "She'd defend Larry Lee, saying that he'd been 'the nicest little boy.'" But York had actually met Larry Lee when Larry Lee was just a child and would visit relatives who lived near York's family. He recalled that Larry Lee always looked unkempt and untended. He often had a lost, vacant look in his eyes, even then. Not at all the "nicest little boy" that Ruby remembered.

York had kind words for Larry Lee's estranged wife. "Sara tugged on everyone's heartstrings, and she was more than willing to do anything needed to help bring Larry Lee to justice." He talked about the abuse Sara had reported experiencing at the hands of Larry Lee. "She was terrified of him. Sara was a sweet girl—*real confused*, but somebody you'd like."

York said he'd *known* Larry Lee was involved in Michelle's murder, but back then he couldn't rule out Chas either, not with the way he was acting during the investigation.

Then York told Sasha about his investigative file, the one he'd compiled during the months after Michelle's remains were found: interviews, statements, documents. "I had a book on that thing," he said, a look of frustration on his face. He claimed that his memories had grown fuzzy on some of the details of the two-decade-old cold case, so that file would come in mighty handy for Sasha's research. But there was a problem: the file was missing.

When York retired, he took copies of certain unsolved case files with him, as was standard procedure. The file on the Michelle Anderson case was one of them. A few years back the captain of the KPD Major Crimes Unit called York wanting to borrow York's copy of the file. They were reviewing old cases and couldn't find the KPD copy of York's Michelle Anderson investigation. York was happy to hand over his files. Later, he heard that they had located the KPD copy, but he never got his copy back, and now neither of the files could be accounted for.

Although, York told Sasha, the case was *technically* the TBI's, so they should have some documents on file. He suggested Sasha start there. He also suggested she track down FBI agents DeVuono and Steed. In the meantime, he'd keep trying to get his KPD file back, but he warned Sasha that it didn't look promising.

At the end of the interview, Sasha gave York her card. "I'm glad somebody's following up on this," he noted as he shook her hand. "I'll be glad to help in any way I can."

5. <u>INVESTIGATING THE INVESTIGATION</u>

After meeting with Anita, Doug, and Investigator York, Sasha returned home knowing she had her work cut out for her. But more importantly, she had a purpose. She began this project thinking that if there was enough information available, she might write a story about it. But now there was more than a story—or even a book—at stake. There was justice. Justice for Michelle and any other woman who'd had the misfortune of crossing paths with Larry Lee Smith.

Sasha decided to take a two-prong approach to her research, which she squeezed into the hours around her demanding job as a clinical program director. She needed to investigate Larry Lee Smith, that was obvious, but she also needed to investigate the investigation of Michelle's disappearance and murder. She started by reaching out to the Tennessee Bureau of Investigation, like York had suggested. But she hit an instant road block. TBI records are confidential, she was told over the phone. Information on an open case could not be released without a subpoena, and a case was not closed until it was solved. She wasn't allowed phone access to any human to argue otherwise, and all emails were ignored.

The FBI had officially closed their Domestic Police Assistance case on the Michelle Anderson murder investigation in 1991. So Sasha filed a Freedom of Information/Privacy Acts request for the records from their closed Michelle Anderson file. This lead seemed promising, though she had no idea how long it would take for the file to arrive.

Even though York told her that the Knoxville Police Department had lost their files on the case, Sasha decided to reach out to them anyway, to introduce herself at least. She had a feeling they would be communicating a lot in the future. She started by emailing Lt. Doug Stiles of the Crimes Against Persons Unit. She sent him an overview of the Michelle Anderson case, indicating pertinent dates and developments. She concluded with the question:

> If a fifteen-year-old female didn't return home under suspicious circumstances, would it be standard procedure to presume she was a runaway and do no search?"

Lt. Stiles emailed back the same day:

> That is a hard question to answer. I need more information please.

Sasha answered:

> I have a lot more info and yet there are pieces that I am just now filling in. Michelle did not return home one night in 1987. Detective McNair identified her as a runaway even though no one else felt that she had. So, in essence, there was no investigation into her disappearance. Her remains were found two years

later and there was some investigation then, but the ball had been dropped a long time.

Lt. Stiles replied:

Very interesting. I've never heard of this case before. Jerry McNair has passed away, any other detectives involved? Where did they find her body? Please let me know when you come to town.

With contact made at the KPD, Sasha began looking into Larry Lee. She had some dates and case numbers from his Georgia Department of Corrections prisoner information page. She used those to follow Larry Lee's trail of court activity leading up to his incarceration. A visit to the records room of the DeKalb County Courthouse in Decatur, Georgia, yielded the two-volume transcript of Larry Lee's 1990 trial for the kidnapping and assault of Amanda Sanders.

The transcripts included Larry Lee's police statement, Amanda Sanders' Victim Impact Statement and court documents from Larry Lee's 1982 conviction for the kidnapping and rape of Katherine McWilliams in Florida. *Katherine McWilliams:* Sasha now had a name for the Florida victim to whom Anita had alluded.

The detailed first-hand accounts of two of Larry Lee's victims, as well as his own words spoken on the witness stand, provided much insight into the saga and psyche of Larry Lee Smith, whom she now understood to be a serial rapist with a predictable pattern. She had little doubt in her mind that if he was released from prison, he would strike again.

If Sasha wanted to learn what had transpired in the past, then she would have to continue talking to those who'd once been involved. Based on the documents she'd gathered so far and her interviews with Anita, Doug and York, she compiled a database of people she needed to interview: victims, witnesses, family members, and investigating officers. Many of the people on her list had retired, moved or married. Sasha wasn't a law enforcement officer, a private investigator or any other person whose occupation gave her access to special databases. Fortunately, she could turn to the internet for help. She had several websites and social networks at her disposal (Facebook proved especially useful). As details became available, she added them to the database. Her "Who's Who" list quickly grew to nineteen people.

In an effort to reconstruct what had happened twenty-plus years before, Sasha first turned to those who knew Michelle best.

6. <u>DIFFERING DETAIL</u>

Anita had provided the number of Michelle's best friend, Marci, with whom Sasha scheduled a meeting. Prior to departing for Knoxville, she called York to touch base. He'd be out of town that weekend, he told Sasha, but he had some news.

Just the day before, he'd served divorce papers on Chas, someone whom Sasha very much wanted to talk to, but hadn't located yet. No one seemed to know what had happened to him until York's timely encounter. Chas was staying at a friend's house on Blount Avenue in South Knoxville. York said that when he'd approached him, he'd brought up the subject of Michelle's murder. "Either you did it or Larry Lee Smith did it," York told Chas.

"Do you think he'd talk to me?" Sasha asked, encouraged by this news.

"I'm sure he would."

"Do you have a phone number?"

"Call me back this time tomorrow. I'll have it for you."

After two unanswered attempts, an early-morning call caught Chas at home. His roommate answered the phone and passed it over.

Oh, yeah, a half-awake Chas said, York had told him to expect this call. Sure, he'd be glad to talk to her. Sasha told him when she'd be in Knoxville and they agreed to meet.

The interview had been scheduled for a Saturday afternoon at Sasha's hotel, but Chas had been avoiding her calls all day. Sasha had been calling him on her drive to Knoxville to advise him of her expected arrival time, but really she was making sure their meeting was still on, that Chas wasn't going to back out. That had been his pattern all those years ago when York and DeVuono had tried to talk with him. He'd initially agree, then become evasive.

Sasha arrived at her downtown hotel adjacent to the Knoxville Convention Center, built on the site of the 1982 World's Fair, and tried Chas's number again. The interview was scheduled to begin in fifteen minutes. And again she got his machine. But this time she changed her message:

"Hi Chas. Sasha Reynolds again. Just wanted to let you know that I've checked in. Room 306. I've left several messages. Not sure if you've gotten them. But listen, that's fine. If I don't hear from you soon, I'll just head your way. York gave me the address."

That last part wasn't exactly true. York had told her that Chas lived on Blount Avenue, but offered no further details about the address. And Blount Avenue is a long, winding road.

Sasha's bluff, however, paid off. Within ten minutes the phone rang. It was Chas. He said he'd been sick. The doctor had him on strong antibiotics. "Could we reschedule for tomorrow?"

"Sure, we can do that," Sasha responded. "Ten o'clock?"

"Okay."

"Hope you feel better, Chas. See you then."

* * *

Nine-thirty the next morning, the phone rang. It was Chas. The thing is, he explained, he didn't have a car or a ride. "Could you come to my house?"

"Absolutely," said Sasha. She paused. "Can I get that address?"

As Sasha pulled into the gravel drive, Chas recognized the sound of the turbo diesel engine in her sedan. It proved a nice ice breaker as he hashed over the merits and engineering of the car. He opened the screen door and held it as they entered the small, comfortable living room and settled into chairs to begin their talk.

Sasha hadn't known what to expect, but she found Chas friendly and talkative. He had a people-pleasing demeanor and often broke into a sudden, deep-throated laugh. When Sasha began asking about Michelle, he offered pieces and recollections of that night and the period that followed, although, he acknowledged, some memories had become a little fuzzy.

Most of Chas's stories focused on the drama of his adult life, replete with addiction and domestic violence and a tendency to make excuses for the latter. Chas was quick to tear up. He'd had a lot of pain, he said, and most of it was currently due to the impending divorce from his second wife and her restraining order against him.

He was addicted to alcohol and cocaine, he admitted, but he'd been clean almost a year. In addition to being diagnosed with cirrhosis and hepatitis C, Chas reported that he was recovering from a serious fall at work eighteen months earlier. At the time, he was only three months into his second marriage. He was on a balcony spray painting a ceiling when he fell twenty-three feet to the floor below. After being unconscious for nearly a week, he'd spent another six weeks in intensive care.

It was September eleventh—a date he remembers for a whole other reason than terrorist attacks—when she left him. He'd totaled his car later that same month in an effort to do himself in. In court, his wife had refused his apology letter. Now, the divorce papers.

Chas had been praying that the papers wouldn't come, that maybe his wife would change her mind, but then up walks a nightmare from his past, Investigator Randy York. Chas had just finished working in the flowers in the side yard and was sitting at the table on the shady front porch eating Cocoa Crisps and reading his Bible when York pulled up. Chas saw the badge, the radio and an envelope of papers and felt the weight of disappointment.

"I already know what it is," he said as York approached from the car.

"What is it?" York made him guess before handing over the dreaded documents.

York's duty done, he switched topics to the cold case of Michelle Anderson. He told Chas about Sasha Reynolds's research into the matter. Chas said that he would cooperate in any way needed; he wanted to clear his name. He would talk to *anybody,* take another polygraph, *whatever,* if it would help.

But after agreeing to meet with Sasha, he'd had second thoughts about doing so. *Do I even want to talk to this woman?* he asked himself. *Is it any of my concern, my business?*

Then he reasoned that he owed it to himself and to Michelle's family to help in any way that he could. After explaining all of this to Sasha, he paused and considered his words. It wasn't so much that he owed it, he explained more clearly. He wasn't feeling *burdened.* He wasn't carrying any *weight* around—he didn't want Sasha to get the idea that he was implying some kind of guilt—but if he could help in any way, he would.

Chas told Sasha that he did feel guilty for being drunk that night, for not standing up to Michelle—"even though she was angry"—for letting Larry Lee drop him off first. Still, Chas clarified, he thought Michelle was being driven home.

After she disappeared, he could sense the "animosity" of Michelle's family, that at the very least they thought that he had "abandoned their daughter." That's one of the reasons he searched for Michelle with them so consistently for so long. He wanted them to see that he cared.

But it was in this part of Chas's account that he offered up a detail differing from the version he'd given to Anita and the others more than two decades before.

When Chas first told the story about the intoxicated Michelle, semi-conscious in Larry Lee's upstairs bedroom, he'd said their whole fight started because she called out the name of *another* guy. He said she'd called for *Mike*. Yet now, these many years later, Chas casually mentioned that Michelle called out for *Tommy*. This might have been considered a small and insignificant detail, but these were the names of two people who'd had significant—but very different—roles in the life of teenage Michelle. Mike was the boyfriend of Michelle's best friend, Marci. So Michelle calling out his name had the potential to cause suspicion and jealousy—and perhaps that was Chas's intention—but no one paid much attention to that detail. Marci trusted Michelle completely and Michelle had never shown any romantic interest in Mike. With Michelle missing, no one cared what name she'd called out.

But *Tommy* was a different story. Tommy was Marci's younger brother, and everyone knew that Michelle liked him. The summer before Michelle disappeared, rumors had floated around that Michelle and Tommy had hooked up (a story fabricated, by strange coincidence, by Larry Lee Smith). In

Chas's mind, Tommy was his rival for Michelle's affections. He was the guy she would have been with if she could have been, if he wasn't locked up in a juvenile detention facility out near Crossville. She'd made plans to go visit him with Marci the next day. So if she had, in fact, called the name Tommy instead of Mike, this could have had a profoundly different impact on the drunken, jealous, violent Chas. *Mike* would have made him angry, maybe a little confused, but *Tommy* would have thrown him into a full-blown rage.

Sometime in the year after Michelle's disappearance, and after the videotaped interviews on Anita's carport, Chas and his new girlfriend, Venus, ran into Anita and her boyfriend, Ted. Ted took Chas aside and told him that he'd watched his interview. Ted pointed out that Chas was laughing on the tape. He accused Chas of acting like the whole thing didn't matter.

"I think you did it!" Ted yelled at him.

"I thought we were gonna fight!" Chas told Sasha. His voice became louder and more defensive as he talked about his behavior on the day of the videotaping. "You've got a bunch of teenage boys over here making jokes, getting high, and a cop over here fucking with us. [Chas mistakenly believed Vance, the videographer, was a cop.] It's serious. A death. A tragedy. If I could have been more mature, had more composure, but..." His voice trailed off.

Chas leaned forward in his chair and rested his forearms on his knees. Then he shifted the subject from Michelle to his murdered younger brother, a topic that seemed easier for him. Chas explained that he felt a similar type of guilt in each case. He'd gotten angry with his brother, Bobby, for telling Venus that Chas was "drinking too damn much" and becoming just like their father. "Something I *did not* want to be." So he'd refused to hang out with Bobby, who was gay, and Bobby's new friend, Melvin.

"Hell no," Chas recalled saying when he turned down his brother. His chin began quivering and his eyes filled with tears. "Hell no."

Bobby never made it back. He and Melvin got into an argument and Melvin killed him, dumped his body on the side of the road and stole his truck. In another strange coincidence, his body was found near Crossville.

Chas had lost two people close to him in one year, both murdered. In both cases, he felt he could have done something, saved their lives, but in both cases he wasn't there. And in his last moments with Michelle and Bobby, he'd been angry with them, fighting, yelling, saying things he could never take back. And then they were gone.

In the two years following Michelle's disappearance, Chas never met Detective McNair—"Never talked to him," he told Sasha. But in the months after Michelle's remains were discovered he was questioned a number of times by York and Agent DeVuono, who also administered a polygraph exam. "I tried to do everything I could during the investigation. I told them what I did, who I was with, what we did after Michelle didn't come home. I gave blood samples, urine, pubic hair, and hair from my head."

"When you took the polygraph and it reportedly showed deception, did you know about that?" Sasha inquired.

"No. They were on the tip of saying that. The examiner told me that I was lying, that I had at least some knowledge. I really didn't."

At age nineteen, the year after Michelle vanished, Chas had a child with Venus, who later became his first wife. It was in that relationship that he earned his reputation for getting rough with women, at least when drinking. It was this growing reputation, in part, that made Anita and others even more suspicious about his behavior the night Michelle went missing. Eventually, his violent behavior sent Venus and their son packing. She moved out of state to be with her family.

Chas had another son with another girlfriend. He was a teenager now, at the house on the day of Sasha's visit. Through more tears, Chas explained that this son is the only family he has left. He said he'd tried to understand what Michelle's family had gone through.

Chas told Sasha that he was glad he'd kept the appointment with her and that their talking had given him a sense of relief. His teenage son came out with their small pet dog and Chas introduced him to Sasha. He seemed like a nice kid.

"Well, thanks so much, Chas," she said. "Hope you continue to heal." She stepped out onto the front porch and headed toward her car. She had to get back to her hotel. She'd already scheduled another interview.

For the past seven years, Marci had been the owner of a maid service. She'd called ahead to tell Sasha she was running a few minutes late; she needed to help her crew finish a job. When Marci arrived at the hotel room, despite the passage of more than twenty years, Sasha recognized her from her videotaped interview, though her wavy hair was now more blonde than sandy brown. Michelle's former best friend still possessed the same sense of self-assurance that was already evident in her teenage years. Now in her late thirties, she was a wife and mother of two teenage sons.

When Sasha first contacted her, Marci wasn't sure what help she could be. She hadn't been with Michelle, Becka, or Chas in the latter part of the night and she'd never met Larry Lee. Sasha explained that as much as anything, she just wanted to hear Marci's thoughts about what might have happened to her late best friend. Marci said she'd share what she knew.

Marci and Michelle had met at school a year and a half before that night. The two girls hit it off right away despite Marci being a couple of years older. They were pretty much inseparable, she recalled. Marci stayed over at Michelle's house a lot.

There'd been around twenty teens in their adolescent clique, gathering in one venue or another, goofing off, drinking alcohol and sometimes smoking pot. She and Michelle could hold their liquor. They could kill a fifth, walk a straight line and do it again, she confided, amazed herself at their tolerance. "I tell people now that I had a drinking problem when I was a teenager. My father's an alcoholic, so that's probably where I get it," Marci noted. "I gave my mom a lot of grief when I was young; I know I hurt her. Stupid teenagers. You think you know it all. She tried to give me a curfew, but when I was drinking, I didn't want to come home."

But Michelle's disappearance had changed all that. It wasn't typical of Michelle to go off to someone's house, the way she had with Chas to Larry Lee's. Michelle was trusting. She didn't know a stranger. She thought everyone was good. Marci knew Michelle would not have made that choice if she'd had less to drink. That part tortured Marci. "I didn't touch alcohol again for years and years," she said. She'd been scared straight by the chance encounter that had befallen her best friend.

Marci had nightmares, *bad* nightmares, for a long time. *"I still have nightmares,"* Marci told Sasha. "I see Michelle in a neighborhood somewhere, after twenty years, like she's just been there all along."

Marci and Mike married the year after Michelle's disappearance and tried not to look back. She focused on raising a family. She'd done her best to move on, to live a satisfying and productive life, but she still had strong opinions to express concerning the investigation into Michelle's murder.

"I just never understood how Larry Lee Smith was not charged," she said. "He was supposedly interviewed and admitted he gave her alcohol. She was a minor. He was the last person to be seen with her. How could they not have charged him with *something?*"

Marci didn't know what role Chas might have played that night, with his drinking and his temper, but she believed Larry Lee had killed Michelle. She always had.

Just like the other teenage witnesses that night, Marci had not been contacted by the police after Michelle disappeared. She'd never met Detective McNair. She had gone down to the Knoxville Police Department twice after Michelle's remains were found: once to be interviewed by Investigator York, and then a short time later to identify her hooded, yellow- and white-striped sweatshirt which Michelle had borrowed, found among the thick leaves on the forest floor still cradling her disconnected bones.

When asked about her brother, Tommy, Marci said he always seemed to be in trouble back then. That's why he was incarcerated in a juvenile facility in Pikeville, the Taft Youth Development Center. But Michelle was crazy about Tommy, Marci said. They'd visit him at the center every month. They were going to visit him the day after she disappeared. Marci claimed that she knew Michelle better than anyone, and it was her opinion that Michelle and Tommy were in love. She'd heard from some of the kids with Michelle at the party that night that she'd been saying she wanted to go to Pikeville to see Tommy (whether she was talking about her impending visit the next day or if she planned to go sooner is unknown).

The road that led to Pikeville, Highway 68, passed

by Crossville, a half-mile from where Michelle's remains were found. Knowing this, Marci pieced together her own nightmare scenario. She believed that after Larry Lee dropped off Chas, Michelle asked for a ride up to Pikeville so that she could see Tommy. In her angry, intoxicated mind, this seemed like the thing to do in the middle of night, especially after a fight with—and possible sexual assault by—her boyfriend. Larry Lee, taking advantage of the situation, had obliged. Somewhere along the way he'd stopped the truck, raped her, killed her, and then dumped her body on the wooded hillside off Highway 68.

"*That* would have been a reason to take her up there," Marci observed.

7. <u>THE SURVIVORS</u>

Hello? answered a melodic voice with an enthusiastic, girlish quality to it.

"Hi, is this Amanda?"

"Yes. It is."

"Hi, my name is Sasha Reynolds. This call might seem a little strange," she cautiously began. "I'm doing some research into the 1987 disappearance and murder of a girl in Knoxville, Tennessee, named Michelle Anderson. Larry Lee Smith, the man who assaulted you, was giving her a ride home, but she never made it."

"Oh, yes. That monster. I remember hearing about that case during the trial."

"I wondered if I could meet with you to talk about what happened to you. I'll come to Atlanta."

"Ahh..." Amanda said, thinking it over. "Sure. I could do that."

Amanda and her boyfriend arrived at Sasha's hotel room and the three got acquainted over pizza delivered in. Amanda said she knew that Larry Lee was to be released from prison; she'd followed his annual parole hearing outcomes on the

Georgia DOC website, but hadn't corresponded with the Georgia Department of Pardons and Paroles in years. After talking to Sasha on the phone, she'd hoped that he was going to be prosecuted now for the disappearance and murder of Michelle. That was what she remembered hearing all those years ago. Back then, a number of people had hoped that would happen.

Sasha filled Amanda in on the status of Michelle's case, and they revisited the events of October 13, 1989.

Following the assault, Amanda recalled, she'd been "a nervous wreck." For a while she became afraid to go anywhere alone, especially at night. She no longer felt safe in her car; she didn't drive it for weeks. Even stopping to pump gas in daylight felt too frightening. Seeing someone who resembled Larry Lee would send her into a panic, causing her to flashback to the moment of the assault.

Sleep became difficult; sleeping alone in a room was impossible. It was the choking dreams that haunted her. She had them nearly nightly for years. "I'd wake up in the middle of the night not breathing—gasping, crying and shaking," Amanda recalled, tearing up as she talked about it. When she learned Larry Lee was about to get out, the dreams started again.

Already high-strung and emotive by nature, the assault impacted Amanda's self-esteem. Although she had been the vulnerable victim—attacked by an impulsive serial rapist—Amanda felt somehow ashamed. But she didn't confront the shame or her pain. For as long as she could, she ignored them, buried them deep. For her anxiety, she medicated. In time, she came to understand that this was not the best way to deal with her trauma and eventually sought professional counseling.

She and Sasha walked through the trial and discussed the significance of Katherine McWilliams showing up to tell her story. "It was brave of her to come up and testify after all that time," Amanda noted. "I'm sure it helped him receive a twenty-year sentence."

Then she paused, again becoming reflective: "He took my innocence... He took my trust. I still get angry when I think about it."

Funny, friendly and down-to-earth, Katherine McWilliams was easy to be with. The auburn-haired beauty seemed totally at ease in her jeans, bluejean jacket and boots as she and Sasha talked over sandwiches in Sasha's hotel room in the North Carolina city where Katherine, her husband and kids had been living for more than ten years. Sasha filled Katherine in on the details of Michelle's case, and Katherine shared thoughts and recollections about hers, a hint of her native Brooklyn still audible in the shape of her words.

Katherine had not been easy to find. It was from Anita that Sasha first heard of Larry Lee's conviction for the kidnapping and rape of a teenage girl in Florida five-and-a-half-years before he'd encountered Michelle. But Anita was never given a name or a date or even an exact charge in that matter. From the court records of the Amanda Sanders case, Sasha had learned the Florida victim's name. She then made additional progress online in tracking down Katherine's married name and current city and state of residence. She had then reached out to Katherine through Facebook:

> I am doing research on a cold case. The primary suspect is a man named L. L. Smith. If you are the correct person, I believe you had an encounter with this individual in 1981. If you understand the meaning of this communication, I would like to interview you. If I have contacted the wrong person, I apologize.

* * *

Less than six hours later, Sasha had a response:

> I know exactly who you are writing about and I would be willing to help you in any way I can. Call me when you're ready.

As Sasha listened to Katherine tell her story, she noted that the spit-fire element of Katherine's personality was still strong, though tempered by years of ever-wiser living. Katherine explained that she'd dealt with her feelings about the rape pretty thoroughly back when it happened. So it surprised her that just the day before, while thinking about this meeting, she'd broken down in front of a friend. She said she'd had a long, emotional cry, and it was all related to the rape.

"Obviously, you're not over it," her friend had observed.

"But I don't think I swept it under the rug," Katherine told Sasha. When Sasha had first contacted her and told her that Larry Lee was soon to be released, Katherine had looked him up on the prison registry. A rush of emotions had come over her, although Katherine wasn't sure why. They had been swirling ever since. "At some point," she said, "I think I forgave him. I mean, I had my chance to go to court."

Still, her sudden immersion back into the circumstances of the case had opened an old wound. Katherine reflected on that night and how she'd handled Larry Lee. In light of Amanda's bold, daytime escape from their common captor, Katherine felt a small need to justify her strategy of compliance, although it wasn't being questioned. Then, out loud, she reminded herself that Larry Lee's assault on her was very different from the assault on Amanda. Amanda had been attacked in broad daylight in a busy urban setting where a witness had intervened. Katherine had been alone with Larry Lee, in an apartment, in the middle of the night.

"You were fourteen," Sasha reminded her. "Only fourteen. Your wisdom was amazing. You were still such a little girl!" Katherine's intuitive cooperation was instinctively clever, Sasha stressed. She explained that a power rapist such as Larry Lee will usually exert only the amount of force necessary to gain control and submission of his victims. If Katherine had not cooperated, Larry Lee might have severely injured her, or worse.

After the incident, Katherine finished high school in Florida, then moved back and forth between there and New York before settling in North Carolina in the late 1990s. She'd gone through a few bouts of the blues over the years, but overall, she felt her life was really very good. She was happily married to a good guy who made a good living. She had a daughter away at college and two handsome sons. The family took weekend getaways as often as they could. And she and her mother, who now resided in the same city, were very close.

Katherine expressed great compassion for Michelle's family. "I could just imagine her fighting back," she reflected, speculating on the assault that must have led to Michelle's death, "especially when she'd been drinking."

For Katherine, the thing that had been the hardest to let go of—the thing that she blamed herself for—was that she'd put herself in such a dangerous situation to begin with, that she'd accepted a ride with a stranger named Larry Lee. "It was difficult to forgive *myself*," she said.

8. <u>STEED</u>

FBI Special Agent Grey Steed arrived at the Starbucks in West Knoxville dressed in khakis and a blue shirt and wind breaker that accentuated the blue-green of his eyes. He was tall and handsome with graying hair and a friendly, no-nonsense demeanor. He reminded Sasha of Gary Cooper.

They ordered some coffees and settled into a couple of chairs by the window to talk. After his retirement from the FBI, Steed had launched a business in Knoxville, Grey Steed & Associates, where he offered services in forensic accounting, investigations and as a bankruptcy trustee. He informed Sasha that the FBI had officially closed their Domestic Police Assistance case on the Michelle Anderson murder investigation in 1991, but he remembered it clearly.

Steed entertained Sasha with some interesting tales about his history as a special agent and the series of cases and circumstances that eventually led to his being involved in the Michelle Anderson investigation.

Kidnappings and homicides were not his forté during the bulk of his FBI career. Raised in Nashville, Steed graduated from college with a degree in accounting and went to work for a large CPA firm before accepting a position with the Bureau. For seven years he was an agent in the White Collar Crime Program in the Chicago FBI field office. During those years Steed worked on some prominent cases in the national news, including the 1982 Chicago Tylenol murders, which claimed seven lives.

In the Tylenol case, FBI code-named TYMURS, Steed's job was to track fugitive suspect Jim Lewis and his wife as they moved frequently and changed identities using false social security numbers. After that operation, a case of white-collar crime in Knoxville demanded his expertise.

Jacob "Jake" Franklin and Cecil "C. H." Butcher, the Butcher brothers, were larger-than-life figures in the cultural landscape of Knoxville and East Tennessee in the 1970s and early 1980s. Born and raised in Union County, just north of Knox County, their father ran a general store and served as president of a bank where the brothers cut their teeth in the banking business.

In the late sixties, the Butcher boys began buying stock in numerous Tennessee banks, and their banking empire and influence grew. Jake Butcher founded United American Bank (UAB) and C. H. founded City and County Bank (C&C). Jake Butcher's UAB handled over fifty percent of Knoxville's commercial loans.

But the Butcher brothers brought more than banking services to the citizens of Knoxville and East Tennessee; they brought flair, flamboyance, and vision. In the late 1970s, when Sasha first moved to Knoxville, UAB's new Plaza Tower, a twenty-seven story, glass-sided high-rise on Knoxville's Gay Street, was a symbol of opulence, progress and a city moving forward. It remains Knoxville's tallest building. City and County Bank's Riverview Tower, built by C. H. in the early 1980s, is Knoxville's second tallest building.

The exceedingly handsome Jake Butcher, often in the news, was a major player in bringing the 1982 World's Fair to Knoxville. Held over a period of six months, the Knoxville International Energy Exposition, as it was dubbed, attracted more than eleven million people to the mid-size city on the banks of the Tennessee River. It was deemed one of the most successful world fairs ever held.

The prosperous Butcher brothers had secrets, though. It was these secrets that Agent Steed was brought in from Chicago to uncover. On November 1, 1982, the day after the Knoxville World's Fair closed, Federal Deposit Insurance Corporation bank regulators raided the twenty-nine branches of the Butcher brothers' banks. A paper trail of bank fraud in the form of illegal loans, forged documents and other evidence led to lengthy prison sentences for both brothers.

After the bank-fraud investigations and prosecutions were over, Steed stuck around and soon found himself drawn into a murder investigation with many parallels to Michelle Anderson's. In September 1984, Rosalyn Goodman—called Rosie by her family and friends—a thirty-five-year-old mother of two from Memphis, had driven across the state alone in her 1970 yellow Volkswagen beetle to spend a few days backpacking in the Cades Cove area of the Great Smoky Mountains National Park.

Cades Cove is a lush meadow ringed by mountains. Tourists drive its eleven-mile loop, leisurely stopping at the functioning grist mill and restored historic churches and log cabins along the way. Trails lead off for day hikes, and visitors can register to backpack overnight in the majestic mountains.

That's what Rosie Goodman did on that September day. When she didn't return home days later, as scheduled, the family alerted police. Her car was discovered at a bus station miles away, cleaned of all fingerprints and other identifying evidence with a cleanser-like substance. Two months after she disappeared, her skeleton was found by hikers. Three years later, the case remained unsolved.

Sasha had been living in Knoxville when Goodman disappeared and remembered the story of the murdered Cades Cove hiker. She'd followed the case in the local paper and on the news. It was a story that had troubled her greatly: this young mother, described as a free spirit, murdered by an unknown assailant in the peaceful sanctuary of the mountains.

At the FBI office in Knoxville, Grey Steed's desk happened to be nearby the agent assigned to the case, which had by then grown cold. They'd gotten a single lead years before that ran into a seeming dead end. A maid at a local rundown hotel claimed that she had met Rosalyn Goodman when she brought a man staying there back to pick up his camping gear. The FBI agent initially assigned to the case had obtained a picture of the man in question, taken during the grand opening of a new Bob Evans Restaurant in town, where the man had been working. In the photo, he is standing among a group of fellow employees along with *the* Bob Evans.

Harry Steven Mercer was this man's name—only it wasn't. The real Harry S. Mercer was a man in Texas. No one knew who this guy, using Mercer's social security number, actually was. "Close it," the other agent's supervisor instructed. "We'll never solve it."

"Let me have a shot at it," Steed said.

"What can you do?" the supervisor asked.

"I know from having worked the Tylenol case that I can get a warrant for this individual, John Doe, for using someone else's social security number."

"So what?"

"Well, if he was using someone else's social security number there, he used it other places, and we'll start tracking him."

The case was reassigned to Steed and that's what he did, track John Doe and his wife—also using a bogus social security number—all over the country. They were moving every three weeks and going from one fast-food restaurant job to another. Grey Steed got arrest warrants for both of them, but they stayed just ahead of him. He resolved to try a different tactic.

Steed decided he would get the case profiled on *America's Most Wanted,* then a relatively new show he'd seen only a few times. With this in mind, he planned to watch an episode that very evening. Yet the special agent would be in for a big surprise, because profiled in this very episode for another crime was his guy, John Doe. Turned out that his guy was among the "U. S. Marshall's 15 Most Wanted," for a rape and robbery in Florida. Real name: William Hewlett.

Now Steed had an accurate identity for the guy. He just didn't have any proof. "We had a pile of evidence on a guy who'd last been seen with Rosalyn," Steed explained, "just like the Michelle Anderson case. And also like Michelle's case, we had a pile of bones that animals had picked clean, so we couldn't even prove the cause of death."

Steed tirelessly worked the Rosalyn Goodman case for the next nine months. John Walsh's crew from *America's Most Wanted* flew into Knoxville and filmed a segment on the murder and the search for the fugitive. A viewer from Pearlington, Mississippi, near Gulfport, called the show to say that William Hewlett had been to her office. She was told to call the U.S. Marshall or the FBI if he came around again.

Hewlett didn't know he'd been profiled on the show. "So, sure enough," said Steed, "he backtracked to this place. The caller then slipped across the street and phoned the FBI." Hewlett was arrested.

"Now I had a guy in custody in Gulfport, Mississippi, that I thought had killed Rosalyn Goodman," Steed continued, noting again the parallels between the cases, "but I didn't have any proof of that, and he was going to be held by the U.S. Marshall for the rape in Florida. So I flew down to Gulfport."

"There's nothing to be gained by me talking to you," Hewlett told Steed at the beginning of their meeting in the Gulfport jail.

"Well, William, that's not really true," Steed countered, searching for an angle to entice the murder suspect. "The difference is that I can get you federal time for the murder of Rosalyn Goodman as opposed to you going back to the state prison for the rest of your life." It was the same offer Steed later made to Larry Lee.

Hewlett pondered Steed's proposition, contemplated his odds. "I'll tell you what I'll do," he finally said. "When I get to Knoxville, I'll solve cases that you don't even know about." So the FBI flew Hewlett to Knoxville where agents met with him and his court-appointed attorney. Hewlett pleaded guilty to the murder of Rosalyn Goodman. Said he'd raped her before strangling her with a piece of cord. Hewlett also confessed to a number of other rapes and crimes committed under multiple aliases in thirty-five states.

Steed received accolades for solving the Rosalyn Goodman case. So when the less-experienced FBI Special Agent Joe DeVuono began working on the disappearance and murder of Michelle Anderson, seasoned agent Grey Steed was assigned to be his training agent. And that's how Steed went from CPA to FBI, from crunching numbers to catching killers.

Sipping his coffee, Steed wasted no time in transitioning to the story at hand. He reflected on Larry Lee's discussion and demeanor the day that he, DeVuono and York had traveled to the DeKalb County jail to interview the prisoner following his conviction for the kidnapping and assault of Amanda Sanders. "The thing I remember most about the interview that day was that Larry Lee was trying to play games," Steed remarked, "trying to break his routine by talking to us, but not really giving us anything. He kept saying that he didn't do it, but that he might have some evidence that could help us. He was very cocky."

He discussed the difficulty in building a case against Larry Lee after Michelle's remains were found, and how difficult it would be to reopen the cold case in the present. "The problem is that the case wasn't treated properly on the front end by the investigating officer. Even if they had treated it properly, it wouldn't have changed Michelle's fate. There would be a circumstantial case against Larry Lee Smith that, without DNA or something that the DA would have built a case on, it's anybody's guess what would have happened. People don't realize how much of the district attorney's budget it takes to try a case in court."

Despite the many roadblocks ahead of them, Steed pledged to support Sasha in any way he could. "It's horrific that these predators are out there," he said. "They're always repeat offenders, the ones you have to worry about."

The conversation turned toward Joe DeVuono. Echoing the sentiments of nearly everyone who'd had any contact with DeVuono, Steed described him as a "super caring guy with a big heart." Sasha informed Steed that she hadn't yet spoken to DeVuono. She knew he'd relocated in the early 1990s and kept in contact with Anita and Sara for several years afterward, although they eventually lost touch. Sasha tracked him to the FBI field office at O'Hare Airport in Chicago, his hometown. But when she'd called that FBI office, she learned that DeVuono, too, was now retired.

"Well then," Steed said, "I think Joe will be willing to talk to you. I'll give him a call."

9. <u>MEANS, MOTIVE & OPPORTUNITY</u>

The week following Sasha's meeting with Steed, she received an email from Joe DeVuono:

> Grey Steed told me that you are researching the Michelle Anderson case and may be interested in speaking to me. If so, you can email me at this address or call me…. That case meant a lot to me; it stayed with me over the course of my career. I'm happy you are bringing it to light. What Anita and Sara went through is more than anyone should ever endure. By the way, how are they?

Sasha emailed back right away, and a time was scheduled for their call the next day. At the agreed-upon hour, her phone rang. "Hi. It's so nice to finally talk to you," she'd enthused to the retired special agent. "I've heard such favorable things about you."

Sasha praised DeVuono's diligence in his efforts on Michelle's case two decades before. "Your going to Atlanta, tracking Larry Lee there and contacting the assistant DA in the Amanda Sanders case, informing her about his history, was amazing," Sasha continued. "You were the link. You made them aware. That's huge!"

The tone of DeVuono's voice was warm; he laughed easily. And he laughed now at the idea that his work behind the scenes back then was such a revelation. "Yeah, it was kind of unofficial," DeVuono confessed. "But it made me feel better, actually, because of our lack of success in Knoxville."

For Sasha, the opportunity to talk shop, to probe the theories and possibilities of what had happened on the fateful night, was a privilege. She wanted to pick his brain, primarily in two areas of the cold case: what DeVuono thought about the treatment of Michelle's case as a runaway for so long after her disappearance and what his opinion was about the role Chas might have played that night.

After getting the go-ahead from his supervisor, DeVuono's first official interaction in Michelle's case had been with KPD Detective McNair. By nature, DeVuono is not a disparaging kind of guy, but even he had difficulty being diplomatic when it came to the KPD investigation. "Certainly, I wasn't critical," DeVuono recalled, "but I was surprised that the KPD was treating this case as a runaway. I couldn't believe this guy [Larry Lee] had a criminal history as a sex offender and that Michelle's disappearance wasn't being looked at as a potential kidnapping. There was some indication of an abduction. The indication was that she was last seen with a guy who had a history of sexual assault. It was pretty obvious to me."

But DeVuono didn't think all the weight of the mismanaged case rested solely on the shoulders of the late detective. McNair had supervisors, those to whom he answered. The case should have been transferred to the unit that covered kidnappings and homicides, he reasoned. A good detective assigned early, getting search warrants, could have made all the difference in solving the case. "When York got involved," he added, "it was like night and day." Now, years later, with missed opportunities and missing case files, the likelihood of ever achieving justice in this very cold case seemed remote.

"My instinct told me that Chas had more knowledge and possible involvement," DeVuono added. "I'm not saying he killed her or intended to hurt her, but I believe he knew something that he didn't tell. His lack of real cooperation led me to believe he had more involvement. And my feeling was influenced by his reaction when we tried to polygraph him. He'd had two years to build up some psychological wall to deal with the guilt."

Still, when DeVuono and Sasha Reynolds combed through the known facts, they concluded that Larry Lee alone had the means, the motive and the opportunity to have caused the death of young Michelle Anderson. They walked through each one.

Means: transportation. Larry Lee had a truck in which to assault and rape his victim and then drive her body out to the remote frozen hillside. By his own account, he had dropped Chas at his grandparents' house before driving off alone with Michelle, allegedly to give her a ride home. She never made it. His claim that he'd actually dropped her back near Chas's grandparents' house hours later seemed weak, illogical and highly doubtful.

Just supposing she had been dropped off at Chas's, Chas had no vehicle, although his brother had a truck. In the videotaped interview six months after Michelle's disappearance, Chas claimed his brother, Bobby, was in Texas when Michelle went missing, although Anita believed Bobby was in Knoxville around that time. If he was, why did Chas lie? Of course, none of this could be explored after Bobby was murdered just a few months later.

Then there was the fact that Chas lived with his grandparents. The house wasn't huge; Chas reportedly shared a bedroom with his grandfather. Where was he going to undress Michelle and murder her before catching a ride to cart her body off to the remote location an hour away?

Motive: Of the last two people to see Michelle alive, one of them was an impulsive, disorganized, violent, opportunistic serial rapist of young girls. Larry Lee had struck out with Becka that night, so he focused instead on Michelle, whose profile was a complete match to that of his other victims: young (15), small (size 5; 5' tall), attractive, vulnerable, and accepting of a needed ride in his truck. Neither Chas nor Larry Lee excelled in the area of natural intelligence, but one was a decade older, a practiced sexual deviant, and sober. No doubt, to some degree, Larry Lee was just playing it by ear, waiting for another opportunity to strike.

Chas had a drinking problem and a temper. And he was drunk the night Michelle disappeared, while Larry Lee was not. By both Larry Lee's and Chas's accounts, Larry Lee had carried the passed-out fifteen-year-old upstairs to a bedroom. What a friend twenty-six-year-old Larry Lee was to the eighteen-year-old Chas, whom he had just met that night, to be so supportive and interested in Chas having a sexual encounter with his young, unconscious girlfriend.

What was the payoff for Larry Lee? While a goofy, drunken Chas might have thought his deviant host was just being this cool guy, Larry Lee no doubt had ulterior motives of his own. He'd forced his estranged wife, Sara, to have sex with other men while he hid in the closet and watched. Maybe he'd hoped he could watch Chas and Michelle in the same way. Or maybe he thought he could get in on the action. Or maybe he was already scheming for a reason to drive Chas home first and get Michelle alone.

Chas claimed that he was trying to get "intimate" with Michelle upstairs, but she wasn't cooperating. Given Chas's known history of domestic violence when drinking, it's likely he got rougher than he admitted with Michelle, which supposedly sent her darting down the stairs and out the door. Suddenly Larry Lee was cast into the role of rescuer. Very convenient. Splitting them up by making Chas sit alone in the back of the truck and dropping the unwitting, intoxicated boyfriend off first would fit Larry Lee's modus operandi.

"Of course, Larry was a great manipulator," DeVuono reasoned to Sasha. "He could have easily created a scenario where he gets Chas and Michelle together with the ultimate aim to get Michelle alone.... All he had to do was work with the group, buying drinks and hanging out with them until he got them where he wanted."

Opportunity: What if Chas's role in the whole affair had been more than a drunken argument with Michelle? What if he had assaulted her in some way, sexual or otherwise? Then it seems unlikely that Larry Lee would have given Chas the cover story of taking him home first and then driving off alone with Michelle. So DeVuono and Sasha figured that last part, Chas being dropped off alone, was the truth. The part about dropping her back at the end of Chas's street later seemed more like an afterthought, something Larry Lee concocted when no other explanation would work. By saying he dropped her back at the corner of Cherry and Jefferson, at her request, at four in the morning, he attempted to shift the focus back to Chas, or at least away from himself. But with no investigation by the KPD after Michelle's disappearance, just about any story would have allowed him to get away with murder.

If Larry Lee did assault and rape Michelle (and everyone with knowledge of the case believed he had), it was difficult to conceive that he would have allowed her to live. Perhaps Larry Lee had learned a lesson in Florida, where he'd let his victim go and thought he'd covered his tracks. He'd been wrong, and served over two years in prison for his mistake. With Michelle, there would have been no way to turn back, if he'd raped her; no way to cover his tracks, if he'd allowed her to live. DeVuono and Sasha entertained the idea that, at the very least, he might not have intended to kill her. Michelle might have fought back when Larry Lee went for her throat—as he was nearly always reported to do in his assaults—and her choking death might have been accidental.

"If that's what Larry Lee did," Sasha concluded.

"Right," DeVuono said. And he ended the interview with an ominous warning: "He needs to be dominant and aggressive over young girls. He still needs to be watched."

10. <u>SARA</u>

Not long after Sasha interviewed DeVuono, she received an uplifting email from the retired FBI agent that reflected his reputation for goodwill:

> I enjoyed our conversation very much. By shining a bright light on Smith and bringing pressure to bear on Knoxville PD to reopen the case, you have done a great service to those who have suffered so greatly through Smith's actions, Anita and Sara especially.

Anita and the investigators had all spoken highly of Sara, but nobody knew her current whereabouts or anything about her present circumstances. They hadn't seen or talked with her in years. So locating Sara in plain sight was a complete surprise. She was listed in the Knoxville phone book under Sara R. Smith.

Sasha dialed the number.

"Hello?"

"Yes, hi," Sasha responded. She introduced herself and explained why she was calling. Sasha hadn't known what to expect from Sara, but there was no reason for concern;

Sara was still as good-natured and friendly as everyone had described. She told Sasha she had moved in with an elderly aunt and uncle in North Knoxville. She was helping take care of them. She and her three small canine companions occupied a room in the basement. "Kind of like Cinderella," she joked.

When Sasha asked about the Michelle Anderson case, Sara answered excitedly, "You know, I was just thinking about her the other day! Oh, please tell me you got more developments on that, 'cause he's getting out. You know that, right?! Anything that I can do to help, please count me in. Whatever you need me to do on this case, I'll do. With everything he did to me, I know he did something to her. He's a *baad* boy, and he does not need to be on our streets."

Despite battling several addictions and surviving a history that would wreak havoc on anyone's body, Sara was still pretty. She wore her dark-and-shiny hair pulled back in a ponytail. "Sorry for my appearance," she said in the deep, raspy voice of a forty-five-year-old lifetime smoker, apologizing for being in her work clothes: jeans, sneakers and a sweatshirt. She'd caught a ride to the hotel straight from work—she didn't have transportation of her own—where she was employed part-time as a pet groomer. She was working her way up from shampoos to cutting. It was a new career for her, one of many. The owner was giving her on-the-job training. "I like it," Sara said. "I've got three Pomeranians of my own."

Sasha offered Sara some take-out food, but Sara claimed she was too nervous to eat. "I do love work," she said self-consciously, making small talk as she tried to settle in. "That's all I do. I worked as a truck driver for four years. Been to all forty-eight states at least ten times and Canada and Mexico. You don't like smoking, do you?"

"Well... it's a non-smoking hotel," Sasha responded. "We

can go down to the parking garage."

The concept seemed to surprise Sara. "I'll be okay," she uttered and braved a smokeless interview, during which she sometimes launched into a deep and rumbling cough.

"Well, I'll be honest with you," Sara confessed. "I have some mental problems—post traumatic stress disorder, bipolar disorder, anxiety." She described the diagnoses she'd been given and explained that she'd been a patient at the local mental health center. "Smoking helps relax me. I don't have health insurance. If it wasn't for Cherokee Health Systems, I don't know what I would do." Sara rattled off a long list of medications that were, she explained, essential to her daily coping. "I've just got so much stuff in my head, not just from Larry Lee but everyone. I have nightmares every night."

It wasn't difficult to get Sara to tell her story. She'd been telling it for years. She'd reduced a lifetime of pain and chaos to a series of scenes and symptoms regularly repeated to doctors, investigators, social workers and mental health staff. It was a troubling and compelling tale to tell: neglect in the crib, rape at age five, addiction by twelve, pregnant and married to Larry Lee by age fifteen. She gave Sasha a synopsis of her life, including her marriage to and captivity by Larry Lee. Eventually, she felt relaxed enough to unwrap her sandwich and open her bag of chips.

"So, how did you get in this," Sara inquired, turning the tables on Sasha. Sasha then shared her own history related to the case.

"What time is it getting to be?" Sara eventually asked. She was fidgeting. Sasha could see she was seriously in need of a cigarette—or something more—but not willing to say so. "I don't know how much longer I can stay. I take care of my elderly aunt and uncle."

They called it a wrap, and Sasha drove her home. But she would meet with Sara several more times on her trips to Knoxville. She wanted to get past Sara's unconscious soundbites, her oft-repeated scripts, her guardedness and sense of shame. Usually, Sasha would pick her up and continue the discussion over dinner. Sara admitted she wasn't always sure how she felt about probing the past; sometimes she felt relief and sometimes she felt back in the nightmare.

Sara had maintained a relationship of sorts with her son, Joey, who was raised by his grandmother, Ruby. And through Joey Sara had also reconnected with the daughter she'd given up for adoption at six-months-old. When the girl turned eighteen, Joey had reached out to her. Sara described her relationship with her kids as "good" and produced pictures of some of the grandchildren—she had five and one on the way, Joey's wife was pregnant—but Sara's contact with them was sporadic. Her daughter had a close relationship with her adoptive mother. But physically, in the pictures, both Joey and his half-sister resembled Sara; they'd inherited her dark hair and elements of her good looks.

Although Larry Lee had not come after Sara again—not after he'd fled to Florida, gotten arrested, served time and then returned to Knoxville—she never stopped looking over her shoulder. The beatings, captivity, and sexual and emotional torture she'd experienced at his hands had left a permanent mark.

No therapist at the mental health center had ever been successful in guiding Sara through that or any of her other trauma. The meds were her fix, those and the alcohol she still drank, sometimes in copious amounts, more often than she admitted. Sara was accident prone and getting "falling-down-drunk" only exacerbated the matter, the evidence being the numerous scars, pins and plates that held her body together. If only the intrusive memories and thoughts would stop. If only her brain would give it a rest, and her mind would be still.

Sara felt deep empathy for Anita and the rest of Michelle's family. She was a compassionate person by nature and she knew the nature of Larry Lee. In the early years after Michelle's remains had been found, Sara ran into Anita a couple of times at a little club off North Broadway. Anita would quietly slip in alone and give her endless grief over to the inhibition-releasing power of the brew. On those nights, Anita would cry as the drink unleashed torrents of pain.

"I felt for her so much," Sara recalled sadly. "I knew how he was and what he was capable of, and there was nothing I could do about it. I felt helpless, completely helpless. I just knew in my heart, and I still know, that he did it. There's no doubt in my mind."

Sara did help in the investigation following the location of Michelle's skeletal remains. She'd never met Detective McNair, of course; he'd never attempted to contact her. But Sara had worked with KPD Homicide Investigator York and FBI Special Agent Joe DeVuono. Everyone who'd worked with Sara had praised her warm and generous nature. They could see that she was "a mess"—she'd readily admitted as much herself—but she also had an innate integrity, a core of genuine goodness that stood out, with a sense of humor and irony thrown in.

For Sara, Joe DeVuono's genuine acceptance and nonjudgement of her was uplifting. He appreciated her assistance and felt her pain. "I loved that man to death," Sara said. "He was very gentle and kind and made me feel at ease. And he understood. I mean, he was just awesome. He really wanted to get Larry Lee."

Sara was a survivor. Her addictions kept her spinning like a hamster in a wheel, but she held on. And she'd gained some insight into the dysfunction that had dominated her life, beginning as a child in the home of her neglectful and abusive mother.

"It's a pattern," Sara told Sasha. "It happens that way. I come from a long line of incest. Beatings and torture, even. That's why I was so gullible for Larry. Because I'd always been treated like shit. Always! I mean there was never a day I wasn't treated like shit by my mom, her boyfriends, my uncles, my cousins, even my brothers! It's always been there. I thought that was normal. I thought that was how people treated one another. Hell, I didn't have a clue for years."

One evening, as they finished a nice meal at a local restaurant, Sasha showed Sara some case-related photos on her laptop. As she scrolled through the images, up popped a picture of Larry Lee. It was an older image, grainy, a scan of a photocopy of a mug shot. Regardless of quality, Larry Lee's eyes peered menacingly and directly back at them.

"Oh, this one," Sasha said and began to explain that it was from Larry Lee's 1989 arrest in Georgia. But when she turned toward Sara, she was surprised to see tears pooling in Sara's eyes.

"It just looks so much like him," Sara said, choking back the tears. "That's what I see in my dreams."

Sasha encouraged Sara to allow those tears to flow, then reframed the circumstances for her. "Remember," she told Sara, "you're in control now. He doesn't have power over you anymore."

Sara's tears slowed. "I need a cigarette," she said.

11. <u>RELEASE</u>

Kidnapping is a felony known as one of the seven deadly sins under Georgia's state-sentencing guidelines. Conviction of one of these sins results in a minimum sentence of ten years served without the possibility of parole. During the sentencing phase of Larry Lee's 1990 trial for the kidnapping and assault of Amanda Sanders, the judge had informed him that because his term was longer than five years, he had a right to have his sentence reviewed by the Judges Review Panel. As an interested party, Anita received notice in 1991 that Larry Lee's case had been reviewed by the panel and his sentence upheld.

Ten years later, at the halfway mark of his twenty-year sentence, Larry Lee first came up for parole. Anita and other family members bombarded the parole board with letters and emails and ensured that he stayed behind bars. They continued their efforts each year his early release was considered. But now Larry Lee neared the completion of his twenty-year sentence. In August 2008, nine months after Sasha first made contact with her, Anita received notice from the Georgia Board of Pardons and Paroles that Larry Lee was being considered for their prison work-release program, a nine-month transitional plan leading to parole.

Sasha joined in the family's letter-writing campaign protesting any kind of early release. She crafted a letter to the attention of Ms. Shalandra Robertson, Director, Georgia Corrections and Parole Board Office of Victim Services, in which she carefully organized her research and laid out Larry Lee's criminal history. She covered his previous conviction for rape in Florida and emphasized that he remained a person of interest—in fact, the primary suspect—in the disappearance and murder of fifteen-year-old Michelle Anderson in Knoxville, a crime that occurred before his Georgia conviction. Citing verifiable sources, including the various people she had interviewed, Sasha profiled Larry Lee as a serial rapist with a strong, impulsive desire to violently dominate women. Most importantly, he would offend again.

While Sasha and Anita awaited the board's decision, Sasha made some calls to Pinellas County, Florida, and DeKalb County, Georgia, both places where Larry Lee had been convicted of sex crimes. She learned that in neither state would Larry Lee have to register as a sex offender. In Florida, his sexual assault was committed before the passage of laws creating the sex offender registry, so he wasn't required to be on it. In Georgia, the same condition applied, but there his conviction was actually for kidnapping, albeit committed during an attempted sexual assault, but not a sex offense by itself (he'd been found not guilty of the attempted sodomy charge in that case even though his lawyer had argued that he had been unsuccessful in his efforts to force Amanda to perform oral sex on him, thus acknowledging the criminal attempt to commit aggravated sodomy; the not guilty finding was somewhat baffling).

On December 5, 2008, two months after the last

notification, Anita and Sasha received a letter from the Georgia Corrections and Parole Board Office of Victim Services:

> The Board has determined that Inmate Smith is not eligible for the work-release program. However, the Parole Board has voted to proceed with parole in this case and feels strongly that inmate Smith receive intensive supervision upon his return to the community. Inmate Smith will be placed on Electronic Monitoring immediately upon release. You will be notified once the Board has set the actual parole date. The notice will include the name and telephone number of the chief parole officer assigned to supervise the case.

Then another ten months passed with no further news or updates from the Georgia Parole Board—not until Tuesday, October 13, 2009. A light rain fell on East Tennessee that fall day, with temperatures climbing into the low seventies. Anita attended the funeral of her father. He'd passed away the previous Sunday after struggling with a long-term illness. When Anita returned home, the message light on her answering machine was blinking.

She pressed play and listened to the brief message. It was from the Georgia Board of Pardons and Paroles. Larry Lee Smith had been released from prison, twenty years to the day after he'd kidnapped and assaulted Amanda Sanders in Stone Mountain, Georgia. Neither Anita nor Sasha—or anyone else, for that matter—had received prior notification. Anita called the Office of Victim Services and asked why Larry Lee had been set free. The person on the phone said it was because he'd served out his full twenty-year sentence. Anita also learned that there would be no work release and no electronic monitoring.

"It sickens me," she said in an email to Sasha. "At least my dad didn't have to hear the news."

Sasha immediately put in a call to Randy York, who, in turn, called Deputy Chief Gary Price at the KPD. Larry Lee Smith was bad news, York alerted Price, and he was probably headed back to Knoxville. It was at this point that an ironic twist of fate came into play: Tennessee may have been the one state where Larry Lee got away with rape and murder, but by returning there now, he came back to the one place he had to register as a sex offender.

"Tennessee passed legislation a couple of years ago," Deputy Chief Price explained to Sasha in a subsequent phone call. "We require anyone residing in the state to register regardless of the date of their conviction of a sex offense. I checked the Tennessee Sex Offender Registry and determined that Smith is in compliance with requirements and has registered."

Larry Lee Smith, the serial rapist and murder suspect, was now a free man and back in Knoxville.

Part Two
Connecting the Dots

12. <u>TRACKING LARRY LEE</u>

When Larry Lee was released from a Georgia prison in October 2009, he had to navigate all new terrain in a family system almost completely altered. His brother Brad had died while he was in prison. A half-sister, Carrie, who also lived in Knoxville, had committed suicide. Larry Lee's son, Joey, whom he hadn't seen in more than a decade, was grown, married, and also a father; Larry Lee had a granddaughter he'd never met. Joey and his wife, Natalie, lived in Ruby's old house on Fern Avenue. They were well aware of Larry Lee's history—the Georgia part, at least—and wanted little to do with him. They especially didn't want him around their daughter. Larry Lee moved in with his mother, Ruby, now seventy-nine-years-old and living in nearby Sevier County, southeast of Knoxville.

Larry Lee had reentered a world drastically changed—two decades into the digital age. Sex offender registries were available online, accessible in almost every home, and Larry Lee was on one. He was under someone's official radar at all times, meaning that he was obligated to report certain aspects of his personal data and any changes in residence or employment.

His page on the TBI Sex Offender Registry (SOR) showed his picture and included a physical description, his home address, date of birth, date of registration, date of last update, driver's license state and number, vehicles owned (or to which he had access) and their related tag numbers, employer(s), and dates and types of sexual crimes.

Sex offenders registered with the TBI are grouped into two broad categories: Violent and Non-Violent. Offenders deemed to fall into the violent category remain on the registry for life. By virtue of Larry Lee's 1981 Florida conviction that qualified him for the Tennessee registry— the kidnapping and rape of Katherine McWilliams, pleaded down to "attempted sexual battery"—Larry Lee was not grouped with the violent offenders, although violence was clearly a part of his pattern. If he didn't reoffend by 2019, ten years from the date of his release, Larry Lee would be off the registry altogether.

After Larry Lee's release, Sasha contacted KPD Deputy Chief Gary Price about the cold case of Michelle Anderson. In a series of email exchanges she reviewed the history of the case: Michelle's disappearance, the treating of her disappearance as a missing person—a runaway—by Detective McNair and the KPD, and then the finding of her remains two years later in Cumberland County when virtually all forensic evidence was gone. Sasha told Price that she'd met with York, discussed his work on the case some twenty years before, and had learned that York's investigative file was missing from the KPD. She inquired as to whether the file had been located and offered to meet with someone there to share what she had learned about Michelle's case and the recently released suspect, Larry Lee Smith.

Price wrote a polite and official-sounding response:

> As you recall, Michelle's remains were discovered in another county close to Knoxville, so the Tennessee Bureau of Investigation assisted that county with the homicide investigation. Investigator York did interview numerous people to assist the TBI after her remains were found.... We have not located the [Investigator York's] file to date, however, the official file would be kept by the TBI, since they would be the official investigating agency. Lt. Doug Stiles is the supervisor over our Violent Crimes Unit and Cold Case Initiatives. He would be glad to meet with you.

The Deputy Chief's message had been copied to Lt. Stiles.

Not long after first making contact with Anita, Sasha had briefly corresponded via email with Lt. Doug Stiles. He'd told her then that he'd never heard of the Michelle Anderson case but was interested in learning more about it. At the time, Sasha had been a novice to the case, but since those earlier communications, she had gathered much additional information. Now she was ready to share what she knew in an effort to stir some interest in this old and unsolved murder. After a couple of introductory emails, followed by a few attempted phone calls, Sasha finally had Lt. Stiles on the phone.

At first, she wasn't sure how open to be regarding McNair's inadequate investigation into Michelle's disappearance. Doug Stiles' father, Tommy Stiles, had been a police officer before him, a homicide detective. Tommy Stiles and Jerry McNair had been close. Doug Stiles had grown up coming to the station with his dad, and McNair had been like an uncle to him.

"I've heard some stuff about his work," Stiles said of his father's late colleague, "but I thought a lot of him. The only thing I don't like about this is that it [the lack of an initial investigation] will all be blamed on him."

The last thing Sasha wanted to do was alienate the KPD lieutenant before she'd even met him. She drew a deep breath and chose her words carefully. "I understand," she said. "He was a nice guy, I agree. I mean... it's not *all* about him."

"Okay!" Stiles said, suddenly shifting to an upbeat, take-charge tone of voice. "Let me know when you're coming to town and we'll get together."

The elevator dinged, the door slid open and Lt. Stiles appeared. He was tall, handsome and commanding, with dark, tightly curled hair, graying on the sides and top. Sasha joined him in the ride to his second-floor office where a Sgt. Walker, smaller in build and with an air of order and precision about him, awaited. Both men were dressed in suits. Stiles took his jacket off, hung it over the back of his office chair and rolled up his sleeves before taking a seat behind his desk. Sgt. Walker grabbed a seat along the wall and turned it toward Sasha.

"Okay," Stiles began in his professionally polite manner. "What do we have?"

Sitting across the desk from Lt. Stiles, Sasha felt that she needed to address the matter of the late Detective McNair. "You said that you were bothered that McNair might be singled out or blamed..." Sasha started to explain to the lieutenant.

"I kind of regret having said that," he politely cut in and the subject was dropped.

So Sasha launched into her story. She shared what she'd learned about the history of the now-cold Michelle Anderson case and everything she knew about convicted serial rapist Larry Lee Smith. She informed the officers about the trial transcript from Georgia, updated them on the people she'd talked and met with, including the investigators on the previous investigation, and the people she still wanted to locate. Lt. Stiles didn't say much, but he took notes. She made a point to emphasize Larry Lee's pattern in the sexual assaults, the similarities between them. With one major difference in this case: Michelle was dead.

"He'd learned his lesson," Stiles surmised. He referred to Larry Lee having allowed his earlier victim, Katherine, to go free. Larry Lee thought he'd covered his tracks, and then he got fingered by her, arrested and sentenced to prison.

Sasha had brought a lot of her research with her. She shared several documents with the detectives, and Sgt. Walker stepped out to make copies. She had deliberately cultivated no expectations in advance of this meeting, but it was her opinion, as it came to a close, that it had gone reasonably well. Lt. Stiles seemed alerted to and concerned about the gravity of the matter—the danger of Larry Lee back in the community.

"Well," he concluded, with a half-smile. "Let's just solve this." Sasha raised her eyebrows and laughed. His demeanor was professional, his vibe authentic. She liked him. Maybe, she thought, something would develop from all of this.

A larger-than-life statue of Sevier County native and country music legend Dolly Parton stands on the courthouse square in Sevierville, the county seat. A block away from the star's statue is the Bruce Street office of Chief Detective Jeff McCarter, with the Sevier County Sheriff's Office. Sasha had contacted the sheriff's office to determine to whom Larry Lee would be reporting as a registered sex offender residing in that county. Detective McCarter was the man.

In McCarter's wood-paneled office, complete with a mounted bass hung high on one wall, Sasha provided the stocky, middle-aged detective with a history of the Michelle Anderson case and the other known crimes of Larry Lee. He made notes and reviewed the timeline, tapping his index finger against his mustache as he studied it. "He's disorganized," McCarter finally pronounced in his Southern Mountain dialect.

Detective McCarter was referring to Larry Lee's pattern of abductions and assaults, noting that the serial rapist was impulsive and did not stalk his victims or plan his attacks far in advance. Like nearly every other detective in the area, McCarter was a graduate of the University of Tennessee National Forensic Academy, the premier school of its kind in the country. Leaning back in his office chair, still stroking his mustache absentmindedly, McCarter observed: "Twenty years in prison. We don't know what he's like today."

Sasha gave the chief detective copies of the documents related to the Florida and Georgia convictions. Only Larry Lee's Florida conviction, involuntary sexual battery (1981), was indicated on the TBI's Sex Offender Registry. All-in-all, not a very clear picture for the community of this violent sexual predator in their midst. "Had Larry Lee mentioned these other crimes?" Sasha asked.

When the offenders reported to him, McCarter explained, he rarely got into their pasts, their crimes. "Of course, they're all innocent," the detective mocked. "I just want you to know right off the bat, I'm innocent, they'll say. Then they'll tell you some lawyer talked them into pleading guilty.

"And the momma thing," McCarter continued. "Do you know how many of these guys show up here with their momma! I'm talking fifty-years-old, forty-years-old. They show up here to register with their mommas. It's kind of a running saying around here: Chester Molester brings his momma with him. You'd be surprised.

"I do talk to them," McCarter clarified. "I have a pretty good rapport with them. They do like me. I'm nice to them. I'm cordial. And they say to me: 'I appreciate you being nice to me. Not everybody treats me well.' I don't argue with them. I tell them: 'You follow the rules, no problem. You violate this and you won't like me anymore.'"

Detective McCarter updated Sasha on his contacts and communication thus far with Larry Lee, who'd moved in with his mother on Alpine Road in the Seymour community and had been "very compliant so far." Larry Lee had reported to him twice: once to register, and the second time a month later to tell him that Ruby had given him her 1988 Chevrolet Celebrity. So far, Larry Lee hadn't found work.

"I'll definitely have a renewed interest in him," McCarter told Sasha. "I may start sending someone out to check on him a little more frequently. With a lot of these guys, it's a domination thing.

"I'm just going to be very honest with you. Bottom-line, my role at this point is to monitor him. Monitor. That's not even a good word. We don't monitor. We register them. We verify that they do live there. The law says we have to do that once a year. We try to do that a little more often, twice a year or so. Smith reports in yearly. I've told people this before: Is the Sex Offender Registry to keep people from reoffending? No, it's so if they do reoffend, we know where to go to find them.

"I've got a mapping program that we developed here in this department. Got every sex offender plotted on it. If my patrol people get a call about a missing kid, the first place we'll go is the nearest sex offender.

"Can we guard Larry Lee Smith? No. I've got one hundred

registered sex offenders. I'm surprised some of them don't have electronic monitoring with ankle bracelets."

13. <u>NEW EYES</u>

In the months following Sasha's meeting with the KPD's Lt. Stiles and Sgt. Walker, she tried to stay on their radar, to keep a flag waving from the sidelines: Don't forget about this case! But she would soon learn that the KPD rarely handled cold cases. They didn't have the time, budget or resources. They didn't even have a cold-case investigator.

Then Sgt. Walker surprised Sasha with an especially encouraging phone call. He reported that the investigative file compiled years earlier by retired Investigator York had been located. A meeting was going to be convened to review it. They were going to contact the TBI. Sasha was ecstatic. She wanted to call everyone she'd met while researching the case and share the good news, but she decided to wait until she'd heard more. Past experience had proven that promising leads don't always pan out. Her caution turned out to be correct. Weeks passed, and no meeting had taken place. Turns out, the file had not been found. False alarm.

Another month or so passed and Sgt. Walker called again, friendly and apologetic. There had been four promotions in his department, he explained. They were operating on a skeleton crew. But, he added hopefully, it looked like the KPD might finally get a cold-case investigator. That was the last time Sasha had contact with Sgt. Walker.

Sasha was worried the case had hit another dead end. Then one evening she arrived home late from work and found that she had an email from Lt. Stiles, which simply said: "Call me when you get a chance, please." It was too late to call by the time she read the message, so Sasha had the whole evening to allow her imagination full rein. Such a cryptic line, and unlike any she had previously received from the lieutenant. Sasha wondered if something significant had developed in the case.

She called Lt. Stiles the next morning. He had news: the KPD now had a cold case investigator named Jeff Day. "This case has been on my mind a lot," Stiles said. "I'd like this one to be the next one we investigate." Lt. Stiles was sending Investigator Day to meet with Sasha at her home in Tuscaloosa, Alabama. Day wanted to review the materials she had.

Sasha was excited and hopeful about this development, yet still cautious after the missing-file false alarm. She decided that no matter the outcome, she had to email Anita. Hopefully it would comfort her to know that something was happening, new eyes were looking at her daughter's old case, no matter how much of a long shot it might turn out to be.

"Great news!" Anita replied.

Before Investigator Day arrived, however, Sasha received more good news, of a sort. The FBI's notes on its closed Michelle Anderson case finally arrived. Much of it had been redacted, but in those notes was another clue to a mystery that had bothered Sasha since she'd first received Dr. Bass's files: what had happened to the collected forensic evidence?

The physical evidence collected at the recovery site had been handled by three different law enforcement agencies: the Federal Bureau of Investigation, the Tennessee Bureau of Investigation and the Knoxville Police Department. Initially, the TBI had collected the evidence. In a Knoxville News Sentinel story published four days after Michelle's remains were found, Lt. Charles Coleman, then head of the Major Crimes Division at the KPD, indicated that the TBI had turned the clothes and jewelry recovered at the site over to the KPD. (Marci remembered going downtown to the Knoxville Police station when she was called in to identify her sweatshirt which Michelle had been wearing.) The University of Tennessee Forensic Anthropology Center report, issued by Dr. Bass and his team, indicated that the clothing collected at the site had been transported from the KPD to UT and from there would be sent to an FBI lab for analysis. Nobody Sasha talked to could remember for sure if this had actually been done.

But the FBI files Sasha received confirmed that the evidence had been sent to the FBI lab in Quantico, Virginia. The files stated that the lab had then returned the evidence to the KPD, by registered mail, along with written reports and recommendations. What had happened to that evidence once it got back to the KPD, no one knew. And the decades-old notes couldn't tell anybody where the evidence was now.

A few days later, KPD Investigator Jeff Day was on his way. It's a five-hour drive from Knoxville to Tuscaloosa (historically spelled Tuskaloosa, the one Sasha always preferred). Like so many of its southern counterparts, Tuscaloosa retained its Native-American name even after the Creeks, Choctaws and Cherokee were forced from their lands following passage of the Indian Removal Act under

President Andrew Jackson in 1836. Just five years before that, in 1831, the University of Alabama had been formed about a mile east of the young town.

Day checked into his hotel the evening before the scheduled morning meeting and took a drive around town, having never before been to Tuscaloosa. He was especially interested in seeing the campus of the University of Alabama, home of the Crimson Tide. Sasha had lived in both Knoxville and Tuscaloosa—more than a decade in each—and experienced the religion of SEC football firsthand. Day is a Tennessee Vol; his blood runs Big Orange, not Crimson Tide red. Still, he had to admit that the stadium was something to behold and the UA campus emanated a beautiful Deep-South charm.

The next morning, he crossed the Black Warrior River, passed through the charming, artsy streetscape of historic downtown Northport, and pulled into Sasha's driveway a few minutes early for their nine a.m. meeting. Of average height and build, Day wore the collar of his beige shirt unbuttoned beneath a blue sport coat. His close-cropped hair framed a pleasant face with a ready smile; his demeanor was friendly and outgoing.

"Hi, thanks so much for coming," Sasha said with genuine gratitude, shaking his hand.

"Glad to be here," he replied.

Sasha and the newly-assigned cold-case investigator gathered around an oval-shaped dining room table where they spread out Sasha's materials. Sasha found Day to be congenial and open to her questions. She learned that he was a North Knoxville boy. His mother, Brenda, had known Anita when they were kids in school. He was near the age Michelle would have been, had she lived. As a youngster, he had attended the same church as Anita's cousin, Susan.

And like his boss, Lieutenant Stiles, Day had followed in his father's footsteps to become a Knoxville Police officer. Jerry Day had been Chief of Detectives before he'd retired. There were a number of perks to this position that Day liked: the hours weren't bad, usually daytime and fairly flexible, leaving evenings for the wife and three kids or moonlighting as security. "It takes a lot for a family of five," he said.

The only thing he didn't like about being labeled a cold-case homicide investigator was the word cold. He didn't want families of victims to associate that word with him. But other than that, and the fact that he was the only cold-case investigator of a hundred unsolved cases at KPD, he liked the gig just fine.

To expedite a review of Michelle's case, Sasha gave Day her "Who's Who" list of people involved with the investigation—the names and identities of nineteen people related to the case: victims, witnesses, family, and law enforcement. Day quickly absorbed the facts and timeline as Sasha went on to describe the pattern Larry Lee had exhibited in the commission of his crimes, his modus operandi: offering assistance to attractive, petite young girls and women in a time of need, getting them alone, then choking and hitting before raping them.

"I'd love to nail a guy like this," Day remarked. He said he'd also love to see the look on Larry Lee's face when they showed up at his house to bring him in after more than twenty years, "Even if all he said was, 'I want an attorney.'" Sasha explained that Larry Lee had a history of lawyering up, at least he did in the early years of this investigation, when Ruby's money paid the fees. "These days," Day said, "it would likely be a public defender."

Still, he explained with some regret, the case would be hard to prosecute. "In real life, once the lawyers get involved, they don't even talk to the cops. It's difficult for us to prosecute murders unless they're almost open and shut. Without a confession, it's going to be hard."

Day would have to decide how and when he was going to approach questioning Larry Lee. If he went to his home, Day could talk to him, but it would likely be unproductive. If he brought Larry Lee in to the station, Day would have to Mirandize him, and Larry Lee would probably ask for a lawyer, and that would be that. Tight choices.

"Most of these cases, I won't be able to solve," Day said. "They're cold for a reason. A case like this, oh my God, it'd make my job worthwhile. If I ever get with the DA and get this case going..." His voice trailed off.

"The biggest challenge in this case is the absence of hard evidence," Day continued, "especially DNA." DNA evidence was increasingly the magic ticket in the effort to clear out cold cases. And in a number of the cases that Day was working simultaneously, it had done just that. But at this point, no known DNA evidence existed in the Michelle Anderson case.

Yet Sasha wondered if there might have been DNA in the still-zipped, hip-section remnants of Michelle's nearly-disintegrated size 5 Levi's, the ones with the still-readable label inside the waistband, discovered by the forensic team buried in leaves among her remains—but now missing along with the other forensic evidence carefully collected years ago. From the location of the bones inside the jeans, Dr. Bass and his team had been able to conclude that Michelle's body was abandoned there minus underwear (in addition to the missing shoes and socks). Someone had dressed her in a hurry before placing her on the cold forest floor.

Sasha didn't know a lot about DNA or whether it survived that long, but she reasoned that the semi-protected fabric in the crotch portion of those blue jeans, shielded by layers of thick, waxy oak leaves, possibly held a dried reservoir of bodily fluids. Whoever drove Michelle's body to the remote location had probably raped her either before or perhaps during the taking of her life. So the fibers in those Levis might hold chemical clues about Michelle's last hours.

But, of course, the forensic evidence was still missing. Sasha told Day what she had recently learned, that the evidence had supposedly made its way from the FBI back to the KPD. Day said he would look into it, as well as York's missing file. He was also counting on the TBI to have some records on the case. Sasha told him how she'd had no luck with the TBI, but Day assured her that he'd be able to get the files from them (if they still existed).

As the meeting came to a close, Sasha touched on McNair's investigation in the crucial first hours of Michelle's disappearance. It was near the end of McNair's career, Investigator Day pointed out, making more of an observation than a point. Day never knew McNair, but his father had commented on what a nice guy the late detective was.

"Now, I'm going to be honest with you," Day said to Sasha. "Runaway juveniles are very common. We get a lot of them. We don't blast an alert."

He was referring to an AMBER Alert, named for Amber Hagerman, a nine-year-old who was abducted and murdered in Texas in 1996. AMBER evolved into an acronym: America's Missing: Broadcasting Emergency Response. AMBER Alerts use a broad array of media to blast an alert of a child abduction fast and far, around the world, if needed. Police departments currently use an assessment tool to determine the likelihood that a teen ran away. Investigators ask relevant questions: problems at home, clothes or backpack missing, and so on.

Sasha pointed out that just to have had the community recognize that Michelle had been abducted—back when she'd first disappeared—would have been a soothing balm to her bewildered and desperate family.

"You can pretty much get a sense immediately of whether a kid is a runaway or not," Day noted. "The TBI won't issue an AMBER Alert unless certain criteria are met. We have training every year. But *Michelle's* case would have been a classic AMBER Alert, even if Larry Lee wasn't a sex offender."

As Sasha showed Investigator Day to the door, he expressed gratitude for the head start her research had given him. "I really appreciate this," he told her. Before he left, he turned and added a final thought, something, perhaps, that had been bugging him all day: "Smith likes his victims just old enough to be sexually attractive but young enough that he can manipulate them. I wonder how many more are out there."

14. <u>THE LONE NOTE</u>

The day after Michelle went missing, Anita and Doug stood opposite Larry Lee in the Western Heights apartment he supposedly occupied with his girlfriend, Maryanne. She was away in Florida with her son, he explained. Yet in the two years that Michelle remained missing, and the more than twenty years that her case remained unsolved following the finding of her remains, Maryanne was rarely, if ever, mentioned again. No law enforcement officer working the case explored who or where this person might be. If she existed at all, she was marginal to the case of a murdered Knoxville teen. But Maryanne Parker was real, and she knew a *lot* about Larry Lee.

When the redacted FBI notes had finally arrived in the early fall of 2010, there was one memo that stood out from the rest, unrelated to the *known* crimes of Larry Lee. For a while, Sasha gave it little attention, being drawn to the *obviously* more relevant information contained in the other memoranda. But periodically she would glance at the lone note, puzzling over its meaning and its message.

This lone memo, initialed by FBI Special Agent DeVuono

and his supervisor, described a booking report obtained from the Collier County, Florida, Sheriff's Department, dated 8/29/85—a year and four months after Larry Lee had been released from the Florida prison for rape. Collier County, whose seat is Naples, is several hours down the gulf coast of Florida's peninsula from Pinellas County, where his kidnapping and rape of Katherine McWilliams had occurred. Yet Collier County is just south of Bonita Springs in Lee County, home to Larry Lee's father and stepmother when he moved to Florida in 1981.

The nature of the crime and the identity of the victim were redacted. Certainly if it were another sex crime, Sasha reasoned to herself, she would have already heard about it from York or DeVuono. What was the 1985 Collier County arrest of Larry Lee for? Some petty crime? Was it worth her effort to probe?

Finally, Sasha resolved to check it out and contacted the Collier County Sheriff's Office. Through the Clerk of Courts, Criminal Division, she obtained documents that included the name of the victim: *Maryanne Parker.* The documents also contained her date of birth (a year younger than Larry Lee), the charges (burglary of an occupied dwelling and sexual battery), and the outcome in the Collier County Criminal Court (the victim had refused to testify).

Sasha had trouble tracking down Maryanne Parker, so she reached out to DeVuono, who, since retiring from the FBI, had obtained an Illinois private investigator license. DeVuono quickly replied with a probable address in Florida. Sasha used it to contact Maryanne by mail.

She explained that she was researching a cold case in Knoxville and asked Maryanne to describe her history and relationship with Larry Lee Smith, including what happened when she pressed charges against him in Florida and then didn't follow through.

Maryanne replied. She wrote that although the mere mention of Larry Lee's name in Sasha's letter brought on "bad nightmares," she would comply with the request and describe her experiences and her history with her sadistic ex-boyfriend.

She'd met Larry Lee in early 1985 when she walked into the Circle K convenience store where he worked and they struck up a conversation. He seemed like a nice-enough guy, so they began to date, which evolved into a relationship.

At first, Larry Lee was kind and treated her and her toddler son well. Then she stumbled upon his prison-release papers and asked him about them. He gave her the same story about "statutory" rape that he had given his family. Her intuition told her to get away, but Larry Lee could be convincing, and he convinced her to stay. He was a "changed man," he told her.

Then one day Maryanne walked in on him telling her two-year-old son to "suck my pop." Larry Lee had stuck his penis into a bag of sugar and was trying to entice the toddler by saying, "Want some pop? Here it is in my lap. Take a big lick."

Maryanne immediately confronted him, screaming at him.

"It's a game," Larry Lee said.

"You're sick," she responded. That led to a huge fight and Maryanne kicked him out. Despite her outrage, she didn't call the police.

But Larry Lee didn't take rejection lightly. Just past dark on a humid Florida night, he returned, broke through the latched door on Maryanne's screened porch, and attacked her. He beat her, choked her, and then raped her—all in front of her son. Then he sauntered out the door.

This time, Maryanne mustered enough courage to call

the cops. Larry Lee was arrested that night, but by the time the court date rolled around some months later, Maryanne declined to testify. "After I filed," she explained in her letter, "he came to me and said that if I didn't drop the charges, I wouldn't see my son ever again, except in a box, if they could identify the pieces. So I dropped everything in fear of my son's and my life."

In no time at all, Larry Lee had Maryanne back under his control. He even convinced her to return home with him to Knoxville. For the first few months they stayed in his basement bedroom at his mother's house. But Ruby, who'd gained custody of Larry's son, Joey, wasn't too keen on having another family downstairs.

To get this new girlfriend out of her house, Ruby helped Maryanne apply for the public housing apartment in Western Heights, the one Larry Lee lived in when Michelle disappeared. Maryanne's recollections of Ruby were very similar to those shared by Sara. "I tried not to upset her," Maryanne recalled, "but if you sneezed wrong, she would lose it: *Shut up! Keep it down! Get out of my house!*"

For a while after Maryanne moved into her own place, Larry Lee backed off a bit, gave her some space. She and her son were doing okay, but then he staked his claim again. "Larry Lee came back around, told me things were going to change." It wasn't a false prediction.

"Larry Lee made my life hell—getting me into drugs, forcing me into prostitution and making me have sex with other men while he hid in the closet to watch. Then he'd say he didn't trust me, always accused me of things. Larry Lee was violent. He beat me and my son. He told me that if I told anybody what he was doing to me, I would die.

"And to make sure I understood him, Larry Lee drove me to a dead-end road out near Sevierville. He had a knife and pulled out a gun, some rope and tape. My son, John, was asleep in the back seat. Larry Lee said that John could either be without his mom or he could join me, but that no one would be able to find us for a long time."

Larry Lee put Maryanne to work at a notorious Knoxville brothel known as Hazel's, named for its founding madam, Hazel Davidson. Hazel had been a bold, beautiful and flamboyant fixture in Knoxville's party scene from the 1940s to the 1970s. She pursued well-heeled men who paid for her time and her favors, and she also kept connections to the city's underworld. Married five times, her name became linked in 1968 to the still-unsolved murder of the wife of one of her prominent suitors, Knoxville businessman Harry Busch.

But as Hazel Davidson aged, she transitioned from "playgirl" to madam, running the busiest and most popular brothel in town. At Hazel's, a stylishly furnished and decorated bordello, beautiful young women served the clientele, which included cops, attorneys and drug dealers.

Larry Lee's estranged wife, Sara—still stuck in a desperate downward spiral—also worked at Hazel's. She saw Maryanne there and felt sorry for her. She understood what Maryanne was going through, what a controlling, twisted monster Larry Lee could be. She could tell that Maryanne was terrified of him.

One day he showed up outside Hazel's to pick up Maryanne, but she resisted leaving with him. He tried to force her into his vehicle, and she began crying and begging him to stop. Sara'd had a bit too much to drink, and she'd had more than enough of Larry Lee. So she propped herself against the car, raised her left foot, removed the spiked heel from it with her right hand, and began pounding him over the head with it.

"Ouch! God!" Larry Lee yelped. He put his hands up to

block the blows. He didn't want to attract attention and risk a confrontation in front of Hazel's. And Ruby had custody of Joey, so she would be very upset if he made a public scene with Sara now. He cursed and threatened both women, but he left.

"I only had that one chance, and I took it," Maryanne wrote. She fled back home to Florida just after the holidays, in the first days of the new year, 1987, shortly before Michelle ran into Larry Lee and was never seen alive again. "I bought a bus ticket and my son and I stayed on that bus for three days. It has taken me most of my life to forget Larry. He ruined my life," she confided to Sasha. "I don't want to relive it again.

"Sara helped me change my life, the first change of many. She was my only friend and I never forgot what she did for me and my son. Larry Lee Smith is not the type of human being that needs to be free. He is better off behind bars where they know how to treat men like him, give him what he deserves."

15. <u>CHANNEL 6 NEWS</u>

In the fall of 2010, when KPD Investigator Jeff Day began looking into the cold case, twenty-three years had passed since Michelle Anderson's disappearance and death. No one who knew the facts of the case doubted the guilt of Larry Lee, but the limited and lost physical evidence remained a barrier to proving it in a court of law. Neither the investigative file compiled by retired KPD Investigator York nor the forensic evidence collected by Dr. Bass could be accounted for. So… where to begin?

On the way back from a prison interview related to another cold case he was working, Day stopped by the TBI office in Crossville to meet with the agent assigned to Michelle's case. Jim Moore had been the TBI agent assigned back when the remains were found, but he'd been promoted not long afterward. He was replaced by Tommy Callahan, who had been hired away from the Highway Patrol. For the next two decades, the case had belonged to him. At the time of Day's visit, Agent Callahan was weeks away from retirement himself. Like his KPD counterparts, Callahan wasn't sure what had become of the physical evidence; he didn't even know it was missing. But he agreed to make copies of *certain* case documents for Day, who wondered silently why the TBI was being selective in their sharing, since the KPD was actually handling the investigation.

In the meantime, Day began following up with the people on Sasha's "Who's Who" list. After his meeting with Sasha, he spoke with York and interviewed Anita, Sara and Chas, each of whom reiterated the familiar details they'd already shared with Sasha. Only Dr. Bass would add something new.

Day made an appointment to meet with the retired forensic anthropologist in South Stadium Hall, underneath Neyland Stadium, where the Anthropology Department has been located in former dorm rooms at the University of Tennessee for close to forty years. Day followed Dr. Bass into a room lined with shelves of long boxes from which he slid out box FC 89-01 and placed it on the large wooden table before them. Bass removed the lid and Day's eyes rested on some small bones and other pieces of forensic material, items Dr. Bass reasoned might one day yield damning evidence. That day might have finally arrived.

When a family requests the return of remains after a forensic examination, as Michelle's family had done, certain bones or other material, which might eventually help determine the cause of death in an unsolved case, can be withheld. Inside box FC 89-01 were some bones—mostly finger and toe—and nails. Dr. Bass had determined that at least two of the nails might be from Michelle's fingers.

Shortly after Day met with Dr. Bass, he had lunch with Anita. He gave her the news about the remains Dr. Bass still had, including the nails. Michelle would have fought back, Anita assured him. It was a long shot, Day told her, but he would send those nails off for DNA testing. That was exciting news to Anita.

For his next move, Day decided to run a cold-case

television piece on Knoxville's WATE Channel 6 Evening News. When he told Sasha his plan, she was thrilled, but also wondered what Day hoped to gain by it. Everyone familiar with the case seemed to believe that Larry Lee was guilty. "So what will the angle of the TV spot be?" Sasha asked Day, "or is it just to reopen the cold case?"

"Usually we do these stories if we don't have a suspect and need the public to call in," Day said. "So, I don't know if it will help or not." But he had a feeling about this.

Anita was highly in favor of the television feature. All these actions and developments once again brought a glimmer of hope that Michelle might get justice. But Anita declined to go before the camera—a decision she'd made after some internal struggle and a flashback to the television interview she'd given back in 1989, when she'd declared that she'd like to kill whoever was responsible for her daughter's murder.

"It is still so hard to verbalize what I really feel," Anita confessed. "Sasha, you know that. No, I told Jeff I don't want to be interviewed on TV. Been there before and found it very uncomfortable. I feel guilty that I declined, like I'm failing Michelle by not doing it. But I don't know why they would need my mug on TV. Just another poor, pitiful victim. It breaks my heart when I see families being interviewed. I just think it's such an invasion."

The segment aired on the six o'clock news on Thursday, February 24, 2011, and ran for three minutes and twenty-four seconds. It opened with a graphic behind WATE 6 News anchorwoman Lori Tucker that read "COLD CASE" and featured police crime-scene tape angled across the bottom of the screen.

"Tonight a Knoxville Police investigator is carefully looking at a cold case involving the disappearance and murder of a teenager more than twenty years ago," Tucker said. The graphic shifted to a map of eastern Tennessee with a picture of Michelle on the right. "In January 1987, fifteen-year-old Michelle Anderson from Knoxville was reported missing. Two years later her body turns up in Crossville. Police believe Anderson was murdered and have a person of interest. Six News reporter Mona Nair has more on the case."

Nair appeared on the screen, a hint of her native Indian accent flavoring her earnest delivery. "This is the story of a Knoxville teenager who went out to a party with her friends. Police say they found an older man who helped them buy alcohol. Investigators say she was last seen leaving in a truck with that man. Two years later her body turns up in Cumberland County."

The graphic showed another striking studio portrait of Michelle, taken not long before her disappearance. Day's voice broke in: "She was a pretty popular girl, pretty outgoing."

The image changed to the red-brick Tacoma Trail house that Michelle's family lived in at the time. Nair continued,

WATE's Mona Nair reports on the reopening of the cold case.

"Michelle Anderson's case first came to investigators as a report of a missing teenager. Police say the fifteen-year-old left her home in 1987 to go to a party with some friends." The picture panned right to a young Michelle leaning against a palm tree, a photo taken on a family vacation. "Sometime that night police say she met this man, Larry Lee Smith"—the image switched to Larry Lee's TBI Sex Offender Registry photo—"who helped the underage group buy alcohol, then stayed with the crowd."

Investigator Day appeared on camera, seated in the KPD conference room. Mona Nair sat opposite him. "Jeff Day is still putting together the pieces of this story, but what he says they do know is that Smith was last seen dropping off the rest of the group at this intersection,"—the screen showed the intersection sign at the corner of Cherry and Jefferson—"then leaving with Michelle still in his truck."

Michelle's high school picture appeared while Day narrated: "What happened after she left with him, I'm not

Mona Nair interviews Dr. Bill Bass regarding the discovery and retrieval of Michelle's remains twenty years before.

sure. Only he can tell us."

Next Mona Nair sat down with forensic anthropologist Dr. Bill Bass in the living room of his condo. "Two years after Michelle was missing, Dr. Bass was called to Cumberland County." The screen image changed to a close-up photo of Dr. Bass and his team of experts in January 1989, excavating at the recovery site of Michelle's remains. "Dr. Bass was the forensic anthropologist for the Tennessee State Medical Examiner's System at that time."

"A man walking his dogs outside Crossville in Cumberland County discovered some skeletal remains," Bass recounted.

"Dr. Bass says the jewelry and dental records found at the scene helped quickly identify the remains as Michelle's," Nair said. "They believe she'd been murdered." Another recovery-scene photo showed red rectangular flags marking the locations of Michelle's scattered remains. "But with two years of decomposition it was tough to get evidence that would link the body to a killer. With the bones they did gather, investigators say they weren't able to narrow down an exact cause of death either. They could tell that she hadn't been beaten or stabbed." The screen image now rested on the picture of a smiling Michelle wearing the striped shirt with the turned-up collar and the crab medallion pendant, the one used in her "missing child" posters when she'd first disappeared.

Voice of Dr. Bass: "Could have been strangled, could have been smothered, could have been drugged—some drug used that rendered her unconscious or caused death."

The screen image now changed back to the TBI Sex Offender Registry photo of Larry Lee. "Since Michelle's body was found," Nair said, "Smith, the last person she was seen with, has spent time behind bars for a case of sexual battery in Georgia." The camera zoomed in closer on the image of

Larry Lee. "Today he is a registered sex offender living in Seymour. It's a case police still hope to solve." The segment wrapped with Day informing Nair that the KPD had some new evidence they hoped would help them break the case.

Sasha knew he was talking about the possible DNA on the nails, but he didn't specifically mention that in the piece. She let out a deep sigh of relief to finally see the case portrayed in an accurate way in a public forum. No more of this garbage about Michelle being dropped off at the corner of Cherry and Jefferson. No. She'd ridden off into eternity in the truck of Larry Lee Smith, who, Sasha later learned, happened to be watching Channel 6 News the very night the piece aired.

Sasha emailed Day right after she watched it:

> I really liked the TV spot. All the early reports always repeated the same nonsense about Michelle last being seen "when a friend dropped her at the corner of Cherry & Jefferson." This one paints a real picture. She drove off with Larry Lee, and it named him! Yes! Progress!

Day quickly replied:

> At least the truth is out. I've been by his place a few times. I just have to decide if I want to bring him in before the DNA test is back on her nails, or wait. Either way, he will have to come in and talk.

16. JOEY

Joey Ray Smith has a big heart, a quick wit, a firm and confident handshake and a sharp tongue which he can fire off pretty hastily if he thinks he's been given a reason to— and sometimes it doesn't take much. It was one of the first things Sasha learned about him after she'd made contact.

In Sara's talks with Sasha, she'd made several references to her son, Joey, whom she spoke to occasionally. "He's a good kid," Sara said. "He's *nothing* like his father. He won't have anything to do with him."

Joey was now thirty years old and living in the Fern Avenue house with his wife and daughter, with another child on the way. Sasha had driven by there one day when she was in Knoxville. She just wanted to see the place. She guided her vehicle down the narrow, sidewalkless street and stopped before she reached the house. But the high elevation of the snug street and the absence of any trees or bushes in front of the houses made remaining discreet a challenge. She'd been there only a minute or so when Joey's wife, Natalie, walked out into the small front yard. Her gaze was poised and direct. She wasn't afraid, or if she was, she contained it well. Can I help you? she seemed to ask through her arched eyebrows. It hadn't been Sasha's intention to alarm this assertive and protective young wife and mother.

"I'm doing some research into an old matter," Sasha said.

"I think I know what this is about," Natalie said. "He's bad. He's not allowed to come around here. We're moving. We bought another house."

Sasha was caught off guard. Whenever she had contacted people associated with Larry Lee or Michelle Anderson, they usually expressed surprise (or relief) that someone was still interested in that old case. But Natalie knew exactly why Sasha was there, even if she didn't know exactly who Sasha was. Sasha would learn that police had been checking into the possibility that Larry Lee had been doing some work in South Knoxville too close to a daycare, a violation for a registered sex offender. Nothing came of that investigation, but word got around, because Natalie kept a few preschoolers along with her own child at the house. A couple of pieces of outdoor play equipment dotted the tiny front yard. It wasn't really a daycare; Natalie was more like a babysitter. But a neighbor who knew about Larry Lee had printed flyers and distributed them throughout the neighborhood. Natalie knew her family was being scrutinized, which is why she and Joey had decided to move.

"Please tell your husband that I'd like to talk with him," Sasha said, handing Natalie her card. "If he's willing. No pressure."

"All right," Natalie said, putting on a cordial but guarded smile. "I guess I could do that." It was a crazy long-shot, and as Sasha expected, Joey didn't call. But now he knew she was around and wanting to talk with him; she had established that much. Sasha wanted to know what Joey knew—what he believed—about the crimes of his biological father, and how those crimes had been handled within the family.

After the chance encounter with Joey's wife, Sasha located him online. She could see some of his online communications, in which he sometimes displayed his sharp-tongue, cutting banter and quick, caustic wit. He also posted numerous loving messages to and about his wife, his kids and his grandmother-turned-adoptive-mother, Ruby.

After the television spot ran on the WATE 6 news, Sasha reached out to Joey through a work email address he'd listed on his Facebook page. She attached a link to the news feature and sent the following message:

> Joey, I've been researching this case for a couple of years. I would like to speak to you briefly and ask a few questions. I don't want to intrude or upset you, but I need your insights into a few issues. Please.

Within a few days she had a response:

> I was seven when this happened... I'm not sure what kinda help I could be seeing as I disowned him but your [sic] welcome to call me anytime after five and before nine.

He included his cell phone number.

Nine years earlier, when Joey was twenty-one and his biological half-sister—the daughter Sara had given up at age six months—was eighteen, he'd searched for and found her. On the date of the scheduled meeting with Sasha, a Sunday, Joey and Natalie had attended the funeral service for his half-sister's adoptive mother, who'd died suddenly. Joey had been a pallbearer at the funeral.

"Sorry for being late," he apologized as he and Natalie took a seat in Sasha's hotel room. "I'm a stickler for being on time."

They were a handsome couple. Joey was of average height with a strong, stocky build. Sasha had seen a picture of Joey and Sara seated side-by-side when Joey was about eleven and Sara twenty-six. She could see that Joey had his mother's eyes and dark hair. Yet his wavy mouth and sloping nose resembled those of Larry Lee.

"We've met before," Natalie joked to Sasha. In the fifth month of her second pregnancy, she looked lovely, her complexion lightly freckled, her make-up understated and tasteful. Natalie's light-brown hair, layered in a stylish cut, came to just below her shoulders, and her straight-from-the-funeral attire was low-key.

The common denominator of this encounter was that both Sasha and Joey wanted answers. It was the only reason Joey had agreed to come. He knew, of course, about the Georgia kidnapping for which Larry Lee had done twenty years. And he'd heard something (very little really) about the case in Florida, but he'd never heard about the Knoxville case of Michelle Anderson—or the fact that his father was a suspect in her disappearance and murder—until he saw the cold-case feature on the news.

Joey recalled Larry Lee leaving town all those years ago. Ruby had switched rooms with Joey shortly after she'd gotten custody, giving him the bigger of the two bedrooms on the house's main floor. In 1987, the year Michelle disappeared, Joey was six, going on seven; he remembered because he was just old enough to walk to Pippen Elementary. His father came into his bedroom one night to say good-bye. He told his son that he was heading over to Georgia for a while.

If Joey's childhood recollection of events is correct, that would mean that sometime during that first year after Michelle disappeared, Larry Lee left town for Georgia. But he was back in Knoxville by the time Michelle's remains were found in early 1989. Joey was then eight and knew nothing, of course, about that case. But he knew about a cut brake line, because the family talked about that in front of him. Seems Larry Lee had gotten into his truck one day, discovered that he had no brakes, and crashed into a house down the hill at the end of the street. After that, Uncle Brad stayed with them until Larry Lee left town again.

Sasha asked Joey to describe his relationship with his father before he left town. Joey couldn't recall having much of one. He remembered playing with the kids across the street, but he couldn't really remember spending time with Larry Lee or him even being around all that often. It seemed to him that Ruby sent Larry Lee off to do things a lot of the time. "I never really understood that," he said. "I just thought it was normal."

"Do you think she was sending him away because of you?" Sasha asked.

Joey squinted his eyes as he pondered. "Looking back? Yeah."

If Ruby was feeling protective of Joey around Larry Lee in the first years she had custody of her grandson, she'd apparently relaxed that standard by the summer of 1989, after Michelle's remains were found, the summer Joey turned nine. He recalled spending several weeks with Larry Lee in Lawrenceville, Georgia, before he became homesick and returned to Knoxville. He remembered that Larry Lee drove a black hatchback during that time (the AMC Pacer identified in his assault of Amanda Sanders) and took him to the laser show on Stone Mountain with the carved men atop carved horses galloping out of the rock.

The timing of that summer visit would have been between Larry Lee's July "battery" of young Caroline Bronti in Lawrenceville and his October "kidnapping and assault" of Amanda Sanders in Stone Mountain. Larry Lee came home to Knoxville a time or two after that summer, Joey recalled, but by the following spring—just after the trial—he was told that his father was going away and wouldn't be back for a long time. Few details were offered, and the subject would not be discussed again until Joey happened upon a video tape six years later.

Larry Lee's older brother, Brad, lived next door to Ruby. His sister, Nancy, and her kids lived on the other side. So Joey always remembered his aunt and uncle being around. Brad was tall, dark and engaging. At six feet, he was a half-foot taller than his little brother. He was also a wild, abusive alcoholic and a petty criminal who sometimes burglarized houses, dealt drugs, and stole air conditioners out of new construction for the copper they contained. Like his little brother, he was frequently in need of legal defense.

Brad had served a stint in the Marines, but he'd been discharged for selling cartons of cigarettes out of the commissary in Korea. No one ever told Joey that story; he'd found his uncle's discharge papers. No doubt Brad's lifestyle was far from the model Joey needed, but he was the only consistent father-figure Joey ever had. "He tried to show me some things," Joey said, a crooked grin spreading across his face. "*Some of them*, I'm not sure why he did."

Larry Lee had always looked up to his *bad-ass* brother, four years his senior. A *bad-ass* was something Larry Lee aspired to be. When he bragged of his drinking prowess, he was actually talking about Brad. When he claimed he'd been wounded in combat—as he'd done with Katherine McWilliams right after he'd raped her—he'd again been talking about Brad. Although the latter story wasn't true for Brad either. Brad had been shot in the ankle by a KPD officer as he scaled a fence behind his mother's house.

To anyone outside the family, Brad always took up for his baby brother, but he would confront Ruby for always defending and protecting him. "He's your brother," Ruby would remind Brad. A fierce argument erupted between them one day when Joey was young, and it was over Larry Lee. Joey didn't know the exact cause of the conflict, except that Brad was again accusing his mother of babying her younger son. In the emotion-charged altercation, Brad became so enraged that he threw a chair through the living room's plate-glass picture window and into the front yard. Joey was sure a police record of that incident existed somewhere.

Ruby invested heavily in Joey; he became the center of her world. And the way she cared for the center of her world was to provide: to work, to earn money, to give *things*. Materially, Joey wanted for little. Ruby was a hard worker. She often worked three jobs simultaneously: housekeeping, waitressing and overnight patient sitting. To sustain her grueling schedule, according to some well acquainted with her at the time, she sometimes popped "Black Beauties," a then-popular amphetamine supplied by one of her drug-dealing sons.

"She wasn't an emotional person," Joey recalled. "When I would get mad at her, her way of making me *un-mad* would be to buy me something. I liked getting stuff, so..." Joey smiled wryly, then continued. "I loved my mom very much,"—he referred to Ruby as "mom"; she'd legally adopted him when he was twelve—"and she loved her kids, but she wasn't sure how to raise them. She tried to give them everything. Brad went wrong early, and Larry Lee followed. She didn't know how to stop it," he theorized, "so she minimized it."

Emotionally, Joey needed structure and a little more of

Ruby's time. She assumed responsibility for everything he did, no doubt shades of her parenting style with Larry Lee. "When I was growing up, I could do nothing wrong," Joey recalled. "When I set my desk on fire in second grade, she blamed herself, quit smoking and got rid of all the cigarettes and lighters in the house."

Regarding his biological mother, Sara, Joey had grown up feeling disappointed, hurt and resentful toward her. She had visitation, but was only as dependable as her addictions allowed, which was not very much. For a time, Joey became an angry kid. And he had questions about his father, too, but he kept them to himself until his preteen years. When he finally asked Ruby about Larry Lee, her answer revealed that she may have come to terms with the man his father had become.

"Never forget he is your father," Ruby told Joey.

"But she also said that I needed to know my limits in being around him," Joey recalled. "She didn't say that she thought he was *guilty*, but when she told me that, I knew she thought there was some truth to it."

It is hard to imagine that Ruby could have sat in the Georgia courtroom, heard the testimony of Katherine, Amanda and the witnesses, and the summation of Assistant DA Elizabeth MacNamara, and not had a change of mind, a shift in awareness, about the true nature of her son.

When Joey was fourteen or fifteen, he found a VHS tape tucked away in the linen closet. He popped it into the VCR. "It was a TV news report about Larry Lee's trial in Georgia, about him getting found guilty and sentenced," Joey explained. "And it upset me a little bit. I asked my mom what had really happened, and the tape disappeared and never got talked about again."

"What did she say really happened?" Sasha inquired.

Ruby told Joey what Larry Lee had told her—the explanation that he'd offered on the witness stand in Georgia—that it was all misunderstood flirtation. Larry Lee thought Amanda was flirting with him, he put his hand on her leg and she screamed *rape*. "I never believed that," Joey clarified, "because you don't get sentenced to twenty years in prison for touching someone. I never knew exactly what happened."

Ruby also told Joey, after he was grown, that of the five kids she'd raised, he was the only one "she raised right."

"How did she raise you differently?" Sasha asked.

"I don't know," Joey laughed in reply, "because I had my fair share of problems growing up." He speculated that one thing Ruby had done differently with him was to get him out of the neighborhood, placing him in boarding schools and private day schools.

In the twenty years that Larry Lee remained in a Georgia prison, Joey visited him twice. The first time, when he was younger, he'd gone with Ruby. The second time, when he was seventeen, about a year after his Uncle Brad died, he drove down alone in his new car, the one that Ruby had just bought him. Larry Lee told him that his late Uncle Brad was probably his father. It was an accusation Larry Lee had thrown at Sara several times before. Joey was filled with rage. It wasn't the idea of Brad being his father that so offended him—actually, that was kind of appealing, certainly more desirable than Larry Lee—it was his timing. "How could he sit there and tell me that in my face after that person was dead?" Joey asked Sasha. He said he'd asked Sara about it as soon as he got back, and she denied it, just as she had since she first got pregnant. Joey didn't visit Larry Lee again. He made the trip one more time, driving Ruby down, but he waited outside.

It was a stint in the military, Joey reasoned, that helped him mature. "I think the fact that I was raised without my biological parents made me want to do something good so my kids didn't have to grow up like I did," he said. So far, he had succeeded with that goal.

When Larry Lee was released in the fall of 2009, Joey was away on a job and would be gone for several months. Larry Lee stayed away from the Fern Avenue house, living with Ruby in neighboring Sevier County, but she was soon diagnosed with cancer and moved back into her old home so Natalie could help take care of her. As Ruby's cancer progressed, she alternated staying with Natalie—Joey was still away with work—and with her daughter, Nancy, who still lived in Knoxville. Larry Lee sometimes stayed with Nancy, too, although this information was never shared with the officers he reported to as a registered sex offender. He ended up sharing a trailer with an older couple in nearby Blount County, just south of Knoxville. Larry Lee would call Natalie to check on Ruby, but he wasn't welcome at the house.

After Joey returned home, he established the terms for Larry Lee to be able to visit his dying mother: he couldn't come over when Natalie and their daughter were home unless Joey was also there, and he had to be "one-hundred percent honest" about anything Joey and Natalie asked him related to his offenses. Larry Lee agreed.

On one of his first visits, Natalie asked him about his Florida conviction. She wanted to know exactly what happened in that case. Well, Larry Lee explained, he was twenty and Katherine was seventeen. In his "one-hundred-percent truthful" version, he said they were dating and her parents didn't approve, so they turned him in to the police.

At this point in the interview the conversation shifted. Now it was time for Sasha to share some information. Joey didn't know the specifics of any of his father's crimes, which is why he'd agreed to meet Sasha in the first place.

Sasha described Larry Lee as a long-term compulsive liar by habit, so she wasn't surprised he'd lied about the Florida conviction. He certainly couldn't risk telling his son and daughter-in-law the awful truth. Sasha laid out the details in a blunt and straightforward manner. Larry Lee was twenty. His victim was fourteen and needed a ride home. He lured her into his truck with words aimed to win her trust, and then he got her alone, punched and choked her, ordered her to undress, raped her, made her clean-up and cover her eyes, and then he drove her home. She explained that Larry Lee hadn't been charged with *statutory rape* in that case, as he'd told Joey and Natalie. Instead, a plea deal had been offered to him on assault, kidnapping and rape charges in order to avoid the cost of a trial. Larry Lee had accepted, pleading guilty to the lesser charge of *attempted sexual battery*.

Joey sighed. "I want to know a lot of things, but at the same time, I don't want to. You know what I mean?" As disturbing as the other crimes of Larry Lee might be, it was the questions about what happened within the family that haunted Joey the most. Those were the answers he wanted from his father: *Did you tie Sara up in the basement? Did you touch any kids in my family? Did you ever touch me?*

Over the years, Sara had told Joey vague stories about Larry Lee tying her up in the basement and having his way with her. Joey didn't really place much stock in these stories, because he didn't place much stock in Sara. "My biological mother has a lot of imagination," he observed. It wasn't that he believed Larry Lee over his mother—after all, he hardly knew the man—but Sara had lied to him about coming to see him or pick him up so many times that he'd written off her reliability. But at the same time, when pressed, he acknowledged that there was probably some basis of truth to them.

Then there was the question of his older cousin Jenny. She was the daughter of Larry Lee's sister, Nancy. Joey had heard whispers that Larry Lee had possibly molested Jenny when he was a teenager and she was very young. When it came to all of these stories, he said, "I wasn't sure what to believe and my mother [Ruby] wouldn't discuss it. You know, Larry Lee said he would be honest with me. After all this, I want to ask him if he did it."

Lately, Larry Lee had been calling. Joey usually didn't answer, but he'd responded to his father's call a few days after the TV spot ran on the evening news. "I saw you on TV, just so you know," Joey said to him. "Did you see it?"

"I did see it," Larry Lee answered.

"Pretty interesting."

Joey would learn that Larry Lee had been watching the news while sitting with the older couple who had taken him into their trailer. It wasn't long before he had to find a new place to live.

"Had Ruby ever come to see Larry Lee as guilty?" Sasha asked. Natalie shook her head no. She didn't think Ruby had. Although she recalled Ruby's strange behavior one time when Larry Lee stopped by the house early, when Joey wasn't home and Natalie and their daughter had not yet departed. At this point, Ruby was extremely weak and seldom rose from her bed. Yet on this occasion, upon hearing Larry Lee's voice in the adjoining room, she pulled her frail body from her resting place, as if willing it into the living room.

"Granny, what are you doing!?" Natalie asked in shock.

"She's protecting you from me," cracked Larry Lee.

* * *

Joey and Natalie had a couple cookouts in the spring and summer of 2010. They knew that Ruby wouldn't live much longer, so they invited the family to come spend time with her. Larry Lee was invited, too, and he came.

One weekend Larry Lee earned some needed cash helping Joey pour concrete in the Fern Avenue driveway. He mentioned to his son more than once that he didn't know how hard Larry Lee had it. He said a few thousand dollars would sure go a long way to help straighten things out. But Natalie had put her foot down. She said she and Joey had a family to support and there was no way any money was going out of their bank account and into his.

Later, Joey was driving down the 17th Street exit ramp off I-40 in Knoxville and suddenly there was Larry Lee. On the exit ramp. Panhandling. He was holding up a sign that said he needed money for gas. "I debated just driving on by," Joey said, chuckling, "but he looked at me, and I saw him look at me, and it was like: *Okay, I'm gonna stop.* So I said, 'Do you need me to take you to get gas?'"

"No. I can't let you do that," Larry Lee said.

"I'm not just going to leave you here."

"It's my scam," Larry Lee confided to his son. It was one way he got money, acting as if he'd run out of gas, that his truck was on empty.

"I actually asked my wife today," Joey told Sasha, on the day he'd helped bury his half-sister's adoptive mother, "if somebody dies and there's no one to take care of the remains, what happens to them? Because I *won't* pay for his funeral."

There was another cousin, Jenny's younger sister, who Joey thought might be willing to talk. Sasha gave her card to Joey to pass on to her. If she was willing to talk, Sasha would let her make the call.

As the meeting between Sasha, Joey and Natalie came to

a close, the conversation and comments shifted to banter and lighter topics. The couple still had to pick up their young daughter. "How old is she?" Sasha asked.

"Three," Natalie said, giving a proud grin. "The *terrible twos* don't have anything on the *horrible threes*, let me tell you. She is so independent. She won't hold your hand, she won't let you do for her."

"*I do it*," Joey mimicked in his best little-girl voice, smiling, imitating the cute way his young daughter proclaimed her independence.

A couple of days later, before she left Knoxville, Sasha talked again with Joey. He'd spoken to the cousin he'd mentioned, but she declined to talk to Sasha and, instead, cautioned him about doing the same. She was afraid that her children would learn about the history of their Uncle Larry if Sasha wrote about the story.

But Joey also had some good news, he said. He'd picked up Sara the evening following his meeting with Sasha, and after a few drinks, they'd talked more openly about the past than ever before. Joey decided that he would talk to Larry Lee and, *if he did it,* try to get him to confess. A bold, wishful plan.

It was the last time Sasha would communicate with Joey. He decided, it seems, to take his cousin's advice. No doubt he'd said all he wanted to say, perhaps more than he ever intended. The thing that Joey really wanted was more answers, and at that point, he could only get them from Larry Lee, though that was unlikely to happen.

Against the odds, perhaps, Joey had achieved what many never do. He'd become a loving, responsible and available parent. A couple of weeks after her meeting with Joey, Sasha called Sara to check in. Sara sounded upbeat. "Joey said he understood more than he did before. He hadn't realized what all I had gone through and I wanted to thank you."

Joey had even hosted a barbecue and invited Sara. "On Easter Sunday we had a little cookout and I got to see my daughter, my son and all my grandkids. It went real well," Sara said, a soft smile in her voice.

17. <u>FAMILY MATTERS</u>

Sasha opened her laptop early one morning to discover an unforeseen contact from a surprising source:

Hello, I'm Jenny. I would like to talk to you. Call or text ANYTIME please.

What followed was a narrative that Sasha hadn't expected to hear. For Jenny, Joey's older cousin, memories are often hazy. Whole blocks of her childhood recollections are gone. Timelines are hard to keep straight. Some people in her family consider her unstable, unreliable, but they don't realize the psyche-altering trauma she'd endured at the hands of her uncle Larry Lee.

Jenny, born in Detroit, was the oldest child of Ruby's oldest child, Nancy. When Ruby divorced and eventually moved back to Knoxville, only Brad and Larry Lee came with her at first. Nancy remained in Detroit. But relations between Nancy and Jenny weren't always so good. At some point, when Jenny was in elementary school, she joined her grandmother in Knoxville. Again, the memories are fuzzy, but she recalled that Larry Lee wasn't around. At least not at first. Maybe he was back in Detroit. Maybe he was locked up. She couldn't remember. But however long it was, it constituted a happy period of Jenny's youth.

She remembered the time she spent with her grandmother to be the best. Ruby was good to her granddaughter, but not the touchy-feely kind of good. Intimacy and emotional expression were not components of this family's dynamics. *"Do your homework!" "Get off the damn phone!"* were more likely to be heard than, *"How was your day?"* But Ruby smiled at Jenny, made time for her, took an interest in her. She was the center of her granddaughter's world; she was the best thing that Jenny ever had.

Jenny believed that Ruby saw the errors in the way she'd raised her own children—although one of those errors, according to Ruby, was working long hours at multiple jobs, which she continued to do—so she tried to do things differently with her granddaughter. When Jenny came to live with her in Knoxville, Ruby doted on her. She made it to her school luncheons and took her on weekend outings to local places like the historic Blount Mansion in Knoxville. They grew grapes and vining flowers all down the side of the house; Jenny remembers a house full of flowers and toys.

But the days of just Ruby and Jenny came to an end when Larry Lee returned. From where, Jenny didn't know. She also couldn't remember exactly when he came back or how old she was at the time. It was around when her mother came down from Detroit and moved in next door. Maybe. All she remembers is that at some point her sadistic teenage uncle began molesting and then raping her. He told her that she could never tell, that if she did, he would kill her mother and grandmother—his own sister and mother. Only a scared child, Jenny believed him. Larry Lee even had a system. He would knock three times on his bedroom wall—*BangBangBang*—and Jenny knew it was time to go in there, for the terror to start all over again.

When recalling these stories, Jenny used lingering impressions as markers: the brown cable box that sat on top of the TV as Larry Lee lounged on the couch watching it; the color of the shoes she wore when she ran to tell her mother what had been done to her. Jenny couldn't quite remember when she finally told, but she recalled the scene back at her grandmother's house before and after.

Larry Lee knocked three times on his bedroom wall—*BangBangBang*. Sitting in the living room on the other side, a pony-tailed Jenny gasped and jumped simultaneously, a feeling of panic coursing through her tiny mind and body, like a tsunami coming ashore. She stared down at the new blue sneakers with the orange stars, the ones her grandmother Ruby had just bought her. With her heart pounding and her mind racing, she stood up and took a step forward. She knew she had a choice. She could either go into her sick uncle's room, endure another round of torture and torment under his miserable, fat, pimply, sweaty body, or she could escape out the front door.

For once, she chose the latter. But she made it only as far as the porch stoop before she squatted down on the top step, pulled her knees in tight to her little-girl chest and wrapped her arms around her shins. She didn't know what to do. She didn't know if she could go through with it. What if her uncle made good on his threats? What if he killed her grandmother? And worst of all, what if no one believed her? A soft rain began falling and something in her head snapped: *NO MORE!*

When Ruby bought her oldest granddaughter those new shoes, she had told her they would make her run fast. Jenny ran fast now, as fast as she could, to confess to her mother what Larry Lee had been doing to her. *Don't let him catch me,* she prayed as her legs, propelled by fear, raced forward in a slapping flurry toward her destination. At the time, it seemed like a million miles, even if it was only nearby.

Jenny has little recall of arriving, telling her mother everything. Yet she remembers the scene in her grandmother's kitchen when the family gathered there later to confront Larry Lee. Ruby, Nancy and Brad listened as Jenny recounted what she had already told her mother. When she was done, Brad called Larry Lee out of his bedroom. Larry Lee walked into the kitchen with a bed sheet wrapped around his torso in place of a shirt, an unpleasant image that Jenny could never successfully forget. With four pairs of eyes trained upon him, he was questioned about Jenny's allegation. Larry Lee squirmed and made excuses before he confessed to his family that he had, in fact, had sex with his young niece.

To Jenny, Brad had always been a fun uncle, but what he did next made him her *hero* uncle. He grabbed his runty little brother by the throat with his left hand and with the right he wound the sheet around Larry Lee's thick neck. Then he dragged his bound brother outside where he pummeled him fiercely with his broad fists. "You don't do that to my niece," Brad snarled. "Here, Jenny, *kick* him!" Which she did, with her new shoes. Multiple times.

"*Stop! Stop!*" Ruby cried, tears pooling in her eyes.

"You're going to kill him!" Nancy pleaded.

When Brad's hands came to a rest, Larry Lee lay unconscious on the ground, and the matter was closed. It would join an ever-growing list of family secrets, rarely if ever acknowledged again.

"Ruby ignored the ugly parts," Jenny recalled. She had always looked up to her grandmother, so as an obedient granddaughter, she had followed suit; she sealed off her pain and encased it in thick but fragile layers of mistrust and denial.

Eventually, Jenny moved in with her mother, but her grandmother remained the bright spot in an increasingly darkening life. When Sara came to live as Larry Lee's wife in the basement of the Fern Avenue house, back in 1980, she had befriended Larry Lee's ten-year-old niece, who has fond memories of their brief time together. Jenny eventually confided in Sara about the abuse by Larry Lee. Sara felt great compassion for her. Jenny carries a distinct impression of the two of them roller skating together. To young Jenny, Sara just seemed *older*. She had no idea that Sara herself was so young, just fifteen, or that Larry Lee was abusing her, too.

After Sara made her escape, Jenny heard family members tell stories about her drinking and drug use, anything to make her look bad, but they never said anything about Larry Lee's mistreatment of her. And Jenny never knew of her uncle's arrest and conviction in Florida in 1982—when she was twelve—for the kidnapping and rape of Katherine McWilliams.

But she remembers him bringing Maryanne Parker back to Knoxville when he came home in 1986. He had been gone five years, and his niece was no longer a child but an adolescent with a discerning eye. *What does she see in him?* Jenny wondered.

By the time she was a teenager, Jenny had learned to repress her memories. She rarely thought about the inexplicable things her uncle had done to her, but she never coped with them either. There must have been some kind of trigger the day the memories came flooding in. She was eighteen-years-old and driving on the interstate the first time she involuntarily flashed back—and it was bad. Suddenly she was reliving a horrific experience so vividly that she struggled to discern the here and now from the there and then.

She saw the pimples on the rotund abdomen of an adolescent Larry Lee, heard his grunts and noises and the threatening words he uttered to coerce her into compliance, reexperienced his violations upon her body as if they were happening all over again. She had a complete emotional meltdown. Afterward, there was a period when Jenny fantasized about killing her rapist uncle, shooting him at point-blank range.

In therapy, Jenny confronted some of her buried trauma, but it took a long time—well over a decade—before she was able to admit out loud that she'd been "molested and brutalized." She gained insight into aspects of her family's dynamics that she labels "dysfunctional." She also learned that if she didn't let go of the past, Larry Lee would forever have power over her. But emotional stability has remained elusive for Jenny throughout much of her adult years, her moods rolling and tumbling like massive clouds roiling across the sky during a summer thunderstorm.

In a family that shares very little, Jenny, as a rule, was privy to even less. When Larry Lee left for Georgia in 1989, Jenny did not know that his departure was related to a murder investigation. She did know that he'd attacked someone in Georgia and had gone to prison there. But she never knew about any of the other victims. All those years, Jenny thought she and Amanda were the only ones. So the news about Michelle's case shocked and upset the vulnerable, striving-to-be-stable Jenny. She confided as much in an email to Sasha:

> I've had nightmares about Michelle, yelling for me to help her. It was so dark I couldn't find her. I just kept saying, "I'm so sorry. I'm so sorry." I remember him lumbering over me and knowing he probably did the same to her.

* * *

But while learning about Michelle and the other victims stirred Jenny's memories and related emotional pain, the overall process of talking to Sasha and learning about the other victims helped Jenny to move forward, she said, to feel less isolated.

Jenny recognized that her grandmother "coddled" Larry Lee, yet defends the behaviors as those of a mother. But watching her mother and grandmother send money and "care packages" to Larry Lee in prison made her "nauseous," although she kept those thoughts and feelings to herself. In this family, Jenny told Sasha, you learned to "go along to get along."

18. <u>RUBY AND EDSEL SMITH</u>

In a family that stored its secrets—individual and collective—in the deep, dark recesses of silence and repression, information about Ruby's ex-husband, Edsel Smith, was hard to come by. When Sasha interviewed Joey, he admitted he knew almost nothing about the man who was his biological grandfather, except that Ruby became angry at the mere mention of his name. The only way Joey even learned his name was by accident when Ruby rattled it off absentmindedly (as seniors sometimes do) in a list of male family names, trying to get to the one she meant to say to begin with: Brad, Edsel, Larry, *Joey,* she finally said.

"God! I wish you wouldn't do that!" the teenage Joey shot back. *"Edsel? Who's Edsel?"*

Ruby's parents never approved of Edsel Ray Smith, but she married him anyway. Seven years her senior, he'd been a Private First Class during WWII. After the war, they moved from Knoxville to Detroit, where he found good factory work. They had four children together: Nancy, Bonnie, Brad, and Larry Lee.

The first child, Nancy, was born the year they married.

She was followed the next year by a second daughter, Bonnie. Nine years passed before Ruby gave birth to a third daughter, Carrie, whose arrival created a family scandal, because Edsel knew that he was not Carrie's father. Few in the family know the specifics of that story, but Carrie was given up for adoption and taken in by a relative. As she grew up, she remained in contact with her biological mother and siblings. And, despite the scandal, Ruby and Edsel's marriage remained intact. Brad, their first son, was born the year after Carrie. Their youngest child, Larry Lee, came along four years later in 1961.

The union of Ruby and Edsel lasted nineteen years, coming to an end in 1965, the same year that their second born, eighteen-year-old Bonnie, took her own life. Edsel was arrested on suspicion that he had raped his daughter, but he was neither tried nor convicted. He and Ruby divorced, and she moved back to Knoxville with Brad and Larry Lee. The family rarely spoke Edsel's name again.

Jenny told Sasha she knew only that her grandfather had existed and was now deceased, having died somewhere in Florida. Her mother, Nancy, didn't talk about him. Joey recalled hearing that after Ruby left Edsel, but before she moved back to Tennessee, she had some wild times with some characters in Detroit who were supposedly connected to the mob. At some point, Edsel remarried. He and his second wife lived in Bonita Springs, Florida.

When Joseph "Joey" Ray Smith was born in 1980, he had been named after the middle names of each of his grandfathers: Joseph for Sara's father and Ray for Larry Lee's, even though Larry Lee hadn't seen his dad since he was four. After Sara fled with Joey, Larry Lee had some kind of altercation with someone in Sara's family for which he was charged with felonious assault. He was never tried, but it's reasonable to imagine that someone in his family—or perhaps an attorney—suggested he go away for a while. He did. He moved to Clearwater Beach, Florida, where he got another job at a Holiday Inn.

Had he chosen Florida because he thought he might rekindle a relationship with his father, who lived with his second wife in Bonita Springs, a few hours south of Clearwater? Jenny and Sasha both wondered, but they couldn't say for sure.

Less than a year later, in early 1982, Larry Lee was convicted and sentenced to prison for the kidnapping and rape of Katherine McWilliams. He added the names of his father and stepmother to his prison visitation list. Upon his release, he moved to Collier County, Florida, which butts up against Bonita Springs. But in July of 1984, just three months after Larry Lee was paroled, Edsel passed away. The following summer, Maryanne pressed charges against Larry Lee. On the arrest report, he listed his stepmother as his closest relative.

Sasha thought Maryanne Parker might be able to shed some light on the dynamics between the father and his son. But Maryanne knew very little except that the mere mention of Larry Lee's father, whom she never met, sent Larry Lee into a rage. He told her only that Edsel left when he was young and wasn't around when he was growing up. If he gave it much more thought than that, she recalled, he went crazy. In his rage he would throw things across the room or take out his frustration on Maryanne, often with his fists.

But during Larry Lee's stay in Florida, there was plenty of family drama going on in Knoxville to keep his mind occupied on other things. Brad, whose whereabouts were reportedly unknown for a while, was wanted by the authorities, and Nancy, who'd moved back in with Ruby, was in trouble herself. She'd been arrested for receiving and concealing stolen merchandise—lots of it—in a scheme with some of Brad's friends. The loot included guns, valuable electronics and jewels taken from break-ins at five separate homes.

Nancy waived the grand jury and pleaded guilty. She was facing five to ten years in the Tennessee Penitentiary for Women, and although she'd previously spent a few days in jail on shoplifting charges, she was scared. She begged for another chance to pull her life together.

"I am sorry for what Nancy has done," Ruby wrote to the probation officer preparing a pre-sentencing report. "She has had a rough time. I know that she has learned her lesson. And I know she has turned to God for help"—Nancy had begun attending church just after her arrest—"and I believe now she is going to live a good and clean life. I pray that she will have a second chance."

On the date of the hearing, Nancy was granted probation and the "second chance" she'd requested.

But trouble still plagued Ruby's children. One day when Brad was forty years old, he walked into Ruby's house, laid down on the sofa, reminded his mother that his dog had a litter of puppies in his basement, and went to sleep. He never woke up. Jenny told Sasha that she suspected Brad had willed himself to death through his drinking and drug abuse. Others in the family claimed that Brad had, in fact, chosen to end his life.

"Suicide runs in the family," Jenny told Sasha. Carrie, the daughter who had been born to Ruby and an unknown father and then adopted, was another of Ruby's children to die by her own hand. She'd been raised partly in Louisiana but was living in Knoxville in October 2008 when she ended her life.

Joey knew that Ruby had regrets about her kids, the way she'd raised them, the way they'd turned out. And he thought that perhaps she had faced the truth about Larry Lee, even if she never admitted it to anyone. He told Sasha about one conversation in which Ruby had opened up to him, unusual for her or anyone in his family. She told him that being a single parent had been difficult, that she'd been trying to fill both parental roles, but with long hours working multiple jobs just to make ends meet, she hadn't been around as much as she needed to be when her kids were growing up, when they needed her most. The way Joey heard it, she blamed herself for her children's mistakes, and he could tell that Larry Lee was there in the mix. She knew, or at least she'd been told about, the things he'd done: to his niece, to his wife, to all the other young girls. "Grandma *knew* he was guilty," Jenny had told Sasha. "She knew he was."

In early July 2010, on a Monday, Ruby passed away in the Fern Avenue house, surrounded by the remaining members of her family. She was fifty-four days short of her eightieth birthday. "She was ready to go," Joey said, "and it was good... because her pain was finally gone."

Before Ruby died, she had shared a secret with Jenny. She too had experienced abuse as a young girl. Ruby told her granddaughter that she was sorry for all she'd been through, and that she loved her. "People in this family don't often say, 'I love you,'" Jenny told Sasha. "It meant a lot."

19. <u>CASELOAD</u>

Sasha received email notifications whenever there was a change to Larry Lee's TBI Sex Offender Registry page. But her research showed that his whereabouts as reported on the TBI SOR were sometimes unclear or inaccurate. When Larry Lee had to leave his mother's house in Sevier County due to her cancer diagnosis, Sasha received email notifications of changes in his SOR information, but she experienced difficulty accessing his page on the registry. So she sent an email to Detective McCarter in Sevier County, where, at the time, she believed Larry Lee was still residing. It was then that she learned there had been a change in his circumstances and supervision. McCarter informed her that Larry Lee had since moved to Knox County and that McCarter had contacted the Knox County Sheriff's Office (KCSO), and they were interested in reopening the Michelle Anderson cold case. He'd forwarded all the material Sasha had given him on to them, he said.

This was all news to Sasha, and would have been exciting, if any of it sounded right. She explained to Detective McCarter that KPD, not KCSO, had been working the case, and that cold-case homicide Investigator Jeff Day was the officer assigned. "Who is supervising Larry Lee?" she asked. McCarter couldn't answer that question as Larry Lee no longer resided in his jurisdiction.

Sasha looked again at Larry Lee's information on the SOR. It had now been updated to show that he had moved to Blount County, next door to Sevier, but not to Knox.

Sasha called the Blount County Sheriff's Office. She learned that Larry Lee had registered as required, but there had been a "glitch" of some kind in entering the updated information on the registry. Sgt. John James was the man to whom Larry Lee now reported. Sasha left a message on his voicemail, and he called her back the next day.

Sasha introduced herself and tried to get clear on the trail of Larry Lee's supervision. She asked how long he had been on Sgt. James' caseload. More than six months, as James recalled. No, ma'am, he hadn't been told anything about Larry Lee's history when he moved into his area. No, ma'am, he didn't know from which county Larry Lee had moved.

Sasha informed Sgt. James about the Michelle Anderson cold-case investigation and gave him the name of KPD Investigator Jeff Day. Sgt. James said he would like to talk to Day. "Oh yes, ma'am," he said, "you just have him call me."

But Sgt. James then informed Sasha that Larry Lee had come in to his office "just the other day," ironically, to tell him that in three days he was moving *back* to the county from which he came. Sgt. James still wasn't sure which county that was. Sasha told him it was Sevier.

"This guy is dangerous," she said.

"Yes, ma'am," Sgt. James said, "they all are, all three hundred on my caseload."

Sasha informed Detective McCarter that Larry Lee was supposedly moving back to Sevier County. "That's news to me," McCarter replied. "I haven't heard anything about this!"

She sent an email to Jeff Day updating him on her phone call with Blount County Sgt. John James and his request that the investigator call him. Day contacted James the next week, confirming for him the information about Larry Lee's past crimes and his suspected connection to the unsolved murder of Michelle Anderson.

In the meantime, Sgt. James had paid a home visit to Larry Lee, confirming his living arrangements. Larry Lee hadn't moved back to Sevier County after all. He was staying in Blount County with an "older couple," according to Sgt. James' report, in their trailer, where he was given access to a red Ford Mustang registered to a woman by the last name of King, as well as assistance getting a truck and a lawn mower for yard work.

This was just before the news piece aired identifying Larry Lee as a "person of interest" in the murder of Michelle Anderson. Larry Lee had watched it with his hosts. Before long, he was on the move again. This time, he headed back to Knoxville.

In 1970, the same year that floppy disks were invented, student protests resulted in the Kent State shootings, and the Beatles decided to end their musical collaboration, a new two-hundred-twenty-three-room Holiday Inn was built on the edge of downtown Knoxville, just off I-40, near the university, when the boundaries of the city were tighter and smaller. At the time, the four-story building was sharp and modern, with sliding glass doors opening onto every balcony. This was the Holiday Inn where Larry Lee had been employed, along with Ruby, before he'd left for Florida in 1981.

During the decades in which Larry Lee had been in

prison, however, the hotel had transitioned from a quality, overnight inn, to run-down, long-term lodging known as Volunteer Studios, where furnished studio "apartments" could be rented by the week, month or year. It had a pool and an online presence, but its location and condition attracted a level of clientele that included transients, addicts, drug dealers, prostitutes and others who lived their lives hanging by a thread.

Residents smoked cigarettes while leaning in the sliding glass doorways next to torn curtains and sagging shades. They hung over balconies and slouched on scarred and rickety patio furniture. People were assaulted in its hallways. Drug deals were a common sight in its doorways. A place like this, which would accept nearly anybody, attracted registered sex offenders who had difficulty renting anywhere else—so that's where Larry Lee stayed.

How Larry Lee earned money for rent and his day-to-day living costs was questionable. Although he had been out of the Georgia prison for going on two years, he'd never identified an employer. He'd been spotted at the local blood bank a couple of times, and he had that lawn mower and his panhandling scam. It was on a nearby exit ramp that Joey had spotted him begging for money.

In addition to mowing lawns, Larry Lee claimed he made a small income off scrapped metal. But then he was in a car accident and injured his ankle bad enough to require pins and a brace. Soon after, he got a nasty staph infection in the wound. According to a neighbor, Larry Lee began selling and trading the pain pills he'd been prescribed for his injury. He also struck up a pseudo-relationship with a drug-addicted prostitute who lived one floor below him. It was through these activities that Larry Lee came into contact with troubled young women who had no inkling of his violent and checkered past.

KPD Investigator Jeff Day said he liked the idea of Larry Lee moving into Knoxville. "That way I can keep an eye on him." Of course, keeping an eye on Larry Lee didn't fall under the job duties of the cold case investigator. That task belonged to KPD Investigator Krista Sheppard, the officer to whom Larry Lee now reported as a registered sex offender living in Knoxville. Jeff Day gave Sheppard's name and number to Sasha and said he'd filled the investigator in on the history and crimes of Larry Lee.

Investigator Sheppard did not respond to Sasha's phone and email messages. Sasha eventually reached out to the investigator's supervisor, which finally resulted in a response email from Investigator Sheppard; it suggested Sasha visit the TBI sex offender registry website for information and updates.

Working with Investigator Sheppard was clearly a dead end. Sasha would have to put her faith in Investigator Day and hope that, in the meantime, Larry Lee didn't strike again.

Part Three
Beyond a Reasonable Doubt

20. <u>CAN I USE YOUR PHONE?</u>

Larry Lee knew her only by her alias, *Jade*. He first met her in October 2011, when he purchased some drugs from her boyfriend, Tam. Jade's real name was Ayesha Mack. This charming, petite, deeply-dimpled, African-American beauty, the eldest of six children, had run away from her Georgia home at the tender age of sixteen. Now nineteen, she bummed around Knoxville with Tam, her handsome, dread-locked, drug-dealing boyfriend, who was also several years older than her. They crashed wherever they could: friends' apartments, homeless shelters, and the streets, if they had to.

For six months in 2010 they had rented a room at Volunteer Studios, where they got to know many of the local residents. Now they were crashing at the apartment of Larry Lee's companion of sorts, Khristy, a thirty-year-old, drug-addicted prostitute living one floor below him. Khristy let them stay there in exchange for crack, which Tam sold along with a few other illicit substances. Larry Lee was also a client.

Larry Lee liked to call Khristy his girlfriend, and to Ayesha, who'd known them both for only a few weeks, the two were together so much that she thought it was true. But Khristy's addiction was so severe that she'd sell her sexual services for a quick fix. There were times when Tam and Ayesha observed her coming home with a bruised and battered face, which she'd attribute to a john. She'd lost custody of her kids and was supposed to be working to change her life so she could get them back, but not much about Khristy's current lifestyle seemed to support this goal.

On Monday morning, October 24, 2011, Ayesha walked uptown to the central branch of the Knoxville Public Library on West Church Street. There she logged into her Yahoo email account and checked replies to job applications she'd recently submitted online. She was also sending emails to Tam, which he would receive and respond to on his phone.

After about forty-five minutes, something odd happened: Tam stopped responding to her messages. She logged out of her account, gathered her purse and began the one-and-a-half-mile trek back to the apartment building. When she reached Volunteer Studios, she headed straight for Khristy's apartment. Neither Khristy nor Tam were there, so Ayesha went one floor up to the apartment of the man she knew only as Larry and knocked on the door.

"Who is it?" he yelled.

"It's Jade," she answered from the hallway.

"Come in," he said, opening the door. Larry Lee looked terrible. He had been up all night smoking crack with Khristy and their friend David. Then that morning he'd gone to court as a witness at the preliminary hearing of a man named Barry Eugene Evans, accused of robbing Larry Lee of his prescription OxyContin a month earlier. He'd just returned from downtown and taken off his shirt. He wore only a pair of loose, khaki-colored pants held up by one suspender strap; the other strap was broken.

"Have you seen Tam?" Ayesha asked.

Khristy emerged from the bathroom, surprising Ayesha, who hadn't known she was there. "Tam and David got arrested a little while ago," Khristy said. She explained that David had broken into the hotel's laundry machines earlier that day. He'd stolen the change, then walked to Khristy's apartment where Tam was staying. The apartment manager, Kathy Brown, learned of the theft, used security footage to track David to Khristy's apartment, and called the police. When KPD showed up, they arrested David for the theft and Tam for the drugs found in the apartment.

Khristy didn't inform Ayesha that as soon as Tam had been arrested, she'd gone through their things, looking for items to sell or trade. As she stood there, she had Tam's iPod in her pocket; she was on her way to trade it for drugs at another run-down hotel nearby.

Ayesha burst into tears. She felt like the world was always conspiring to keep her and Tam apart. A couple years earlier, she had been arrested for shoplifting, which put her on probation. A quick trip home to Georgia had put her in violation of that probation, and when she returned to Knoxville she had spent time in jail. That time away from Tam had been unbearable. Now, she'd been back with him only a few weeks and they'd been forced apart again. This couldn't be happening.

"Can I use your phone?" she asked Khristy, sobbing out the words.

Khristy hesitated and looked at Larry Lee. "*Uhh*... I'm going to get a phone now," she said.

"Yeah," Larry Lee said. "My phone is out of minutes and I need to make a call, too."

"Well, let me come with you," Ayesha said.

"No..." Khristy said. "Really... I'll be right back."

Ayesha noted that Khristy seemed uneasy, but she was far too distracted by thoughts of Tam's arrest to focus on Khristy at the time. She needed to slow her racing thoughts, sort through this crisis, figure out a plan, but she couldn't halt the flow of tears.

Khristy left and Ayesha slumped down onto a green plastic chair, the only place to sit other than the bed. "Everything is going to be all right," Larry Lee reassured her. His hand touched her lightly on the back. "How about a cup of tea?"

"Okay," she answered softly. He stepped into the bathroom, washed out two cups and prepared the tea. Ayesha's mind remained focused on Tam and her dilemma. She really had nowhere else to go, she reasoned as Larry Lee emerged and handed her the cup of warm liquid.

"Can I get you something to eat?

"No, thanks," she answered in a voice barely above a whisper.

"Well, I'm going to fix myself something to eat," he told her. He opened a can of peas, chopped up part of an onion and heated them together in the microwave. Then he requested that she move from the chair to the bed. He wanted to eat his peas by the table, he explained. "Aren't you going to drink your tea? Did I waste my time making it?"

"No... I'm just letting it cool," she said as she moved to the bed. The double-size bed was minus a headboard, or even a frame, and rested instead on a foundation of evenly-spaced concrete blocks. Ayesha sat at the edge while Larry Lee polished off his peas. *Where is Khristy with that phone?*

After some minutes, Larry Lee suggested they watch a movie. He said it would distract her from her worries, kill time while they waited for Khristy to return. He put in the action flick *xXx*, starring Vin Diesel. Then he turned the volume up—a little too loud, Ayesha thought—and sat on the bed beside her.

"It'll be okay," Larry Lee said again, rubbing her back as tears spilled down her cheeks. He offered her a rolled cigarette.

In her stressed and distracted state, Ayesha lacked the mental energy to analyze what was going on. Yet somewhere in her psyche, warning bells began going off. Khristy had been acting strange. Going to get the phone didn't make a lot of sense, and she should have been back by now. And why was Larry Lee, who was now sitting right next to her on the bed, so insistent on her drinking her tea? A deep uneasiness began to creep up her spine, paralyzing her with fear. She didn't know what to do, so she didn't do anything, just watched the movie, gripping her full cup of tea.

They stared at the TV in silence for several minutes when Larry Lee shifted his focus to a stack of materials on the floor beside the bed. "Can you help me move these?" he asked. It seemed a strange request, but Ayesha didn't know why she should object, or how Larry Lee would react if she did, so she set her cup of tea on the table and bent down to assist.

In a blur, the two-hundred-fifty-pound Larry Lee clamped his hand down on Ayesha's neck. He quickly secured the one-hundred-fifteen-pound girl with his signature throat-choking hold and began slapping her back and forth across her face.

"What are you *doing?*" she gasped, barely able to breathe.

"I'll kill you," he threatened, then pinned her down to the mattress. Using his forearm to maintain pressure on her neck, he reached under the bed and retrieved a chain of neckties, looping the already-knotted end of a blue-gray, diagonally-striped tie around her right wrist. It happened so quickly that Ayesha couldn't determine just how he'd accomplished this. As he tightened the pressure on her throat, he attempted to secure her left wrist with the loop of a golden brown necktie on the other end of the chain, which proved too short for the task.

"Just *cooperate*, Jade, and you won't get hurt," Larry Lee hissed. Ayesha eyed him wildly. She prayed for God to rescue her as her assailant dropped his pants with a flick of the single suspender strap off his shoulder. Naked, he climbed upon her, using the force of his weight to wedge himself between her tightly clamped thighs.

When Ayesha resisted, a horrifying look of crazed lust and anger filled his eyes. "I'll break your fucking legs," he hissed. Larry Lee's hot breath was now all around her; his sweat dripping onto her face and chest as she struggled against his control. But the squeeze on her throat was more than she could resist. Her eyes rolled back in her head and she could feel her consciousness slipping away as Larry Lee tugged off her leggings and underwear and thrust the fingers of his right hand in and out of her vagina.

Then suddenly and unexpectedly, someone pounded on the apartment door. Larry Lee froze. "Nobody's here!" he yelled. "Come back later!"

But he was distracted just long enough to unconsciously loosen his grip on Ayesha's throat. She gasped, sucking in a single breath as her mind sprang to survival mode. She fully believed her very life depended upon this moment, this unforeseen opportunity. "Somebody's here!" she shrieked. "I'll be right there!"

Larry Lee panicked, glanced nervously around the room. He released Ayesha, jumped off the bed and backed away from her. Ayesha never took her eyes off him as she reached over her head with her left hand and unhooked the necktie from her right wrist.

"Jade, I'm *sooo* sorry," Larry Lee said. He was nervous, shaking as he stepped into his pants, slipping the single suspender strap back onto his shoulder. "Everything's going to be okay."

Keeping her eyes locked upon her assailant, Ayesha grabbed for her clothes and cautiously pulled them back on.

"Just don't call the cops," Larry Lee pleaded, but Ayesha didn't say anything. She just continued pulling on her clothes and glaring at her attacker. So Larry Lee changed his strategy. He slid a pocket knife off the table and dragged the green plastic chair to the door, where he sat down to block her exit. "You're not going anywhere," he warned her in a voice low and steady.

Whoever had knocked before didn't knock again. So Ayesha couldn't count on anyone to help her. She began backing toward the sliding-glass door leading to the second-floor balcony.

"Just don't say anything," Larry Lee repeated, shifting yet again to a more pleading tone. "Here," he said, and held out his hand, offering her the knife.

With her eyes still locked on her attacker, Ayesha backed closer and closer to the sliding-glass door. She didn't know what she would do if she got out there. Scream for help? Jump? She would if she had to. But as she neared the balcony, Larry Lee stood, moved the chair away from the door and repeated, "Just don't say anything."

Ayesha eyed the situation cautiously. Larry Lee moved farther away from the door and seemed to be staying back. He had a pleading, helpless look in his eyes. But Ayesha knew he couldn't be trusted. She bolted for the door, flung it open, and fled out into the hallway. She didn't look back as she ran to another apartment where she knew someone, someone who had a phone. Crying hysterically, she called Tam's sister. She told her about Tam's arrest and the assault she had just experienced. "Go to the apartment manager,"

Tam's sister and mother urged.

In the meantime, Larry Lee was in a panic of his own. Still minus his shirt and shoes, he hurried to a nearby apartment where he thought Ayesha might have gone. No one answered the door there, so he returned to his own apartment, put on his shirt and shoes and headed to the front desk. He arrived short of breath, flushed and sweating, shaggy hair wildly askew. Someone there asked him what he needed. He tried to compose himself and said he needed to speak to the manager about his rent being late. He promised to have it soon.

He stumbled back to his own apartment and took care of a few housekeeping details. He emptied Ayesha's unfinished cup of tea and untied a couple of those neckties, tossing them behind the bed. He then returned to the neighbor's whose door he'd knocked on less than thirty minutes before. The occupant was just arriving home. He greeted Larry Lee with dire news: he'd run into Ayesha downstairs.

"What did you do to that girl?" the neighbor said, eyeing him warily. "She's in Kathy Brown's office, hysterical. You better get down there. They're calling the police!"

When Larry Lee arrived at Kathy Brown's office, Ayesha was still visibly distraught, shaking and crying uncontrollably. She had recounted the nature of the assault and Kathy had assisted her in calling 911. When Kathy saw Larry Lee, she instructed the maintenance man, Scott Brown (no relation), to keep an eye on him until the officers arrived.

"You stay right here," Scott ordered.

"Okay, man," Larry Lee said. "No problem."

They moved to chairs outside where Larry Lee, still short of breath, beet red and perspiring, rolled a cigarette. "She wanted me to," he confided to Scott, taking a drag and talking in a guy-to-guy manner. "She asked for it." Larry Lee would continue rolling cigarettes, smoking them one after another, until the police arrived.

21. <u>WHAT SHE SAID</u> HAPPENED, *<u>HAPPENED</u>*

Two uniformed officers, one male and one female, responded to the 911 call. While the female officer talked with Ayesha, the male officer questioned Larry Lee. "Hold out your arms," the officer said, looking for telltale signs of scratches, often found on an assailant when a rape victim has tried to defend herself. Larry Lee held out his arms to reveal the absence of any such marks. He even raised his shirt to expose his bulbous, unscratched belly.

He and Ayesha were transported in separate vehicles to the Knoxville Police Department where Investigator Patty Tipton was on duty. The petite redhead had worked at the KPD for more than a dozen years. She'd been named Officer of the Month earlier that year, in February, in recognition of her quick response and skillful application of emergency first aid to a wounded fellow officer, helping to save his life.

Larry Lee and Ayesha arrived at the police station sometime between three-thirty and four o'clock on that Monday afternoon. They were placed in separate interrogation rooms on the third floor for a long afternoon-turned-evening of questioning, statement taking, evidence gathering, and waiting. Through more tears and shaking, Ayesha related, in as much detail as she could recall, what had transpired earlier that afternoon in Volunteer Studios apartment number 263.

In Larry Lee's interview room, under the watchful eye of a security camera, he must have sensed the mess he was in. He would have been struggling against fatigue and fear. He'd been up all night smoking crack. Then he'd gone to court early in the morning. Then he'd come home and attacked Ayesha. What a day. And now this. As a heavy smoker, his craving for nicotine must have been kicking in something fierce.

Investigator Tipton finished interviewing Ayesha and stepped in Larry Lee's room and began questioning him in a courteous and professional demeanor. When he was younger, Larry Lee had often been shielded from the consequences of his bumbling ramblings by the attorneys his mother hired. They'd told him to keep his mouth shut. He tried that here, advising the investigator that he didn't want to talk to her. But now his mother and her protections were gone, and he started talking anyway.

First he said he wanted to talk—really, *really* wanted to talk—with the Assistant DA handling the case against the man accused of robbing him. He probably thought the DA would be an ally since Larry Lee was testifying for him as a prosecution witness. His request was denied.

When Investigator Tipton asked permission to have KPD Forensic Technician Rebecca Byers swab his hands and scrape under his nails, Larry Lee was accommodating. He gave permission.

"What are you looking for?" he asked casually as Byers collected the samples.

"We're looking for Ms. Mack's vaginal secretions on your hands," Tipton replied.

"*Okay*. How will you tell this?"

"Because her DNA will be on your hands."

"Well, what she said happened, *happened*," he explained, seeming to imply consensual sex. "Her DNA *will* be on my hands because I have touched her."

Next Investigator Tipton requested permission to search his apartment, which Larry Lee also granted. "What will you be looking for?" he inquired again.

"She says you tied her wrist with the end of a necktie," Tipton replied. "So, we'll be looking for that."

"I guess that comment I made about being able to take care of her better than a crack dealer really, really set her off," he said. He also alleged that Barry Evans, the man he'd testified against that morning for allegedly stealing his OxyContin, could be behind it somehow. He claimed that Barry and Ayesha could be conspiring against him.

"I didn't expect this to happen at all," he said. "I don't stand a chance."

He had denied that he had in any way restrained Ayesha, but now he'd need to account for the "strap" of neckties, as he called them, which the officers were likely to find. "Do you have my phone?" he asked. The two cell phones Larry Lee had on him when he was taken into custody had been collected, although he wasn't yet under arrest and a search warrant had not been obtained. They were being held with his other property.

"I don't," Tipton replied.

"You've got those phones out there. Can you get those and bring them in here?" Larry Lee requested. "I want to show you something."

Investigator Tipton retrieved the phones, returned to the room, and handed them to Larry Lee. He activated the Verizon phone, which actually had no service; he kept it only for taking photos. He scrolled until he found the numerous images he wanted Tipton to see, images of a naked woman—or women (she couldn't be sure)—bound by the wrists on a bed. Larry Lee explained to her that he'd done this with other women, *with* their permission. He told Tipton that he didn't restrain Ayesha, that she must have heard he was into using the ties from Khristy.

"You'll probably just confiscate it [the phone] as evidence," he said. "I don't force nobody. I pay them." He said that's what he'd done with Khristy, who was among the images on the phone.

When Investigator Tipton didn't immediately respond, Larry Lee asked, "Are you following me?"

"I'm getting you. I'm following you. Because that's how Ayesha would have seen it," she replied, trying to keep up with Larry Lee's evolving story, which had rapidly transitioned from consensual sex with Ayesha ("What she said happened, *happened.*") to a set-up based on her knowledge of what he and Khristy did using the ties and his phone's camera.

"Those straps are under the bed, and they have not been taken out," Larry Lee said. "Believe me, you don't get to them unless you move the bed."

Investigator Tipton retrieved the phones and left the interview room. While she and Byers prepared to go to the suspect's apartment to photograph and collect evidence, the camera in the upper left corner of the room continued to record. Now alone, Larry Lee stood in silence for a few moments, his back turned toward the camera. Then he reflected aloud to no one but himself: "Well, I'm screwed. They're going to put me away for life." He paced back and forth awhile before finally lowering his weary body to the floor, first stretching out, then rolling onto his side and pulling his knees in as close as his rotund abdomen would allow.

* * *

KPD Investigator Tipton and Technician Byers entered Larry Lee's living quarters at Volunteer Studios, signed permission in hand, where they found a scene much as Ayesha had described. Byers bagged evidence and took more than sixty photographs in the dingy, cluttered, stale-smelling, one-room apartment.

They quickly located the chain of neckties—each end tied into a loop just large enough to slip over a hand and secure a wrist—but not under the bed and unreachable, as Larry Lee stated. It had been tossed between the head of the bed and the wall.

As Ayesha had described to Investigator Tipton, the tie on one end, the one that had been looped over her right wrist, bore gray diagonal stripes; the tie on the other end was of a coffee-brown design. In the middle of this chain, two of the ties were disconnected, although the wrinkles and marks remaining on the fabric revealed that they had recently been knotted together.

An empty can of peas sat on the table, along with a bowl and part of a cut-up onion. A pocket knife also rested there beside two empty tea cups, even though Ayesha had been very clear that she did not drink most of her tea. Tea bags were photographed in the trash can. xXx was still in the DVD player. A dark green plastic chair sat by the small table, as Ayesha had reported, but there was now a second green plastic chair on the other side of the table.

Since Larry Lee had asked Ayesha to switch from the chair to the bed so he could eat his peas sitting in the chair, where had this second chair been during the time she'd been in the apartment? On the balcony? Had he pulled it back inside when he'd hurriedly returned to his apartment, untying two of the ties, tossing them behind the bed and emptying Ayesha's cup of tea?

When Investigator Tipton returned to the station, she reentered Larry Lee's interrogation room and held up his phone. "I was wondering if you would mind showing me those pictures again. I'd like to get photographs of them." She handed it to him.

Larry Lee flipped it open and stared at the screen as he thumbed through the images. "You're going to use these against me, *right?*"

"Well, you don't have to show them to me," Tipton replied in an obliging tone. "It's up to you."

Larry Lee continued to hold the opened phone in his right hand as he studied the images it contained. Then he began to subtly move his thumb back and forth between the buttons on the keypad. At one point, the investigator asked him what he was doing and walked around beside him to look at the phone's screen. Larry Lee didn't respond as his thumb continued its mission, but after a few more moments he stopped and handed the phone back to her. When a search warrant was obtained and the phones officially taken into custody as evidence, the images of the bound women had been deleted. They were gone from the phone—but not from the memory of Investigator Tipton.

At eleven minutes past nine—a little more than five hours after arriving at the police station—fifty-year-old Larry Lee Smith was placed under arrest and charged with Class C felony kidnapping and Class B felony rape of nineteen-year-old Ayesha Kiana Mack. Bail was set at $100,000 per charge—$200,000 total—high enough to keep him there for a while.

Larry Lee phoned his sister, Nancy. The news reduced her to tears. But by the time she ended the phone call, she was largely silent about the development, as per Smith family protocol. As Larry Lee was being booked into the Knox County Jail, Nancy went to her brother's apartment and removed all of his belongings.

A call was made on behalf of Ayesha to the Sexual Assault Center of East Tennessee (SACETN), where staff is on 24-hour emergency standby. Formerly the Knoxville Rape Crisis Center, SACETN has been around since the early 1970s, evolving and expanding its services in more recent years. After talking with the SACETN staff, Ayesha agreed to get a physical exam upon her return home to Georgia the next day.

The white T-shirt she was wearing, which had absorbed the sweat drippings and deodorant stains of her assailant, was confiscated as evidence by the KPD as she changed into an alternate top. Ayesha was then placed in a cab and delivered to a local shelter where she would spend the night before getting a bus ticket, provided by a Knoxville ministry, which would take her back home to her mother and younger siblings the next day.

Early Tuesday morning, unaware that Khristy had already sold or traded most of the items belonging to Ayesha and Tam, Ayesha returned to Volunteer Studios. There was no answer at Khristy's apartment, but when Ayesha walked outside to peer through the first-floor window, she saw Khristy inside lying on her bed.

So Ayesha rapped on the window, then walked back into the hallway and knocked on the door even harder and louder until Khristy finally opened it. When Ayesha eyed how few of her belongings remained—even most of her clothing had disappeared—Khristy claimed she'd been robbed, even though her things had clearly been left untouched. Rage boiled up in Ayesha, as did the urge to slam this desperate and conniving crack addict into the wall. But she resisted. Gathering what little was left of her possessions, Ayesha turned her back on this lost soul and the life she represented and caught the bus out of town.

The next day, Sasha received an email from retired FBI Agent Grey Steed:

> I hear Larry Lee has been charged with another rape this week.

Sasha immediately forwarded the email on to Anita, asking if she knew anything about it. Anita did not, so she shot a message to Jeff Day:

> I found out that Larry Lee Smith has been arrested. Do you have any details? Thanks, Anita.

On Thursday morning, Jeff Day confirmed Larry Lee's arrest to Anita and sent an email update to Sasha, in which he shared the following observation:

> Hopefully Larry Lee Smith will be in jail for a long time (although you never know with our justice system). The trial, if it gets that far, wouldn't be for over a year and he won't be able to bond this time I wouldn't think. Good news, although I hate it for the girl, that he is locked away and no one got seriously hurt. I will send you more when I know more. You can go to knoxsheriff.org to view his charges and his mug shot.

Sasha already had.

22. <u>EYE TO EYE</u>

Strolling along the handsome two-block stretch of Knoxville's historic downtown Main Street, Sasha took in the fall beauty. The maple trees lining the sidewalk had shed most of their red and yellow leaves, allowing the early morning sun to shine directly upon the pedestrians and passengers in cars beginning the business day. On the illuminated city skyline straight ahead stood the office towers built by the Butcher brothers, Jake's on the left and C.H.'s on the right.

Larry Lee Smith's preliminary hearing was scheduled for nine o'clock that morning, Friday, November 4, 2011, in Third Sessions Court, Criminal Division, on the first floor of the Knoxville City-County Building, a modern-style structure built in 1979. The courtyard of the building is wide, with inviting steps leading down from the city sidewalk to a walk-way dotted with benches, flowers and ornamental trees. In the mid-1980s, when her casework often took her inside its court-rooms, Sasha had thought of the building as a striking blend of utilitarianism and aesthetic appeal: practical in a soothing sort of way, its glossy brick floors perhaps the most pleasing part.

Anita was working, and there was no reason for Jeff Day to attend a preliminary hearing for Larry Lee on new charges, so Sasha was attending this one alone. She placed her purse on the conveyer belt, passed through the courthouse scanner and walked down the glass-walled corridor into the building from which the Tennessee River, just a block away, can be seen on the other side. As she sat on a cushioned bench in the lobby, waiting for the courtroom doors to open, Sasha glanced at the people assembled around her, wondering who might be the sister of Larry Lee—Sasha assumed she would be there—or his most recent victim. She wondered if anyone was there for Larry Lee. There had thus far been no news, no publicity, about his arrest, even though this registered sex offender was the primary suspect in Michelle Anderson's murder investigation and had attacked yet another girl.

When the courtroom opened and everyone filed in, they were instructed to sit according to the role they had in the proceedings of the day: victims and attorneys on the right side of the aisle, everyone else in the crowded chamber on the left. The room became a sea of gliding figures, floating around and out of each other's way, checking dockets and files, murmuring, requesting permission to speak with presiding Judge Andrew Jackson VI, named for his direct ancestor, the seventh President of the United States.

Before attending the hearing Sasha had checked out some identities and information online. In the courtroom she recognized the prosecutor assigned to the case, Leslie Nassios. In the Knox County District Attorney's office, Nassios' title was officially Assistant District Attorney for the Sixth Judicial District and Division Chief and Violent Crime Prosecutor for Knox County Division III Criminal Court. She'd earned a reputation as tenacious and tough, with a solid record of convictions. A slim, attractive brunette of medium height, she wore a no-nonsense black business pantsuit paired with a VOLS bright-orange T-shirt underneath. This was, after all, pre-game day in Knoxville, home to the University of Tennessee. *Big Orange country*—sacred as law.

Sasha took a front-row seat on the left side of the aisle, just behind the railing separating the gallery from the court staff, attorneys, and inmates. She scanned the active courtroom as other cases were being heard, attempting to determine whom the victim in this case might be—*is she here?*

Other than a general description of the charges and an age for injured party—that turned out to be off by two years—Sasha didn't yet know much about Ayesha Mack or the details of the alleged assault.

While Sasha watched the courtroom proceedings unfold, the handcuffed inmates—both men and women—were led in. They wore prison jumpsuits with wide black-and-white stripes, the black now faded to gray. Sasha thought she would recognize Larry Lee, having seen pictures of him at nearly every stage of his life, the most recent being the mugshot taken less than two weeks before. But she'd never laid eyes on him in person.

As the inmates filled the seats closest to the walls, on the other side of a wood and glass barrier separating the spectators from the prisoners, Sasha still didn't see Larry Lee. When the line ended and it seemed that all the prisoners had been escorted in, Sasha went over to the court clerk to determine that Larry Lee's case was still on the docket. It was, the clerk confirmed; perhaps he would arrive in a few more minutes.

Sasha didn't realize that inmates charged with more serious offenses came last and had their handcuffs attached to chains encircling their waists and wore shackles around their ankles. When Larry Lee and another prisoner shuffled in a few minutes later, they were secured in this manner. From Sasha's seat at the front of the gallery, she had an ideal view of him; he was only twenty feet away. His nearly chin-length hair was thin, snow-white and bushy-curly around his full face. A wiry mustache once again covered his upper lip. He seemed to have difficulty walking. Sasha couldn't tell if it was because of the chains, his ankle injury or his weight. She guessed he was close to 300 pounds now. Finally, he reached a chair, adjusted the chains binding his wrists to his waist and sat down, looking relieved to be done with that struggle.

Once sitting, he seemed relatively at ease in his shackled state. He smiled and chatted, first with the inmate seated next to him and later with his own attorney, a public defender. As he and his attorney conversed, Larry Lee's expression transitioned from attentive and pensive to somewhat amused—he was lightly laughing—but Sasha could tell they were discussing a serious matter. She watched the interactions between the public defender, the assistant DA, and the defendant, and surmised that there was some negotiation taking place.

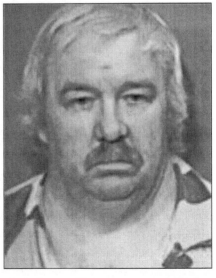

There are strict rules against those seated in the gallery communicating with the inmates—one girl was sent out of the

Knox County, Tennessee, mugshot taken of Larry Lee in October 2011, following his arrest for the kidnapping and rape of Ayesha Mack. He was now 50 years-old.

courtroom by the bailiff for violating that directive during these proceedings—but Sasha couldn't seem to keep herself from staring at Larry Lee. Four years had passed since she'd happened upon that talk given by Dr. William Bass. As a result, she had followed the trail of woe perpetrated by this almost-forgotten serial rapist. She'd compiled a history of his crimes and victims, researched the investigations (or lack thereof), and gained considerable knowledge about this predictable predator. Now here she sat, twenty feet away from him. At first she studied him out of curiosity, then it evolved into a kind of game on her part—an immature game, she acknowledged to herself—because she wanted him to look back.

Larry Lee himself would periodically scan the courtroom crowd. To do so—given the location and angle of their seats—he had to look directly past Sasha, whose eyes were focused upon him. He seemed to be searching for someone (most likely his sister or Ayesha) and acted as if he was unaware of Sasha's scrutiny. She stared at him each time he looked around, but he continued to appear oblivious, as if he didn't notice. Then, on his sixth or seventh courtroom scan, Larry Lee's line of vision shifted focus, and his eyes looked deliberately and directly into hers.

Despite feeling a mild jolt of sudden surprise, Sasha's face purposely bore no expression except for a solemn, unbroken stare. *Who is this?* Larry Lee must've wondered about the identity of the middle-aged woman in a gray suit who was staring him down in the courtroom. There was a mildly confrontational quality to his look, a non-verbal *What!? What are looking at!?* Finally, he scooted his chair far enough to the right that he was blocked from Sasha's view by the angle of the wall, and she chuckled silently to herself.

When the court reconvened after a brief recess, Larry

Lee's public-defender attorney took a seat in the gallery on the same bench as Sasha, to her immediate left. This caught her off guard. She tried to think quickly, to determine how and if she could utilize this sudden opportunity. After a couple of minutes, she scribbled a message on her yellow, college-ruled tablet: "You are representing Larry Lee Smith?" She pushed it toward him. The attorney with wavy brown hair and wire-rim glasses read the note, looked up at Sasha and nodded in the affirmative.

In a hushed tone, she whispered: "Is his case going to be heard?"

"It's going to the grand jury," he replied. The preliminary hearing was being waived. In this crowded, open courtroom, testimony in this case would no doubt be riveting. The grand jury would be a quieter route, sparing the victim.

"Do you know about his other crimes?" Sasha whispered.

"I know that he has had other charges," the public defender responded. In a low voice Sasha quickly told him about the Michelle Anderson case and touched on the others. Out of the corner of her eye, she saw Larry Lee scoot his chair so he could watch his attorney converse with the woman who had earlier been so focused upon him. Sasha wondered how far the attorney would allow this to go. She reached into her briefcase, retrieved one of her cards and extended it toward him. He held up his hand. "I really shouldn't." Instead, he pointed out a young, dark-haired woman on the other side of the courtroom, indicating that Sasha would probably want to speak with her.

Sasha stood and made her way toward the woman. She was leaning against the rail and talking with courtroom staff while supporting a stack of files in the bend of her arm. Her name was Kim Strike. She was the Victim Services Coordinator in the Violent Crimes Unit of the Knox County

District Attorney's Office, and she answered to Leslie Nassios, the prosecutor assigned to Larry Lee's case.

It was nearly noon and the courtroom had fewer people in it now. Kim Strike joined Sasha a few rows back. She informed Sasha that the most recent victim and her mother were cooperating; they'd been present in the courtroom that morning but were gone now. Sasha then shared a brief description of Larry Lee's criminal history and her research into the Michelle Anderson murder. She requested permission to create a timeline of Larry Lee's offenses for the prosecutor. Ms. Strike expressed endorsement of that plan and agreed to inform her boss of their discussion.

As they talked, Sasha faced Ms. Strike on the bench, her back toward the prisoners on the other side of the courtroom. "Does he know who you are?" Strike asked, glancing over Sasha's shoulder in the direction of the prisoner.

"No, he doesn't."

"Because he's looking over here," Strike said. Sasha felt pleased about that.

23. <u>TIMELINE</u>

S asha set to work creating the timeline for Knox County Assistant DA Leslie Nassios. She saw it as a method of conveying information in an orderly, chronological and concise manner. She wasn't an insider in the investigation, but despite the KPD's reopening of the Michelle Anderson cold case, Sasha remained the holder of the majority of information and knowledge—for better or worse—regarding Larry Lee Smith. She'd been collecting it for nearly four years now.

Sasha wanted Nassios to possess a complete picture of this perpetrator. She wanted her to feel moved and motivated to bring an end to the sexual crimes of this broken man who would never be able to control his deviant, violent impulses. Maybe it was a fantasy to believe that he would ever be charged for the kidnapping, rape and murder of Michelle, but if Nassios really understood who he was, maybe she could bring his predatory ways to a grinding halt.

Sasha began with Larry Lee's adolescence and compiled a list of his known victims, covering more than thirty years in the life of this very disturbed individual and his journey through the legal system. It ended with the most recent assault. Sasha inserted herself into the timeline—at the time she became involved—including her attempts to revive the Michelle Anderson cold case, which seemed to have cooled once again.

When completed, the timeline ran for eight-and-a-half pages. Sasha both mailed and emailed it to Nassios, with the accompanying cover letter:

Dear Ms. Nassios,

I have been researching and writing about the crimes of serial-rapist Larry Lee Smith for several years. My interest began with the unsolved kidnapping and murder of Michelle Denise Anderson in Knoxville in 1987.

Enclosed is a timeline summarizing much of what I have learned about this man and his victims. I hope the timeline is helpful to you in gaining insight into the history and nature of Mr. Smith. The world is a degree safer with his incarceration. I realize that you are prosecuting only the current case, but I hope this information will be of value.

If I can be of any assistance, please let me know.

Sincerely,
Sasha Reynolds, LCSW PIP

A few weeks later, Sasha got an email response:

Hello Ms. Reynolds,

Thank you for your interest in Mr. Smith's case. I will appreciate any information you can forward to me related to this matter.

Leslie Nassios, Assistant District Attorney

Sasha had forwarded Anita a copy of the timeline and

the letter. When she forwarded Nassios' response, Anita was encouraged by the knowledge that a prosecutor in the Knox County District Attorney's office was aware of her daughter's cold case. She sent an email to Nassios that very evening. Nassios promptly responded with an offer to meet with Anita, and they scheduled an appointment.

Anita felt nervous before her one-on-one with Nassios. Here she was again, opening old wounds, wounds that had never fully healed. But she had high hopes Nassios could help.

At their meeting, Nassios noted that it was unusual for her to have responded to an email as she had to Sasha's, someone who was *writing* about the case, a "kook" for all she knew. She also admitted that, due to her heavy case load, she had not yet read the entire timeline. So she asked Anita to walk her through Michelle's story. Anita tried as best as she could. She started crying only a few sentences in, but she powered through, even if she was an emotional wreck by the end.

Nassios was supportive and compassionate with Anita and assured her that she would follow up on Michelle's case. Buoyed by the meeting, Anita left feeling guardedly hopeful.

On Tuesday, January 17, 2012, five days after Anita's meeting with Leslie Nassios, the Knox County Grand Jury met to hear the basis of the prosecution's case against Larry Lee Smith for the October 24, 2011, kidnapping and rape of Ayesha Mack. The following witnesses were summoned before the grand jury: the KPD Custodian of Records for the 911 calls, the investigating officers, the victim, Volunteer Studios staff, and staff from the Sexual Assault Center of East Tennessee.

The victim, though, was not present. On the official police report of Ayesha's assault, her address was listed as "Homeless." (She and her boyfriend had been living with

Khristy in exchange for drugs.) So Ayesha's subpoena had been mailed to Ayesha's mother, but the address on file was incorrect, the subpoena was returned, and Ayesha didn't get notice to appear before the grand jury.

Fortunately for the prosecution, the grand jury still determined there was enough evidence to indict Larry Lee Smith on charges of Aggravated Kidnapping and Aggravated Rape. He was bound over for trial.

They'd surpassed this hurdle, but Nassios was concerned that her office might be losing the cooperation of its most important witness, who was now living with her mother and siblings south of Atlanta, Georgia, close to two hundred miles away.

KPD Investigator Jeff Day saw Larry Lee's indictment as an opportunity. With a return to prison looking inevitable, Larry Lee might be willing to cooperate on the Michelle Anderson cold case. So two days after his indictment, Larry Lee sat across from Jeff Day in an interrogation room in the City-County Building, the session being videotaped. Retired KPD homicide Investigator Randy York watched from a nearby viewing room, out of the inmate's sight.

Day started off by discussing Larry Lee's current charges. Larry Lee put forth a cocky defense, expressing confidence that he would get off, that Ayesha—*Jade*—wouldn't follow through and testify. He said this more than once. When they moved to the Michelle Anderson case, Larry Lee sang the same old song about dropping Michelle off at the corner of Cherry and Jefferson. Day pressed for details, pushing for something new, something different, something altered, but after four hours of questioning, Larry Lee still stuck to his story. When Day introduced the subject of DNA, he thought he detected a flinch on the part of the prisoner, but that was all.

Yet there had been a moment near the end of the interview when the investigator thought that the suspect just might cave. Larry Lee had reportedly lowered his head as his eyes became teary, and he mumbled that he felt "responsible" for Michelle. When the KPD Investigator followed up by asking what he meant, Larry Lee asked for his lawyer.

When it was apparent that the interview was unlikely to produce any results, Day played his final hand. Retired KPD Investigator York stepped into the room. "Hello, Larry," he said. "It's been a long time." Larry Lee squinted at this newcomer while his memory cells reconfigured. More than two decades had passed, but few people had aged as little as York. "White as a sheet" is how York described Larry Lee when he realized who was standing there, the investigator who'd made his life miserable all those years ago. Larry Lee immediately requested to leave the interview. He had nothing else to say.

When told about the interview later, Anita confided to Sasha that she wasn't quite sure she believed the part about Larry Lee's tears. She had become skeptical of everything and everyone. She believed that others just told her what she wanted to hear.

With Day's interview yielding no results, Michelle's case cooled down yet again. Communication between Sasha and Anita with the KPD cooled down with it. Neither Sasha nor Anita knew if the nails had ever been sent for DNA testing, although both repeatedly inquired. Clearly, no new case-altering developments had occurred. Even Nassios, who initially showed an interest in the case, had little time to devote to it. She had her hands full with other cases and in making sure Ayesha was going to show.

Nassios eventually made contact with Ayesha. The

prosecutor then asked Anita's permission to give Ayesha her number with the hope that Ayesha would reach out to her and be encouraged to follow through in the case.

A few days later, while driving, Anita received a call. The connection wasn't perfect, but as Ayesha launched into her story, Anita quickly realized who it was and pulled over. Ayesha cried as she described her ordeal. "I thought he was going to kill me," she said. "I really did. I couldn't breathe. I felt my eyes rolling back in my head." Anita cried as she listened. It became an overwhelming emotional experience for both women. Ayesha told her how scared she'd been and how sorry she was to hear about Michelle.

Ayesha wondered aloud why fate had delivered her to the path of someone like Larry Lee. Yet of one thing she seemed certain. There had been a sign in this traumatic event—that knock on the apartment door. As her eyes were rolling back in her head, and her rapist's sweat was dripping onto her face, that knock changed the course of events. It was that *thump-thump* that caused Larry Lee to pause, allowing Ayesha to take a breath and yell out to the anonymous knocker.

Yet when Ayesha's voice rang out, no answer came back in reply, and nobody stood before the door when it was cast open as she fled some minutes later. It was as if the hand of God had reached into the long hallway of Volunteer Studios and rescued a strayed member of His flock. That's how Ayesha's mother saw it, she explained to Anita. Ayesha was beginning to see it that way herself.

At the end of the conversation, she promised Anita she would show up for the trial. "There's no way I won't be there," she said.

24. <u>PRIOR BAD ACTS</u>

In June 2012, Joey Smith's cousin Jenny contacted Sasha with tragic news. Sara Smith had died suddenly from a stroke. She'd had a hard life, endured unspeakable horrors at the hands of her own relatives and sadistic husband, and then coped with those horrors through drugs and alcohol. At age forty-eight, all her years of hard living seemed to have caught up with her.

Sasha was distraught that Sara wouldn't see Larry Lee come to trial. She couldn't imagine Larry Lee's twisted saga coming to an end without Sara around to see it. She located Sara's obituary on the funeral home's website, which allowed visitors to share photos. She uploaded a photo she had of Sara and Joey, taken when Sara was in her twenties and Joey was a pre-teen.

Sara's short obituary contained a descriptive statement of clear and accurate truth: "She was a loving, caring person and kind to everyone." But Sasha felt that this description left out the most important detail of all: Sara Smith had been a survivor. Despite her inner pain, she'd remained warm, compassionate, and generous to others, family and friends alike. Sasha could take solace only in that Sara's troubled mind, plagued as it was by repulsive memories and perpetual nightmares, was finally at rest.

Due to an unspecified "conflict," Larry Lee's public defender had been excused and a court-appointed attorney, Mitch Harper, had taken his place. In July 2012, Harper, a former assistant district attorney who had since gone into private practice, filed a motion for a hearing, but no one seemed to know what the hearing was about. Sasha called the criminal court a number of times to see if any additional paperwork had been filed clarifying the subject of the motion. None had, but the case remained on the docket, so she made the several-hour trip to the courthouse in Knoxville.

Anita and York agreed to meet her there. More than twenty years had passed since York and Anita had seen one another, but the retired investigator recognized her immediately as she came through the entrance to the City-County Building. He squinted at her playfully and declared, "Haven't aged a bit!"

They walked together to the criminal court one level above. York checked, and Larry Lee's name was still on the docket, but there was no sign of him in the courtroom. Then York spotted Larry Lee's attorney, a colleague of sorts. He strolled up behind Harper, a slender man of average height with hawk-like features and close-cropped hair, and squeezed him on the shoulders, then bent down and asked about the hearing.

Even Harper wasn't sure why it was on the docket, but he said a motion on the case against Larry Lee would not be heard in court that day. This was disappointing news. Sasha had driven hours to be there, and Anita had taken the whole day off from work. She'd been anxious about the hearing, fearful of her reaction at the sight of Larry Lee, the first she would have laid eyes on him in nearly twenty-five years. She had even brought along a paper bag in case she began to hyperventilate.

"Well..." Sasha exhaled.

"Well, indeed!" Anita agreed.

As they pushed through the brass-rimmed glass door to exit the courtroom, they encountered Leslie Nassios preparing to walk in. Anita took the opportunity to introduce Sasha, as the two had never met in person. In this brief interaction, Sasha could sense that Nassios felt great compassion for Anita. Nassios invited them to join her across the hall in the district attorney's conference room.

Now Sasha was about to engage in a face-to-face with the assistant district attorney, prosecutor in the newest case against Larry Lee. *So...* she noted to herself, *this is why we're here.*

Anita and Sasha picked from the blue swivel chairs that encircled the long, shiny, oval-shaped wooden table. Nassios, who wore her dark, wavy hair just below her shoulders, sat facing them on the opposite side.

She focused her attention first on Anita, checking up on her, then turned to Sasha. "I appreciate the information you've emailed to me," she said.

"I'll be glad to share any documents I have," Sasha replied, "anything that you can use."

"Obviously this case will hinge on the victim showing up," Nassios said. "In the beginning she seemed very eager to prosecute. This case is set for September. I've got a murder trial the end of August. I know you'd like answers today, but we just deal with our cases as they come up. We usually wait until a month or so before the trial to start preparing."

The pending prosecution of Larry Lee may have been on her office's long list of cases, but at this moment, it had her full attention. She shifted her focus again in the direction of Anita. "Nothing regarding your daughter is going to come into evidence. You understand that, right? I'm just trying to prepare you."

Anita's eyes filled with tears and she struggled to find any words at all.

The prosecutor's face reflected both compassion and confusion. "Why are you crying?" she asked gently, concerned that she might have upset Anita. "I'm really sorry about your daughter."

"She's held it in for such a long time," Sasha offered. "There's never been any real resolution or closure for the family."

Eventually Anita gained control of the sobs enough to utter some words of response. "I'm just not used to talking about it," she confessed. "It's still very hard."

As Anita's tears slowed and she regained her composure, Nassios continued, stating that unlike Larry Lee's Georgia trial twenty years earlier, no evidence of any prior convictions was likely to be admitted during his new trial. "Larry Lee's previous convictions are not going to come into evidence unless he testifies, and *still* the court may make a ruling that it's too similar in nature to what he's charged with and too prejudicial for that to come into evidence."

What a difference another state can make. Nassios didn't know the particulars of Georgia's more liberal policy toward the admission of "similar transaction" evidence in sex-offense cases, but she provided a perspective on the way these matters were usually handled in Tennessee. She said she'd be more likely to get evidence of a similar crime admitted if it was, for instance, a drug store robbery and the defendant used a similar kind of unusual note or a type of bomb or asked for a particular drug. "I just know the Tennessee law is restrictive, particularly on sex cases."

She recalled past cases she had tried in which the "prior bad acts"—as these similar offenses were called in Tennessee law—reflected clear "similar transaction" evidence—proof of motive, opportunity, intent, preparation, plan, knowledge, identity, or absence of mistake or accident—but was still not allowed by the presiding judge. In the prosecution of sex crimes in Tennessee, Nassios explained, the admission of evidence of similar "prior bad acts" is very, very rare.

And while the prosecutor lamented those times when she felt she'd met the standard for admission of such evidence and still been denied, she still defended the need for caution. "The reason why a defendant's past history can't come into evidence is because it would be really difficult for a juror to keep that out of his or her mind and try the defendant for the case that's there in the court that day. It would be really hard for that kind of prejudice not to cloud your judgement in a particular case. I would have difficulty setting it aside. *If he raped somebody before, he did it in this case, too.* And so the law errs on the side of the defendant."

Sometimes, Nassios pointed out, all a prosecutor can do with the knowledge of a perpetrator's pattern of past crimes is use it to motivate him or her to strive even harder to win the case. "Will you send me the numbers and information on those other court cases?" she asked Sasha.

"Absolutely."

Nassios then shared more examples of cases she'd prosecuted that had elements in common with the one against Larry Lee, including trials of serial rapists and murderers, and one in which evidence had also been lost. She wanted Anita to know she wasn't alone in these experiences. "The incompetency level that we sometimes tolerate..." Nassios observed, letting the thought trail off. Then referring to the lack of investigation when Michelle initially went missing, she said, "I don't know why the detective didn't do more to try to find out where Larry Lee went and *document, document, document.* For some, it's easier to believe that girls ask for it, that they run away."

The discussion evolved to the specifics of the night and early morning of Michelle's disappearance. Sasha, who very much desired to hear Nassios' thoughts on this topic, once again laid out the reported series of events on that last night of Michelle's life, including the involvement of her boyfriend, Chas. "I don't think Larry Lee is the kind of guy to work with anybody," Nassios speculated. "He drove off alone with her."

Then as they talked about it further, the prosecutor proposed a different angle. "What makes you think they both didn't rape her? Looking at all of this objectively and trying to think of what is the most likely thing that happened— and I'm calling upon thirty years of experience dealing with rapists and murderers—I try to figure out how they think, how things happened. In this case, it seems the most likely scenario is she's drunk, she passes out, they rape her, she comes to and she wants to get out. She's coherent enough that she pulls on her pants. She doesn't look for her underwear. She's in a hurry. She doesn't have time to put on her shoes. She makes a fuss and he strangles her to make her shut up. And then he's got a girl he's got to get rid of."

"I've thought about that, too," Anita said.

"And stranglers *strangle*," Nassios continued, "over and over. Now that is something that is unique. They use that mechanism to shut women up, to get control of them."

Larry Lee was most certainly a strangler, Sasha pointed out, a fact he'd proven *over and over* across the decades. "But why would Larry Lee give Chas an alibi by saying he dropped him off first at his house?" Sasha asked.

"Because they're protecting each other," Nassios speculated.

"That was my initial thought," Anita responded. She had developed suspicions about Chas in those first months after Michelle disappeared, and she'd never been able to let them go. "The two stories were just so perfectly... I mean... they were *exactly* the same."

"Their stories are the same until Larry Lee says he dropped Michelle back near Chas's house," Sasha interjected. "He tries to implicate Chas in the end by saying, 'I dropped her off near your house.'"

"Not really," Nassios countered. "Why would he put her at a location *away* from the house?"—a few doors down at the corner of Cherry and Jefferson—"Why would you *not* drop her at the door? That doesn't make any sense. He was actually *helping* Chas by having her dropped off not in front of the house. If he says he dropped her off in front of the house, it's going to be hard for Chas to explain that she didn't knock. The police might not believe that. On the other hand, Larry Lee says, 'I dropped her on this corner'—a dangerous area at a time when who knows who can be out—it kind of absolves Chas from explaining why she didn't knock at the door. How could something happen from the street to the doorway? Do you see what I'm saying?"

Sasha was intrigued by Nassios' reasoning, and she would readily defer to the assistant DA's experienced legal mind. The account given by Larry Lee and Chas of what had happened in Larry Lee's bedroom that night never had the ring of complete truth. Sasha had concluded long ago that Chas had taken advantage of Michelle's inebriated state and either had sex with her while she was passed out or forced himself on her when she was barely conscious. And, at the very least, Larry

Lee enjoyed being a stairway spectator to this event, just as he had enjoyed prostituting Sara and Maryanne and watching from closets while they were with other men.

Still, Sasha had reasoned that Larry Lee's lie about dropping Michelle off at the corner was his way of covering for the fact that she never arrived at Chas's house. And the part about Chas being made to ride back in the cold truck bed—a detail provided in both of their accounts—seemed to fit in with Larry Lee's *modus operandi:* splitting them up before driving off alone with Michelle. That detail, Sasha had determined, brought no additional merit to their respective stories except that it inadvertently lent credibility to the account of Chas being dropped off first, alone, and seemed unlikely to have been made up. Larry Lee was a compulsive liar, just not a particularly skillful one.

"Well, obviously, I think it's *all* a lie because he was dumping her body," Nassios clarified. "But you have to explain, where is the underwear? Where are the shoes? Assuming we ever got enough to take this case to trial, we'd have to prove venue, where the crime happened. Venue is presumed to be where the body is found. She would have to have been kidnapped or harmed in Knoxville, initially, for us to even have jurisdiction. The only way to connect him to her death is to connect him to the location of her remains. That's impossible to do at this point."

Why had Larry Lee chosen the wooded hillside outside Crossville, fifty miles west of Knoxville, Nassios wondered. When Larry Lee's niece, Jenny, had contacted Sasha just months earlier, she'd raised this same question. Jenny had only recently learned of Michelle's murder and that her uncle was a primary suspect. She said she had no difficulty believing Larry Lee capable of Michelle's death, because she had experienced his sadistic ways first hand, but why was the body placed outside Crossville, off Highway 68? Jenny thought there had to be a connection. "He's just not that clever," she'd said. "That's a long way to go with a body... unless she was still alive."

Now Leslie Nassios seemed to draw a similar conclusion: "Larry Lee has some kind of connection to that area. It's too particular. He knew that area. He could have just dumped her body off the interstate."

25. <u>OH, I'LL BE THERE!</u>

The pending trial of Larry Lee Smith was pushed back from September 2012 to Monday, February 25, 2013, sixteen months and one day since his attack on Ayesha. He'd been incarcerated the entire time.

For the past few months, Sasha had been in intermittent contact with Ayesha. The two had been communicating since Ayesha had reached out to Anita some months before. She had given Anita permission to pass her contact information along to Sasha. While Ayesha answered texts, she was less consistent in responding to emails, whether from Sasha, Anita or Amanda Sanders, who also had reached out to her as a fellow victim of Larry Lee. None of them were sure what to make of Ayesha's sporadic responses until Sasha got a surprising email from her on a Thursday evening two days into the new year, just two months before the beginning of the rescheduled trial:

> Hey. How you doing? This is Ayesha. Could you give me a call when you get a chance?

The cell phone number she provided was new. Sasha gave her a call that very night.

"Hey. Thanks for calling," Ayesha responded in her cordial manner. "I wanted to find out what was going on in the case. I haven't heard from anybody in a while. And I want to tell you about this guy who said he is a lawyer coming to my house." She went on to describe how she wasn't home when this attorney stopped by, but that her mother or brother had given him Ayesha's phone number, and he'd called and left a message. When Ayesha called him back, he asked her what happened the day of the assault, and she told him. Then the attorney informed her of Larry Lee's side of the story, that he and Ayesha had an ongoing sexual relationship, and that she had come to his apartment that day in search of drugs. Supposedly, the attorney said, there were witnesses.

Ayesha told the attorney none of that was true. He said he was in his car when she'd called and couldn't take notes. He'd have to call her back. Ayesha decided to contact Sasha first.

"Was this guy's name Mitch Harper?"

"Yes, it was!" Ayesha confirmed.

"He's Larry Lee's attorney," Sasha explained. She was surprised by this news. According to certain law enforcement and public officials who'd had occasion to work with Harper, he usually made adequate efforts to defend his clients, but he wasn't seen as particularly *overzealous*. So what Ayesha was saying he had done on behalf of his client was surprising. But Sasha also understood why Ayesha had talked to him. Ayesha had lost contact with nearly everyone involved in the case and hadn't heard anything for months. She wanted information.

In the time since Ayesha had returned to live with her mother and siblings in Georgia, she'd been working at a fast-food job. It hadn't been the easiest year: she and Tam had broken up and he was on the run, her relationship with her mother remained strained, and the intrusive memories of her kidnapping and rape—as well as apprehension about the pending trial—kept her stressed out and on edge.

Not long after she'd returned home, Ayesha's phone number changed and both she and her mother had lost the names and phone numbers of Nassios' staff. She'd had minimal contact with them up to that point, anyway, so she didn't think much of it. Because Nassios' office had the wrong address on file for Ayesha's mother, Ayesha never received the subpoena. She'd been completely in the dark about the case until she began talking to Anita and Sasha on the phone. So she was surprised to come home one day and find out that this lawyer had dropped by her house while she was at work.

Harper had left his business card with his number, and Ayesha's mother told her to call it. Now she felt foolish for calling Harper back. She was also miffed at her mom for urging her to do so. Sasha reassured the naive, inexperienced teen that it was reasonable for her to be confused, to want information instead of waiting around in the dark.

"It's his job to defend Larry Lee," Sasha explained to Ayesha, "to try to get him off. Mitch Harper is trying to scare you into not testifying. Larry Lee's been telling everyone that you won't show."

"Oh, I'll be there!" Ayesha asserted. "I think about what he did to me every day. I shake if I see someone somewhere who looks like him."

Ayesha said she was uncertain about who, exactly, represented her. The state represented her, Sasha explained, and told her about Leslie Nassios. Ayesha remembered meeting with Kim Strike, Nassios' assistant, when Ayesha and her mother attended a preliminary hearing in Knoxville. That had been back in November 2011.

"I'll email their names, numbers and email addresses to you again tonight," Sasha said. "And I'll contact them tomorrow and give them your new phone number."

"Okay. Thanks. That'll be good."

"Don't talk to him again."

"Oh, trust me, I won't!"

That evening Sasha sent an email to Leslie Nassios and Kim Strike, giving them Ayesha's contact information and informing them about the unexpected visit of defense attorney Mitch Harper. She passed along what he had asked Ayesha and what he had alleged about Larry Lee's and Ayesha's "relationship." She also reported on Ayesha's verbalized commitment to be present for the trial.

Mid-afternoon the next day, Sasha got a courteous and professional reply. Nassios thanked her for the information and informed her that she had spoken to Ayesha that day. She signed off with:

> We are in good shape. I appreciate your help.

Sasha knew Mitch Harper was just doing his job, but she also thought he might need a little education about the client he'd been appointed to defend. Finding an email address for the attorney online, Sasha sent him a message:

> Mr. Harper, Larry Lee Smith has been charged in three rapes (so far, convicted of two) of young girls who needed help, Ayesha Mack being the latest...

She then provided details about Michelle's unsolved 1987 murder and attached a link to the Channel 6 cold-case video that KPD Investigator Jeff Day had initiated.

"Smith is a *power* rapist," Sasha wrote. Then she explained Larry Lee's process, pointing out how he befriends and then assaults young girls, using hitting and choking as his primary means of overpowering his victims.

Sasha forwarded a copy of the email to Anita, who then

composed her own response and sent it on to Larry Lee's attorney as well:

Mr. Harper,

My name is Anita Anderson, Michelle was my daughter. Sasha Reynolds has been collecting information for years, starting out in Michelle's behalf. Smith is a dangerous rapist who doesn't need to be released into society. He was and is the main suspect in my daughter's death. He will probably never be convicted for her murder, but I pray that he will be incarcerated for the rape of Ayesha Mack. At least we will have some peace, knowing that he will be off the streets for another twenty years.

Anita Anderson

Of course there was no reply, but Sasha and Anita felt optimistic that the messages had reached their intended target.

As the trial drew near, Sasha hoped for some media coverage, but there wasn't any, and she wasn't sure how she could help bring this about. In early January 2013, she sent out several emails to Channel 6 reporter Mona Nair, who'd covered the cold-case piece, and to the news director at that station, but she'd gotten no response.

A couple weeks later Sasha stumbled upon a series of articles that ran under the headline "Slaying in Sequoyah Hills: Who Killed Rose Bush?" They told the story of infamous playgirl-turned-Knoxville-madam Hazel Davidson—the former employer of both Sara and Maryanne—who may have played a role in the brutal murder of a prominent businessman's wife in 1969. The businessman had been a paramour of Hazel Davidson; the late madam remained a suspect in the sensational death-by-hire case, which was never solved. The article was written by veteran *Knoxville News Sentinel* journalist Jim Balloch.

Sasha had never heard of Hazel Davidson during the years she'd lived in Knoxville, but during her investigation into Larry Lee, she'd run into the name a number of times. In the first year that Michelle went missing, one of the false leads Anita had followed took her to Hazel Davidson's eponymous upscale brothel.

Sasha decided to reach out to Balloch. She found an email address for him at the newspaper and sent him a message:

> I am investigating and writing about an unsolved murder in Knoxville (not Busch; really enjoyed the articles, though). I am writing to determine if you are still at the paper. I don't live in Tennessee.

Balloch replied the next day:

> Yep, still here.

Sasha responded with a brief email highlighting Michelle's unsolved murder, her own post-2007 involvement, and a chronicle of Larry Lee's other assaults, including the one for which he was about to go on trial. She hoped to stir Balloch's curiosity.

A couple of days later he replied:

> Is the new case here in Knoxville? Where?

Sasha became hopeful and immediately filled Balloch in on the present case and her own research on Michelle Anderson. She expressed hope that he, or someone else at the paper, would cover the trial.

A few days later, she received a response:

* * *

> My memory of the Michelle Anderson case has been
> jogged by a fellow reporter. I once wrote a story about it,
> when it looked like cops were on the verge of breaking it.
> Have you talked to retired KPD Detective Randy York?
> He probably knows more about this case than anyone.

This was exciting. Sasha had read through all of the local newspaper articles pertaining to Michelle Anderson—most of them had been included in Dr. Bass's notes—but she hadn't realized that Balloch wrote one of them. After getting his memory "jogged," Balloch had reviewed the article he'd written at the request of KPD Investigator Randy York in January of 1990. He recalled that he'd been instructed not to use Larry Lee's name in the article, although these twenty-plus years later, he couldn't remember why. Sasha reminded him that it was because Larry Lee had lawyered up and claimed harassment by York and the KPD.

She also reminded him about the trial date and let him know that she would be attending along with Anita and two of Larry Lee's early victims. They would all be there to support the current victim. Sasha ended by asking if Balloch might cover the trial.

Jim Balloch's reply came within a couple of hours:

> Possibly. I have forwarded your original emails to Jamie
> Satterfield, our normal court reporter; but since I now
> remember that I wrote about Michelle's case, I might ask
> her to let me deal with it.

> In either case, we likely would not cover this trial gavel
> to gavel [the trial for a hit-and-run DUI in which several
> people had died was scheduled to begin on the same
> day], but approach it in another way. Maybe one pre-trial
> story connecting Michelle, and a follow-up story after the
> verdict. I'm not sure, I will have to talk to Jamie and our
> editors.

* * *

Sasha forwarded the message on to Anita, who wrote back:

> You continue to amaze me! What cojones! What are your plans, when will you be here and is Bert coming with you?

They began preparing for the pending trial. There was work to do. Anita and Sasha were organizing a gathering with Katherine McWilliams and Amanda Sanders, who wanted to be there to support Ayesha. Over the next couple of weeks, Sasha and Anita finalized plans and set up accommodations.

Once they sent out the invitations, the process of getting everyone on board had been fairly effortless. Each wanted to come for their own personal reasons: they wanted to encourage Ayesha, they wanted to find some sense of closure, but most of all they wanted to support Anita. It was her stated wish to meet these women, these survivors who shared some piece of fate with her precious baby girl.

26. **BAND OF SISTERS**

Sasha and her husband Bert departed for Knoxville on Saturday, February 23, 2013, two days before the trial. After they checked into their downtown hotel, Sasha texted Ayesha, who was being bused in by the DA's office and was scheduled to arrive that evening. Sasha wanted to make sure she had arrived safely.

"I'm here," Ayesha replied.

"We're all getting together tomorrow evening for dinner. Would you like to join us?"

"Yes, I would."

"Great! I'll call you tomorrow."

The next day, Ayesha met with Assistant District Attorney Leslie Nassios and KPD Investigator Patty Tipton to review the evidence and prepare for the trial. In the evening, Sasha and Bert went to Ayesha's hotel and met her in the lobby. "There she is!" Bert said, smiling broadly and extending his hand as Ayesha stepped off the elevator.

"Hi. It's great to finally meet you," Sasha added, giving Ayesha a hug.

"Hi. Yes, it's nice to meet you, too," Ayesha replied shyly, deep dimples punctuating her cautious and friendly smile.

Exiting the front door of the hotel at the close of a sunny afternoon, the trio walked into the cool and breezy evening air just as the sun was beginning to set. Temperatures were sliding from a high in the mid-fifties back to the February forties.

"So, your mom didn't come with you?" Sasha inquired. Ayesha had been put in a hotel room furnished with two queen-size beds in anticipation that she would.

"No, she didn't," Ayesha replied, a pained expression on her face.

"Why is that?"

"I don't know. I didn't ask. She said she wasn't coming, so there wasn't any point in asking." What Ayesha didn't say communicated as much as what she did.

"There's some tension between you and your mom?"

"Yeah, there is," Ayesha admitted, her eyes getting teary. "I needed her to come, but she didn't."

They walked through the entrance of a popular downtown brewpub Sasha and Anita had picked for this occasion. Amanda, Katherine, and Katherine's husband, Steve, were seated at a table just inside the door. Almost simultaneously, Anita and Ted came walking in from the entrance in the back where they'd parked. Perfect timing. Sasha introduced everyone and they moved to an upstairs table along an exposed brick wall.

"Guys at that end of the table," instructed one of the women, and the group pulled out their heavy wooden chairs and sat down to partake in this remarkable assemblage. Entrees were ordered, along with a few glasses of blonde brew, and the women focused in on one another.

While a series of tragedies had brought them together, there was a kind of triumph in this gathering. A culmination of crises encountered and overcome, in one way or another, had resulted in the banding together of these women across generations and decades, even as their private lives had carried on quite independently. They dubbed themselves the "Band of Sisters," and Michelle was always at the silent center of their awareness.

Anita had felt so guilty, she explained, so responsible for the fate of her daughter. But here were these other women— good, decent women—and it had happened to them, too. Their presence made her feel less isolated in her loss, less despair in her self-blame, less alone in the horror and grief she'd had to bear.

"It's wonderful that we're all here together," Sasha said, surveying the faces. "I just wish Sara were here. She would have loved this, and you would have really liked her. Maybe she sees us."

"I wish Sara were here, too," Anita added. "She would have enjoyed meeting all of you and seeing Larry Lee get what he deserves."

"I heard about her today," Ayesha said. During her time spent with Nassios and Investigator Tipton that afternoon, they had reviewed jailhouse phone calls between Larry Lee and his sister, Nancy. In one call, Nancy had informed him about Sara's death. "He was real happy about that," Ayesha said. "He didn't like her at all."

"Oh, I bet!" Sasha responded. "She gave it her all to bring him to justice."

As the food arrived, the women continued their conversation, getting acquainted, at times laughing, at other times tearing up, sharing parts of their individual stories. Sasha would periodically put her hand on Ayesha's back and give it a quick and reassuring rub. It was a gesture that would be repeated by nearly all the women that night and over the next couple of days. The group wrapped around her in protection and support, this brave little girl from the streets who'd overcome her fears to show up for the trial, something Larry Lee had predicted over and over that she would never do.

For Ayesha, the early part of the day spent in preparation for the trial had been full of information and images that she'd yet to fully process in her mind. She knew Larry Lee had hooked her wrist with a looped neck tie, but she hadn't known from where it had come or even how he'd done this; it all happened so quickly. But in Nassios' office, Ayesha was shown the chain of neck ties found behind his bed.

Yet as traumatizing as Larry Lee's sexual assault upon her had been, she hadn't been prepared for the images she was shown from Larry Lee's phone, including a video of Khristy crying while disrobing. After seeing them, Ayesha felt like she'd unwittingly played a part in a mini horror show. She expressed her gratitude that everyone had come out to support her. It might have been too difficult for her to do it alone.

At the other end of the table the men engaged in friendly and casual conversation throughout the dinner, the feeling of camaraderie extending there as well. Overall, a warm and uplifting atmosphere surrounded the gathering. As they brought the evening to a close, some sense of peace pervaded, even as they prepared psychologically for court in the morning. Only Ayesha, alone in her room, nervous about what she'd seen and what she would experience the next day, had difficulty falling asleep that night.

Sasha awoke early the next morning and went down to the breakfast bar to retrieve a couple coffees. She spied the morning paper and its front-page headline: "A new focus on girl's '87 death—Chief suspect facing trial in unrelated case."

Jim Balloch had come through, writing the article himself. He'd called Sasha on Friday of the previous week, updating his information and getting contact numbers for those involved. Sasha bought several copies, rushed back to her room, and enthusiastically read through the article.

"When Larry Lee Smith goes on trial this week for a 2011 kidnapping and rape," the story began, "many eyes from the distant past will be on him. Smith, now 52, is the chief suspect in the unsolved disappearance and death 26 years ago of Michelle Anderson, a 15-year-old Fulton High School student. This week, Smith is facing trial in the aggravated rape of a young adult woman. She lived in the same apartment complex as Smith..."

Sasha was thrilled with the reporting on the story, which highlighted the nature of the assault on Ayesha and included a detailed account of Michelle's disappearance. The article did just what Balloch and Sasha had intended: it linked the crimes.

"The two cases are unrelated," Balloch wrote. "But Michelle Anderson's mother and other family members plan to be in the courtroom. So do a couple of investigators, now retired, who pursued the case over the years. And so does a former Knoxville woman, who is writing a book on the case and whose son was a classmate of Michelle.... Her book, to be titled *Similar Transactions,* will link Smith to several other crimes as well." The long article included comments from Anita, Randy York and Grey Steed.

It had been a long, long time, but finally, there it was, a factual account, in the newspaper, on page one.

Monday

NEWS SENTINEL

Knoxville   KnoxNews.com

February 25, 2013   ★★★★★   75 cents

A new focus on girl's '87 death

■ Chief suspect facing trial in unrelated case

By Jim Balloch
ballochj@knoxnews.com
865-342-6315

When Larry Lee Smith goes on trial this week for a 2011 kidnapping and rape, many eyes from the distant past will be on him.

Smith, now 52, is the chief suspect in the unsolved disappearance and death 26 years ago of Michelle Anderson, a 15-year-old Fulton High School student.

Michelle Anderson

This week Smith is facing trial in the aggravated rape of a young adult woman. She lived in the same apartment complex as Smith. Authorities say she went to his apartment because she needed to use his telephone. She was tied with neckties and raped, then managed to escape when Smith was distracted by a person who knocked on his door.

Larry Lee Smith

The two cases are unrelated. But Michelle Anderson's mother, ███████ Anderson, and other family members plan to be in the courtroom.

So do a couple of investigators, now retired, who pursued the Michelle Anderson case over the years.

And so does Sasha Reynolds, a former Knoxville woman, who is writing a book on the case and whose son was a classmate of Michelle.

Smith previously has been convicted of sexual offenses in Florida and Georgia. The Georgia case sent him to prison for nearly 20 years.

Reynolds says her book, to be titled "Similar Transactions," will link Smith to several other crimes as well.

"I just feel like I have to be there," ███████ Anderson said. "I don't know that anything is ever going to be done about Michelle. But if nothing else, I hope he is convicted (of this) and put away so it won't happen again."

The disappearance of Michelle Anderson generated a number of news stories and widespread

See SUSPECT, 12A

337

27. <u>SHADES OF GRAY</u>

The trial of Larry Lee Smith began on Monday, February 25, 2013. The Band of Sisters and their spouses met in the lobby of Sasha and Bert's hotel, just blocks from the courthouse. They were joined by Anita's cousin Susan and her friend Bobbi. Ayesha had already been transported via shuttle from her hotel and was safely sequestered in the DA's office until her time to testify.

The group walked together down Main Street. When they entered the second-floor courtroom, jury selection was underway. Judge Bob R. "Bobby Ray" McGee, elected as the criminal court magistrate five years earlier, was presiding. He had been raised in Knoxville and was a graduate of the University of Tennessee College of Law.

The group slid quietly onto the pale-oak bench second from the front, just behind the defense table. Larry Lee sat only ten feet away. From the top of his thin, white-gray hair—pulled neatly back into a three-inch ponytail—to the tip of his new, black-gray shoes, fifty-two-year-old Larry Lee was decked out entirely in shades of gray. His shirt, a shiny sheet metal gray, paired with a charcoal-colored tie, was tucked into wide, gray, pleated pants; his belt and hair tie were a complementary black. His pink, fleshy face, now devoid of a shaggy mustache, stood out against this smoky ensemble. Fifteen-plus months of starchy jail food had not been kind to his waistline. Not long after the group took their seats, Larry Lee turned to survey these newcomers. His slow attentive gaze moved down the line. He had a bold, confrontational look about him. A sneer was affixed to his face, which bore no trace of humility, embarrassment or shame. When his eyes rested on Sasha, his gaze morphed to a momentary glare. She was slightly taken aback by the brazen lock of his eyes—*Had he read that morning's article? Did he recognize her from the court hearing more than a year before? Did he know she was writing a book about him?*—but then he continued his visual survey down the bench. *Did he recognize Anita these more than twenty-five years since he'd met her the day after Michelle disappeared?* They couldn't be sure. Just before he'd turned around, Katherine and Amanda had stepped out; the group would have to wait to see if he recognized his victims from decades before.

The jury pool filled most of the gallery benches on the opposite side of the center aisle. Looking over at the individuals seated there, Sasha was surprised to observe that they were entirely Caucasian except for a white-haired Asian gentleman. Ayesha was African-American. *Could this be a problem?*

Sasha found the process of questioning potential jurors absorbing. Knox County Assistant District Attorney Leslie Nassios, dressed in a brown pantsuit with her hair held back by a wide, tortoise-shell barrette, sought to identify and eliminate jurors who might have difficulty seeing past Ayesha's semi-marginal lifestyle. She'd been a runaway teen, lived under an alias, travelled with a drug-dealing boyfriend, and been arrested for shoplifting. Nassios referenced these aspects of Ayesha's lifestyle to probe prospective jurors for any probability they might be biased against her, and therefore unable to empathize with the trauma she had suffered at the hands of Larry Lee. Most denied any bias.

The DA also asked if any of the potential jurors had read the newspaper article that had appeared that morning in the *Knoxville News Sentinel*, the first to link Larry Lee to the unsolved Michelle Anderson case. Sasha had considered it a real victory, but the DA's office wasn't so happy. They had to cull the jurors for any prejudice it might have caused.

Nassios had predicted that jury selection would take two to three hours and she was right on the mark. When it was done, the jury of twelve consisted of six women and six men, one of whom was the white-haired Asian man. The thirteenth alternate juror was also male.

The court took a brief recess and Larry Lee was escorted to a small holding room behind the judge's bench. The remainder of the jury pool had been dismissed, making available the benches on the left. When the court reconvened, Sasha and the group shifted to that side of the courtroom, second bench back, behind the prosecutor's table. Katherine and Amanda returned and sat on the end, closest to the aisle.

As Larry Lee exited the holding room and walked toward the defense table, his gaze landed squarely on Amanda, then moved over to Katherine. All sets of eyes in the group saw it: the flinch, the momentary lapse of the sneer, the quick look of surprise and perhaps mild panic as he recognized who they were. As soon as he sat down, he leaned in to his attorney and Sasha overheard him asking, *"They aren't going to testify, are they?"*

From her new angle, Sasha had a more direct view of Larry Lee, a perfect profile, except for those moments when he glanced nervously back at the group. He also may have been scanning the courtroom for members of his family. As far as Sasha could tell, none were in attendance, not even his sister, Nancy.

When he faced forward, he kept his lower lip protruding outward, which gave him a determined but pouty expression. And he would habitually inflate his upper lip like a balloon before expelling a gust of breath. Occasionally Larry Lee put on horn-rimmed reading glasses to examine case and court documents on the table before him. At those times, looking at him in his sharp gray dress clothes with his neat, silver ponytail, Sasha could imagine him, perhaps, in a different life altogether. *What could he have become, she thought, if he hadn't become a monster?*

The trial got under way with the prosecution's opening statement. Nassios slowly moved in front of the prosecutor's table and paced about the courtroom with a strong and quiet grace. She spoke to the jurors about girls and women, victims who are poor or young or from the "streets." She viewed these victims with non-judgment and respect—the law required her to—and urged members of the panel to do the same.

She explained that the outcome of this trial would hinge on the issue of truthfulness and credibility. Ayesha Mack was—and is—young, Nassios said. She had made errors in judgement. She dropped out of school, ran away from home and was living in a bad environment among some questionable characters. There was no doubt about that. But, Nassios pointed out, this victim was still credible. She had the truth on her side. Evidence and witnesses would corroborate her story.

Nassios then informed the jury that they would learn about the sexual assault of her client, how excess force had been used, and how bodily harm had occurred as a result. She also clarified the definition of rape for the jurors, explaining that the object used in the vaginal penetration did not *have* to be the penis of the assailant; it could be—as it was in this case—his fingers.

The state would show that Larry Lee had kidnapped Ayesha, held her against her will and restrained her with the chain of neckties. He'd slapped her and put his forearm against her throat, resulting in physical harm. The pressure on the victim's throat had been overwhelming; she'd become faint and had experienced painful swallowing for days.

And as he'd pressed his rotund body between Ayesha's constricted thighs, forcing them open while threatening to "break [her] fucking legs" if she resisted, she strained against him and pulled muscles in her groin, causing her to limp for several days thereafter.

Nassios instructed the jurors to imagine the sheer terror of this sexual assault from the perspective of the young, surprised victim as she experienced the violence and looked into the crazed eyes of her rapist attacker, who just a short time earlier had been a friend, or at least a friendly acquaintance.

On the other side of the courtroom, Larry Lee pursed his lips together, smiled dismissively and shook his head vigorously in the negative. He would continue this animated behavior throughout Nassios' opening statement.

When Nassios wrapped her remarks, defense attorney Mitch Harper rose to his feet. "The good part about this case," he said in his native East Tennessee drawl, "is that we're going to agree about an awful lot of things that will be testified to."

He told the jury they would concur that Ms. Mack came to Mr. Smith's apartment voluntarily; that she was told the bad news about her boyfriend's arrest; that she stayed in the apartment even after Khristy left; that while she was there, Mr. Smith tried to comfort her by offering her tea and that

Mr. Smith offered her food. "Now at that point in time that Ms. Mack leaves the apartment is where you get the two diverging stories over what happened in that apartment."

Ayesha didn't leave the apartment because she was scared and upset as a result of a sexual assault by Mr. Smith. No, she was upset because her boyfriend, Tam, had been arrested, and Mr. Smith refused to enter into a prescription-selling scheme with her to raise money for Tam's bail.

And the interpretation of Mr. Smith's statement: "What she said happened, *happened*"—made to KPD Investigator Tipton—was a *misunderstanding*. Mr. Smith did not mean to imply that he had sex, consensual sex (or *any* sex), with Ms. Mack. Mr. Smith was just agreeing that he'd offered Ayesha comfort and, in the process, *touched* her, thereby getting her DNA on his hands.

At the defense table Larry Lee nodded his head in vigorous agreement. The defense did not plan to call any witnesses, Harper explained. There weren't any.

The state had a list of seven subpoenaed witnesses. The first witness Nassios called was Volunteer Studios Apartment Manager Kathy Brown, a competent-looking blonde dressed in a navy-blue business suit. Given the nature and the lifestyles of many who called the apartment complex she managed home, Ms. Brown, and sometimes her head of maintenance, Scott, found themselves in court more often than might be expected of an apartment manager. The Knox County District Attorney's office had come to appreciate the credibility that their testimony and demeanor brought to the witness stand.

Ms. Brown explained that there are one-hundred-sixty-nine units on four floors in the hotel-turned-efficiency-apartment complex. Larry Lee had lived in apartment 263 since May 2011, going on six months at the time of his arrest. On the day in question, Ms. Brown recalled, Larry Lee had appeared downstairs at her office red-faced and sweaty before disappearing elsewhere. Then Ayesha appeared a short time later, crying, nearly-hysterical and saying she had been physically and sexually assaulted by Larry Lee.

Nassios then had the 911 call played for the court. In the quiet courtroom, everyone heard Ayesha's trembling, panicked voice sobbing as she described the assault to the KPD emergency operator. When the recording ended, a somber silence permeated the room.

Nassios then called Scott Brown, maintenance supervisor for Commercial Realty, which owned and operated the complex. He recounted being called to the office on the afternoon of October 24, 2011, and being told to sit with Larry Lee to make sure he didn't leave. So he sat outside Volunteer Studios with "beet red" Larry Lee and waited for the KPD officers to arrive. While waiting, the suspect told him that Ayesha "wanted me to. She wanted it." From the defense table, Larry Lee again pursed his lips and shook his head in disagreement.

On cross examination, Mitch Harper confirmed that what Larry Lee did, while under the watchful eye of Scott Brown, waiting for the police to arrive, was roll and smoke multiple cigarettes but in no way attempt to flee. The maintenance supervisor couldn't disagree with that.

Nassios' third witness was the victim. Dressed in a short white jacket and blue jeans, Ayesha, shaking visibly, took a deep breath and made her way to the witness stand. Some of the people in Sasha's row glanced at each other in nervous anticipation. Nassios began by asking Ayesha to describe her current living situation with her mother and siblings near Atlanta. At first, Ayesha spoke so softly that everyone had trouble hearing her. After a few attempts, she was sufficiently able to elevate her voice and lean in close enough to the mic to be easily heard by the attorneys, judge, jurors and courtroom audience.

After answering Nassios, she went on to recall the events leading to her arrival in Knoxville a couple of years earlier and how she came to meet Larry Lee Smith and to be in his apartment on the day of the assault. From that point on, the story became more difficult for the soft-spoken teen to narrate.

Though she occasionally had to stop to compose herself, she managed to walk the jury through Larry Lee's rapid-fire assault. He had asked her to help him move some things beside the bed, she explained. "That's when he tied my wrist with the tie." Ayesha's chin quivered and her eyes became teary. When she got to the part about the defendant pulling her clothes off, climbing on top of her and thrusting his fingers in and out of her, she broke down completely.

"His sweat was dripping on me," Ayesha sputtered through heavy sobs. "It was just so... so *nasty*."

Sasha glanced at the jurors. Several were wiping their eyes.

When Ayesha calmed, Nassios asked her to describe her injuries after the attack. Ayesha explained that she experienced soreness in her neck, difficulty swallowing, discomfort in her groin and thighs, a limp when she walked, and several days of unusual vaginal discharge.

Nassios thanked Ayesha for her testimony and her bravery and turned the witness over to the defense. Mitch Harper rose from the defense table and walked toward the witness. Despite his challenging of Ayesha's account in his opening remarks to the jury, he was not overtly confrontational with her on the stand. In fact, Harper was almost gentle in his cross examination.

He began by asking if she had gotten a physical when she

got back to Georgia the day after the alleged rape, as she had reportedly told Investigator Patty Tipton she would. After all, Harper said, she'd described having vaginal discharge for days and limping as a result of the defendant's weight upon and force against her thighs. Surely she would have seen a doctor.

"No, sir," Ayesha said.

"Why not?"

"I'm not sure," she said, her voice a near-whisper. "I... I just didn't."

"No further questions, Your Honor."

The next witness to be sworn in was KPD Forensic Technician Rebecca Doell Byers, a young, attractive, chestnut-haired woman dressed in her KPD uniform blues. After earning a bachelor's degree in criminal justice, Byers had completed additional training at the University of Tennessee National Forensic Academy in Knoxville. She'd been employed at the KPD for a couple of years when she accompanied Investigator Patty Tipton to Larry Lee's apartment on the day of the assault.

The photographs taken by the forensic technician were now projected onto the blank white wall on the right side of the courtroom. Everyone stared up at enlarged images of the inside of Larry Lee's efficiency apartment while Byers gave an explanation of each. There were several images of two empty tea cups—empty, Nassios pointed out, even though Ayesha clearly stated that she had not drunk her tea. A bottle of Benedryl, Byers noted, was also found in the apartment.

From the witness stand, Byers then displayed a bag of neckties retrieved from behind the bed. Wearing latex gloves, she took them out and held them up for inspection by the jurors. Nassios pointed out that the ties matched, in color and design, the description given by Ayesha of the ones used to bind her wrists.

Officer Byers also displayed a bag containing a white T-shirt worn by Ayesha the day of the assault, onto which had dripped her assailant's sweat. It had been collected for DNA testing. But DNA testing had not been done on any of the evidence gathered that day. With Larry Lee's statement made to Investigator Tipton that what Ayesha said happened, *happened*—and that the officer would find Ayesha's DNA on him—the state had reasoned that testing for DNA wasn't really necessary in this case. They had assumed that Larry Lee was going to claim consent as a defense.

Next, Nassios called KPD Internet Crimes Investigator Melvin Pierce to the stand. It was Investigator Pierce who had examined the cell phones confiscated from the defendant. There were sixty-four pictures and four videos found on the Verizon phone, but Investigator Pierce reported that the photos of a woman (or women), bound by neckties on Larry Lee's bed, which had been shown to Investigator Tipton on the day of Ayesha's assault, were no longer there.

The sixth witness called by the state was Patty Tipton, Investigator in the Crimes Against Persons Unit at the KPD. The veteran officer, with wavy, shoulder-length hair the color of copper, was sworn in, settling confidently onto the sturdy wooden chair from which she had borne witness many times. Attired in a black pant suit paired with a crisp white shirt, she testified about her interview with both the defendant and the victim in the late afternoon and evening of October 24, 2011.

Ayesha was "upset, shaking, highly distraught," Tipton testified. In her professional observation and opinion, Ayesha's emotional state was consistent with someone who had just experienced a sexual assault. After taking Ayesha's statement, the investigator then met with Larry Lee.

At this point the video of Larry Lee in the KPD interview room was projected onto the wall. It depicted the defendant being questioned by Investigator Tipton and showing her images on his phone, being swabbed by Forensic Technician Byers, and then sitting alone in the interrogation room, at times talking to himself.

From the defense table Mitch Harper rose to begin his cross examination. He noted that the defendant had been cooperative with the investigator, had he not? Tipton confirmed that Larry Lee had been cooperative. So Harper continued, "When Mr. Smith said, 'What happened, *happened*,' did you ask what he was referring to?"

"I *knew* what he was referring to."

"But you didn't *ask* him to clarify."

"No," Tipton answered firmly. "I didn't *need* to. It's what we were talking about: *vaginal* DNA on his hands. I knew what he meant."

"No further questions for this witness, Your Honor."

The seventh and final witness was KPD Lieutenant Steven Patrick, who described the Knox County Jail Paytel inmate phone system into which prisoners are required to enter an assigned, twelve-digit number. Phone calls are then recorded.

The state played a portion of a phone conversation between Larry Lee and his sister, Nancy, captured on the Paytel phone about a week after he'd been arrested. This exchange began with Larry Lee asking her to get a certain phone number stored on a phone.

"Oh, you don't know Daniel's phone number?" Nancy said.

"Right.'

"I don't know when I can get the phone."

"Okay," Larry Lee responded. "Because all I have to do is send word out to Khristy to tell the girl that I'll give her a thousand dollars and—"

"Don't even say *nothin'* like that over *this phone!*" Nancy snapped. Moments of silence followed with neither the defendant nor his sibling speaking, and then the recording ended. At the defense table Larry Lee sat red-faced, sporting a nervous grin and shaking his head.

The state rested its case.

At that point, Harper rose and asked the Court for a dismissal, citing a lack of sufficient evidence to move forward. Judge McGee ruled that the testimony of Ayesha Mack and the corroborating evidence provided sufficient verification to continue with the trial. Then he sent the jury out of the room and adjourned court for the day.

28. <u>THEATRE OF THE ABSURD</u>
Part I: Whoa, whoa, whoa!

On the morning of the trial's second day, Tuesday, February 26, 2013, Bert made the coffee run and picked up a copy of the *Knoxville News Sentinel*. On page three, he saw what he was looking for:

Woman testifies she was attacked:
Convicted rapist contends sex consensual

For these Knox County jurors, it may seem a classic case of he-said, she-said. But what jurors do not know is that Smith has prior convictions in Florida and Georgia for sexual assaults—one of which sent him to prison for nearly 20 years—and is the chief suspect in the 1987 slaying of a 15-year-old Fulton High School student.

The article, written by the paper's court reporter, Jamie Satterfield, described Ayesha's account of being bound, assaulted and raped by Larry Lee, escaping only when someone knocked on his apartment door. And it reported on the defense attorney's opening-statement claim to the jury: "When Smith refused to give her money, Harper said the teenager accused him of rape."

Sasha and Bert made their way down Main Street toward the courthouse on the cold and misty winter morning, where they met up with their group and entered the courtroom together. They were joined by Ayesha and KPD Investigator Tipton, who had completed their testimony. The group had no idea what to expect this second day. The prosecution had exhausted its witnesses and the defense had no witnesses to call. That left only the lawyers' closing statements. Sasha was sure Nassios had successfully presented her case, but she still had doubts. *Had enough been said? Had enough been done? Would the jury be convinced of Larry Lee's guilt beyond a reasonable doubt?*

But Sasha didn't need to worry. Larry Lee was, by nature, a self-destructive character. And he was about to take this trial to an absurd new level.

Against legal advice, Larry Lee decided that it was in his best interest to testify. It was, he explained, the only way to vindicate himself. The judge informed him that no one could prevent him from testifying, but that it wouldn't be held against him if he did not.

"I understand that," Larry Lee responded. "I did think about it, and I'm all alone. There are no other witnesses. Therefore, I'm going to testify."

"You're not suggesting that you've been unfairly precluded from bringing witnesses in," the judge clarified. "They just can't be found."

"There are a few," Larry Lee said, "but this comes down to what she says and what I say. I believe that if I don't testify, I'm going to be found guilty. I want the jury to hear my side of the case."

"The fact is that you will be cross-examined," the judge warned, "and some things can go bad for you."

Mitch Harper quietly consulted with his client.

For Sasha, this was thrilling news. Nassios had told her that Larry Lee would most likely not testify, that he could be destroyed if he did, so this turn of events was an unexpected gift. Sasha watched Nassios, looking for a reaction. The DA remained characteristically composed, but Sasha wondered if she wasn't squirming with delight inside that sharp, navy blue suit.

Harper and Larry Lee wrapped their discussion and Larry Lee was still determined to proceed. So the jury returned to the courtroom and Larry Lee was sworn in.

"Were you born here in Knoxville?" Harper began.

"No, sir," Larry Lee responded. "I was born in Warren, Michigan. I was raised here in Knoxville."

"Okay. When did you move to Knoxville?"

"I believe I was about four-years-old. My mom and my brother and I moved down to Knoxville. My mom was originally from Knoxville. I was raised in South Knoxville. I lived in the same house most of my life over there. My son still owns that house."

Larry Lee calmly answered several softball questions and then ran through the story of how he'd come into contact with Ayesha. As he talked, his demeanor became more confident and laid back; his voice took on a friendly, folksy feel. He said he'd had an accident in his vehicle, back when he was staying in the Seymour community in Blount County, about a year before. He'd rolled it off a hill, injured his ankle. That had required pins and ongoing medical attention, which his sister, Nancy, provided when he moved back to Knoxville. Then he'd gotten a staph infection in the wound that left a hole "big as a dollar bill."

"It was *ghastly,*" he added, directly to the jury.

Larry Lee explained that he'd met Ayesha through her boyfriend, Tamryn Conden, in October of 2011. They just hung out. He talked about fixin' soup and grillin' burgers and chattin' it up with Tam's girlfriend. "And I apologize if I confuse you," he offered the court. He was going to have trouble calling Ayesha by her proper name, he explained, because he just knew her as *Jade*.

"Let me direct your attention to the date that we're talking about," Harper said. "October 24. What did you do on that date?"

Larry Lee sighed. He began his account with a story about making soup for himself and some others.

"Is that a normal kind of thing?" Harper asked. "Are you a cook at Volunteer Studios?"

"*Well...*" Larry Lee said, "in those photos"—the ones taken by KPD forensics and projected onto the courtroom wall—"you'll see that I had a big, 'ol black pot. I like to cook a lot." Then he turned to the jury and added, "I'm a big person. I like to eat."

Larry Lee told Harper he'd made soup that Sunday night on his hot plate and that Khristy, Tam, Ayesha and David had been in his apartment. That's when they watched the movie *xXx*. Then Larry Lee turned back to the jury. "That's an action movie," he said. "The reason I liked it was it had a '67 GTO, which was my first car."

In the gallery, Investigator Tipton gave Ayesha's back a reassuring rub and whispered, "He thinks he's charming. He really does."

Anyway, Larry Lee continued, later that night he'd tried to get everybody to leave because he had to go to court the next morning to testify against the guy he'd accused of stealing his prescription OxyContin about a month earlier. The others left, but David remained behind, and he and Larry Lee ended up staying awake all night. In the morning, David wanted to stay in Larry Lee's apartment to sleep while the defendant went to court, but Larry Lee wouldn't allow it. "I made him leave," he said. "Well, David went downstairs and robbed the washing machines of quarters. He took those quarters to Tam to buy something to—"

His attorney cut him off. "Let me direct your attention to what you said you were doing that morning. You'd been subpoenaed to court for some reason?"

"Yes, I was going to testify against a man by the name of Barry Eugene Evans."

"That was the man you were talking to Patty Tipton about?"

"Yeah, he'd stolen some of my medication about a month earlier." Larry Lee turned toward the judge and asked in a soft voice, "Can I have some water? I haven't talked this much in a long time."

Larry Lee received his water and Harper continued, "And when you got finished in court, what time of day was that?"

"It was around noon."

When he got back to his apartment, he turned on the air conditioner and took off his shirt before Khristy came up and gave him the news about David and Tam getting arrested. She also showed him Tam's iPod, which she was on her way out to sell. Then "Jade" knocked on the door and Khristy darted into Larry's bathroom. When she re-emerged from the bathroom, she told Jade about David stealing the quarters and both he and Tam getting arrested, Tam for possession. Jade started crying and asked to use his phone.

"Now tell the jury about what happened when you and Jade were in the apartment together," Harper instructed.

Larry Lee claimed that the first thing he did was try to comfort the sobbing Jade, touching her on the back and shoulder, making her some warm tea. He had apologized to her, he said, for not allowing David to stay in his apartment while he went to court. Maybe if he had stayed there, David wouldn't have broken into the laundry machines, gone to see Tam in Khristy's apartment, where the surveillance cameras followed him, and gotten them both arrested.

"So, in a roundabout way, you felt *responsible* for Tam," Harper reflected.

"Yeah! We talked about that. I didn't understand at the time, but that kind of made Jade mad. That started it!" The "it" being one of Larry Lee's versions for why Jade was accusing him of rape; she wanted revenge because he'd indirectly gotten Tam into trouble.

Larry Lee claimed that he and Jade discussed what they were going to do for money, and she said she was going to go down to the gas station to make some money. "Let me explain," he said, again turning toward the jury. "That doesn't mean she was going to go sell sex or anything like that. What I've seen her do, she'll go down to the Pilot and she'll panhandle, you know? Guys'll give a pretty girl money in a heartbeat. I didn't think there was anything wrong with that. When I was working, I'd hustle, find spare car parts, get scrap metal and I'd get a kickback out of that. That was *my* hustle."

"So, you were having a conversation about money," Harper continued, "and then what?"

"Then we started talking about Tam, and Jade started crying all over again. I just walked over and held her and said, 'You don't have to worry.' And then we started talking about our clothes." Larry Lee alleged that Ayesha complained about always wearing the same clothes, so he trashed Tam for not buying her any with those Target gift cards that he'd seen a couple people give Tam. "And so I talked bad about him."

"To Jade?" Harper clarified.

"To *Jade*—and that is where I made my mistake, *okay?*" Larry Lee paused, as if he was having some kind of epiphany.

"I've been trying to figure out for months what I did wrong to *really* make Jade mad, and I didn't realize it until yesterday."

"What was that?"

"I was talking *bad* about Tam. Jade loves that boy. And here I was talking bad about him. I'm the biggest monster in the world. I messed up. I'm sorry."

"And what happened after that?" Harper asked. "How did that conversation end?"

According to Larry Lee, Jade pulled a prescription pain pill out of her pocket, put it on the table, crushed it and split it with the defendant. She snorted her half as he licked his off his index finger. Then Jade proposed a plan, a drug-selling scheme. "She wanted me to come up with five hundred dollars to buy crack. Well now, I'm on medication, OxyContin."

"Prescribed to you by a doctor," Harper added. "What did you tell her about your ability to come up with five hundred dollars?"

"I said, 'Whoa, whoa, whoa. This is getting a little ridiculous here.'"

Sasha felt a chill. When she had read the 1990 transcript from the Georgia trial for the kidnapping and assault of Amanda Sanders, she'd seen Larry Lee's words in print. Now, listening to him in person, those words from twenty-three years earlier came to life. His testimony offering an alternate version of events from that of Amanda Sanders, in which he was the innocent victim, was peppered with that same expression: *whoa, whoa, whoa.*

"'Jade, you're my buddy, my friend,'" Larry Lee said he responded to Ayesha, "'but I can't come up with no five hundred dollars.' She said, 'Yeah, you can.' I said, 'I'm already late on my rent. Okay, tell me how.'

"She wanted me to tell this other guy we know by the name of 'T' that if he gave me five hundred dollars, I would have it back to him by Thursday or when I went to the doctor, and if I didn't have the five hundred dollars, I'd give him my 'scrip. And I said, 'No, no, no. You're not going to get me like that.' We got into an argument about it. Eventually she started getting mad at me. I said, 'You're not going to get me like that. I can't afford no felony. That *first* felony will put me in jail.'"

Seated at the prosecutor's table, Leslie Nassios wrote the words "first felony" on the yellow legal pad in front of her, drew double stars beside them, then added the word *bingo* before she twisted around in her chair and briefly locked eyes with her assistant, Kim Strike, seated just behind her on the front row of the gallery.

"What did Jade do?" Harper continued.

"She started crying again. She cried three or four times. She's good at that. She really is. She said, 'I'm going to leave.'" In response, Larry Lee said to her, "'You can leave, but you can stay here if you want to.' And that's when she left."

Larry Lee then testified that he walked from his apartment to a neighbor's, then back to his, then to the front office, where Ayesha had already gone. Regarding the reports that he appeared sweaty and disheveled, he turned toward the jury, laughed and said, "I was getting tired. I'm like a big bear. When I eat, I like to go to sleep... *plus* I'd been up all night."

Then he explained that, once downstairs, he'd sat outside with Scott Brown, waiting for the police to show. "I'm not running," he emphasized to the jury. "I didn't *do* anything." Eventually the police arrived, checked Larry Lee over and transported him to the KPD where he met Investigator Patty Tipton.

"Pretty quickly you indicated you didn't want to talk to her about the facts," Harper said.

"Yeah. I really didn't want to talk to her. I don't know

why. She just made me feel… wrong. But I really wanted to know what was being said." Then, in a hushed tone, he noted to both his attorney and the jurors, "Do you know that I didn't even know, *totally,* what Jade had said until *yesterday?*"

"You didn't seem to have a problem with them swabbing your hands," Harper observed.

"No, because I didn't *do* anything! DNA on my hands? Yeah, I touched her."

"What did you mean by that statement?"

"Jade was my friend. I… I tried to comfort her. I could see what was happening," Larry Lee continued, referring to his becoming a suspect in the eyes of Investigator Tipton. "I wanted to go ahead and get some defensive material in for me. And, I was craving a cigarette. I chain smoke, and it had been a couple of hours."

He turned toward the jury again. "I don't know if you smoke, but it's an addiction."

With that final disclosure, Mitch Harper concluded his direct examination of Larry Lee, and the court took a recess.

noted, t

In

DeK

able

Le

29. THEATRE OF THE ABS
Part II: No, no, n

In preparation for her cross-examination of Larry Lee Smith, Leslie Nassios informed Judge McGee—while the jury was out of the courtroom—that she wanted to *impeach* part of the defendant's testimony. On the witness stand, under oath, Larry Lee had testified that he'd refused to engage in a prescription drug-selling scheme as allegedly suggested by Ayesha. "You're not going to get me like that," he'd testified telling her. "I can't afford no felony. That *first* felony will put me in jail."

In fact, Nassios informed Judge McGee, Larry Lee had two prior felony convictions: one in Florida and the other in Georgia. Each conviction involved the kidnapping and sexual assault of a teenage girl. And now that Larry Lee had mentioned his criminal record—false as he was—he had opened a Pandora's Box. Nassios argued that she was now free to question him about his prior convictions.

Defense Attorney Mitch Harper countered that he didn't believe his client had said "first" felony, whereupon the court reporter reviewed that portion of the trial transcript. Yes, she he defendant had said "first."

contrast to the relative ease with which the former
lb County prosecutor Elizabeth MacNamara had been
to introduce the "similar transaction" evidence from Larry
e's 1982 Florida conviction into the 1990 Georgia trial, the
noxville judge advised caution. This is "dangerous territory,"
McGee counseled Nassios. He granted her permission to
question the defendant with regard to the *existence* of prior
felony convictions—but not to the *nature* of those felonies.

While Nassios may have felt some frustration regarding
Judge McGee's decision, she wasn't surprised. "It's a good
ruling," Sasha overheard her say to Strike when she returned
to the prosecution table. She also told the Court that she had
one other element of impeaching evidence that she intended
to introduce during her cross-examination of the defendant:
additional content of the recorded jail phone calls between
Larry Lee and Nancy.

The jury filed back into the courtroom and Nassios began
her cross examination of Larry Lee.

"Mr. Smith, is it your opinion that a jury's duty is to
determine whether *you're* telling the truth or Ayesha Mack is
telling the truth?"

"I *believe* that's what a jury does."

"And so the issue of Ms. Mack's credibility is a crucial one
to consider."

"No, no. See..." Larry Lee responded, suddenly seeming
flustered. "I'm not calling her a liar. I'm calling her *vengeful*.
But I'm not—"

"Well, let's talk about—"

"She's *credible*. You can be credible on anything and
wrong on something else."

"Was she *wrong* about you sticking your fingers up
her vagina?"

Larry Lee looked stunned. "I did not do that!"

"So she wasn't *credible* when she told the jury about that?"

"She wasn't *truthful.*"

"So you agree with me that whether or not she was telling the truth yesterday is an issue of grave importance in this trial."

"Yeah."

After confirming with Larry Lee that on a number of points he and Ayesha concurred in their accounts, Nassios walked him through them one by one—not completely dissimilar from the methodology of Assistant DA MacNamara in Georgia twenty-four years before.

He agreed that Khristy was a mutual friend, that she was in his apartment on the Monday in question when Ayesha knocked on his door, that subsequently Khristy left and Larry Lee was alone in his apartment with Ayesha for a period of time.

"I would say about an hour," he said.

"And you will agree that in the course of that hour you were wearing a pair of khaki pants."

"Of course."

"And you will agree that you had on at least one suspender. Your suspenders were broken."

"No. I had on a belt," Larry Lee answered.

"So, she's *lying* when she says you had on suspenders?" Nassios asked.

"I'm not saying she was lying. On that she was *mistaken,* because I wore a belt to court that day."

But Nassios wasn't going to let the suspenders go. It painted a picture of the large, domineering, shirtless Larry Lee looming over his tiny victim, dropping his pants with a quick flick off his shoulder of the single functional strap, exposing his naked self in one fluid motion. So she explored the issue of the broken suspender further. Larry Lee agreed that he did, in fact, own a pair of suspenders with a broken strap. They broke, he said, when his sister, Nancy, attempted to wash and dry them.

Nassios asked Larry Lee if he agreed that when police searched his apartment they found items consistent with Ayesha's report, including a knife on the table.

"Two," clarified Larry Lee.

"And... what else?" the prosecutor pondered aloud. "There were neckties, right?"

"Yes."

"So they *did* find the neckties that Ms. Mack described?"

"Yes."

"And there was a loop on one end?"

"The golden tie, whatever you want to call it, was looped on one end and tied on the other end to the other ties. So, I have a question about that," Larry Lee said. "If she untied her hand like you are trying to insinuate, did she also take the time to untie that tie from the other ties?" He was referring to the two disconnected ties in the chain shown to the jurors during Officer Byers testimony.

"I don't know," Nassios replied. "Did *you* not have time to do that while you were there and she went to report the—"

"I don't... I don't... That tie was a dress tie."

"You mean the one you used to restrain her while you were performing sexual acts on her?"

"No, no, no, no." Larry Lee shook his head, too flustered to speak.

"Please explain to this jury why you have three or four neckties tied together and kept under the bed."

"I have no problem with that, because I asked my attorney to let me explain that earlier and he forgot. I did, too."

"Go for it."

Larry Lee cleared his throat. "Khristy and I, as you know, had been seeing each other for a while." He turned toward the jury. "Khristy's thirty years old. I thought Jade was twenty-one, because that was my rules. But Khristy and I have had sex before, and we play games. I'm sure *somebody* in here has read *Fifty Shades of Grey* by now. *We played games!*"

Two women on the bench behind Sasha simultaneously slid down in their seats as they struggled to stifle their laughter.

"There are pictures on my phone," Larry Lee continued, "of me and Khristy and—"

"The ones you showed Investigator Tipton?" Nassios cut in.

"Yes... I don't know what she saw, but I know there were pictures."

"Well, you showed them to her, right?"

He was evasive in his response, but when Nassios questioned him again about the accuracy of Tipton's report, he didn't argue. As she tried to redirect the questioning, he blurted out an additional comment: "I'm just a tease."

"Your Honor, I would ask that you admonish the witness that he is to respond to questions—not engage in theories."

"Just answer the questions," Judge McGee instructed.

Larry Lee agreed that he'd sat outside Volunteer Studios with Scott Brown waiting for the arrival of the KPD officers, but denied telling him, "She wanted it..."

"So that was a lie," Nassios challenged again.

"Yes, it was."

"He sat there in that chair, took an oath to tell the truth and told a lie?"

"Yes, he did. He told a boldfaced lie."

"You, on the other hand, are telling the truth?"

Nassios shifted her questioning back to the scene of the interrogation room at the KPD. "Something you said on direct examination struck me. You said that Investigator

Tipton made you feel 'wrong.'"

"Right off the bat. Yes."

"Are you saying she was not *courteous* to you?"

"I didn't say that. Maybe she was *overly* courteous... She just made me feel wrong. You can tell when somebody's, *Oh, I'm going to get you. That* kind of wrong."

"She didn't coerce you in any way?"

"Nooo."

"So you *voluntarily* talked to her."

"I did and I said several things. I was also craving a cigarette, tired. *Um...* so, yeah, I said several things to her. I wanted to get this over with."

Nassios reminded Larry Lee that he had cooperated when Investigator Tipton requested to swab his hands and scrape his nails. He'd extended his hands and asked what, exactly, they were looking for. The investigator answered him: Ayesha's vaginal secretions. How would they tell this, he'd asked. Because the victim's DNA would be on his hands, Tipton had replied.

"And you said, 'Her DNA will be on my hands because I have touched her,'" Nassios pointed out.

"Her DNA, but not *vaginal* DNA," Larry Lee countered.

"But you didn't *make* that distinction to Investigator Tipton, did you?" Nassios fired back, her voice growing louder. "You had the opportunity to, *right?* You had the opportunity to tell her, '*Look*, I touched her, I comforted her, I gave her a hug, but I *certainly* didn't have my hand in her vagina!'"

"I never put my hand in her vagina."

"So, this was just a *misunderstanding.*"

The flustered defendant fell into a long, loud and clumsy rant, arguing that no DNA testing was done so there was no proof, alleging that Ayesha "probably didn't let them test it" because she knew he was innocent, and claiming that he'd cooperated because he had nothing to hide. "I wasn't guilty," he said. "I didn't do it."

During Larry Lee's rant, Nassios had turned her back on him to look through some notes on her table. When he finished, she continued reading over her notes and said, "Would you ask him to be quiet, Your Honor?"

"Just wait for the next question," Judge McGee admonished.

Nassios then turned and pointed out to Larry Lee that when he had given permission for Tipton and Byers to search his apartment, he'd asked what they would be looking for. Investigator Tipton told him that they'd be looking for the ties Ayesha reported he'd used to restrain her during the assault.

"That's when I said, 'Whoa, whoa, whoa... no, no, no,'" Larry Lee recalled.

"Well, *actually*, what you said was, *'Okay.'* And your next response was, 'Do you have my phone? Let me show you something.' You scrolled until you found the photographs that you wanted her to look at. You wanted Investigator Tipton to see that these photographs were something you did, *right?* Maybe that was how Ayesha got the idea because everybody knew that you liked to do this, right? And you said, 'You'll probably just confiscate this as evidence.'"

"I wasn't thinking like that," Larry Lee said.

"You used the word *confiscate,* and you used the word *evidence.* It didn't come out of *her* mouth," the prosecutor shot back.

"I don't know what I was thinking about but—"

"You were thinking clearly when you deleted the images."

"Ma'am?" Despite the entire courtroom, including Larry Lee, having watched blown-up footage of him moving his thumb back and forth between the buttons on the phone, before the images went missing, he still wasn't admitting that he deleted them.

Nassios moved on to the "strap" of neckties and Larry Lee's explanation to Tipton of what he did with them. "'Yeah, I don't force nobody,'" she quoted him as saying. "'I pay them.' Do you agree you said that?"

"That's right. I said that because I paid Khristy."

The prosecutor returned to the matter of the images on Larry Lee's phone, which Investigator Tipton had asked to see a second time. "She asks for permission," Nassios reminded Larry Lee.

"Yes."

"And you said, 'You're going to use them against me, right?' And she says, 'Well, it's your call. You don't have to show them to us.'"

"And you know," Larry Lee responded in a now-raised voice, "I shouldn't have! If I hadn't brought up the pictures, they would never have looked on my phone. And I feel bad because Khristy was fighting for custody of her boys. And yeah, I admit that I feel really rotten about having shown those pictures."

"Oh, okay," Nassios said. "So *that's* why you deleted them: because you were worried about Khristy's custody suit."

"I didn't say I deleted them! I *have not* said I deleted them!"

This exchange continued on for a few minutes. Larry Lee admitted that the images had originally been there. Perhaps he could have deleted them accidentally, sort of, maybe. "I don't know what happened." He was growing weary. Any semblance of the good-natured swagger he'd brought to the stand was long gone.

"You admit that you deleted potential evidence against you?"

"I don't understand the question. Would you repeat it?"

"If you deleted the images on the phone, you ruined potential evidence against you."

"So now you're asking me to admit that I understand... You're asking me to admit to a *crime?*"

"I'm asking you to respond to my question."

Larry Lee leaned forward in the witness chair, beyond the corner of the judge's bench, and looked in the direction of the defense table. "Where's my attorney at?"

Mitch Harper had watched this entire performance without comment or overt reaction. He did not respond now. If Sasha could guess what he was thinking, it would be something akin to this: *You dug this hole on your own, buddy. I advised you not to take the stand.*

"Just answer the question," the judge instructed.

"I'm still not understanding it."

"Oh, it's not a trick question."

But Nassios moved on. It was time to bring up the "first felony" comment Larry Lee had made on the stand. She repeated it back to him and said, "The fact is, you *are* a convicted felon."

"Yes, I am."

"You have *two* felony convictions, right? One from Georgia, one from Florida."

"Yes."

The jurors, in unison, bent their heads forward and began scribbling on their writing pads.

"So, there's no question about dealing drugs and getting your *first* felony conviction."

"My first felony conviction in *Knoxville* would put me away for life."

"*I'm sorry.* It was just the *location.* Let's move on then to your conversation with your sister, Nancy, on December 1, 2011, when you're trying to get her to make your bond and you tell her: 'You know my doctor has already said he's going to boost me, as soon as I come off my probation'—and she's not really interested in that." This was in reference to an additional recorded conversation between Larry Lee and Nancy that had not been played in the courtroom.

"She says, 'Yeah, well…' And you say, 'So, all I have to do is go back to him as soon as I get out of here.' Did that conversation take place?"

"Well…"

"So you admit that you were willing to peddle your prescription drugs in order to make money?"

"No, I deny that. You have to understand what I was trying to say to her."

"Explain it to us. Tell us how you can distinguish that from what you said Ayesha Mack was telling you to do."

"Because me and my sister have known each other for a long time and—"

"She'd never rat you out to the police, right? So you could get away with it."

"Are you going to let me answer the question?"

Nassios cast her eyes upward and turned away from Larry Lee. "How can I *stop you?*" she muttered, not quite under her breath as she strolled toward the state's table.

Larry Lee stumbled and rambled some more, claiming that Khristy had tried to get him to sell his prescription pills previously, but he needed them for the pain in his legs and back. He mowed lawns and scrapped metal for his cash.

"What's the price of an OxyContin pill?" Nassios asked.

"Uhh…"

Nassios didn't wait for an answer and returned to the subject of the defendant's honesty and credibility. She probed other conversations Larry Lee had with his sister during his numerous jail-house phone calls. "Always truthful with your sister?" Nassios asked.

"Not really," he admitted.

Nassios brought up a story Larry Lee had apparently spun to his sister regarding an interaction between him and a judge in which Larry Lee claimed to have eloquently argued for his "constitutional right" to be adequately defended by his previous attorney.

"That was just bullshit," Larry Lee admitted. "I'm sure I've told my sister plenty of tall tales."

"In not one of the nearly fifty jail-house phone calls with your sister did you tell her the story that you told this jury today... that Ayesha was upset with you because you refused to go into a pill-selling scam with her. Right?"

"I wouldn't talk about something like that to my sister. I mean, you know—"

"You never told her that Ayesha was mad at you because on that day you *kind of trashed her boyfriend.*"

"No, I didn't tell her that."

Nassios returned to the issue of Ayesha's credibility—her *believability*—versus that of Larry Lee and challenged him on his various, evolving stories: "I'm going to go over the six different versions you've told witnesses and others about the motivation of Ayesha Mack, the first one being Scott Brown's testimony that on October 24th, while you were waiting outside for the police, you told him, 'She wanted me to. She wanted it.'"

"I would never say *anything* like that about *any* female," Larry Lee protested.

"In version two, when you're with Investigator Patty Tipton, you say, 'What she said happened, *happened.*'" Larry Lee admitted he'd said this, but claimed he *certainly* wasn't referring to rape.

"Right. I mean, 'What she said happened, *happened,*'

could mean it was consensual, right? Kind of like, 'She wanted it.'"

"*No, no no...* I thought she meant something else. Jade's not that kind of girl." He lowered his voice. "She's a *decent* girl."

"She's somebody who would perjure herself and try to put somebody in prison with a false accusation about kidnap and rape. Other than that, she's... *all right!*"

"No, see—"

"Let's go on to version three, the Barry Evans thing—a setup, a conspiracy." Nassios was referring to Larry Lee's theory that the man who had allegedly stolen his OxyContin had conspired with Ayesha against him, even though they didn't even know one another.

"Version four: you told Patty Tipton that Ayesha probably got angry with you when you said you could take better care of her than a crack dealer. Right?"

"Yeah."

"Okay. Well, don't you find it odd that you would say that when your story now is that you all were actually arguing because you *wouldn't* give her money?"

"I didn't mean—"

"Version five: you told your sister on January 14, 2012, that Ayesha was lying about rape in order to figure out how to have a place to stay. Somebody downstairs talked her into it."

"I believed that was a possibility."

"Okay. Version *six* is the story we've heard today. Yes, you touched her, but only in an effort to console her because she was upset about her boyfriend, right?"

"I agree, yeah."

"And somehow, she got *mad* during the course of your contact with her?" When Larry Lee didn't immediately respond, Nassios prompted him. "I'm asking a question."

"Yes."

Nassios then ran through the three theories Larry Lee had presented for Ayesha's alleged anger, why she would go to all this trouble to set him up: he'd said mean things about Tam, he'd refused to go into a prescription drug scam with her, and she blamed him for Tam's arrest. Quite simply, Ayesha was looking for revenge.

The prosecutor took in a deep breath, then sighed. "You'll have to agree with me, Mr. Smith, that you have given *inconsistent* accounts of why she has done this to you. Despite these *inconsistencies,* we are supposed to believe you—and not her."

"I think that's where the jury comes in."

With that, Leslie Nassios turned away from the defendant. She was done.

"Any redirect?" Judge McGee asked Mitch Harper.

"No, Your Honor."

"What?!" Larry Lee exclaimed, staring in shock at his attorney. "That's not right!"

Sifting through papers at her table, Nassios said, "I ask the court to admonish him to be quiet."

Shaking his head and pursing his lips, Larry Lee stepped down from the witness stand and shuffled back to his seat at the defense table. He was trying not to show it, but everyone in the courtroom could see that he'd lost that overconfident feeling.

Sasha leaned over to Bert and whispered, "He should have listened to the judge."

30. <u>THINK ABOUT IT</u>

It was well into the afternoon when the prosecution and the defense presented their closing arguments to the jury. The state went first and Leslie Nassios rose to face the panel of six men, six women and one alternate. Larry Lee sat watching from the defense table, a crooked smile seemingly fixed upon his face.

Nassios led off by restating the nature of the charges against Larry Lee. She reminded the jurors that Larry Lee's penetration of the victim with his fingers still constituted rape, and that according to the law, the severity of Ayesha's injuries, the length of her confinement, and the fact that the defendant had eventually allowed her to leave, did not matter in determining guilt. All that mattered was that Ayesha's freedom, through the use of undue force, had been hindered.

"I want you to think about how that would happen," Nassios said. "Larry Lee Smith on top of that young girl, the bulk of his body on her. She's terrified for her life. She can't breathe. Remember what she said—'the look in his eyes,' crazed with lust and anger. Sweat dripping from his red face onto hers. Think about how she must have struggled to get him off her."

She acknowledged that Ayesha had made a number of questionable choices in her troubled adolescent life—running away with her drug-dealing boyfriend, living in some fleabag place with some shady people. "She's young," Nassios reminded the jurors. And despite a lifestyle lived among those on the edge, the victim remained credible in this case.

Ayesha had provided clear and precise details about the circumstances of her assault, all of which had been corroborated through witnesses and the evidence collected by KPD Investigator Tipton and Forensic Technician Byers. She had been accurate about details at the scene of the crime: the can of peas, the cut-up onion, the movie in the DVD player, Larry Lee's attire with the broken suspender, the balcony from which she had planned to jump, the knife laying upon the table where he had placed it, the tea cups and the tea bags in the trash. "And I have wondered," the prosecutor observed, "why he was so *anxious* that she drink all her tea."

Nassios then emphasized the courage it took for Ayesha to share such an embarrassing personal story with a room full of strangers. "She didn't *exaggerate* her symptoms. She told you exactly what happened to her. And I believe that's why her account is credible. If she was making up the story, she could have told you anything, because as Mr. Harper will tell you in a few minutes, her injuries were not documented by a doctor.

"Your only account is her experience, and what she felt as a result of it. She still sees it: an experience so repulsive and so disgusting to her that it's imprinted upon her mind. Who makes that up? It would have to be a miraculous actress, a marvelous manipulator, a fantastic liar to make up a story like that."

Larry Lee's crooked smile remained firmly in place

throughout the summation. As Leslie Nassios returned to her seat, defense attorney Mitch Harper rose from his and crossed the room to address the jurors. He began his closing remarks by revisiting something Nassios had said. The jury had been instructed by the state to examine the credibility of the victim versus that of the accused. But *credibility*, Harper argued, is indicated by the actions of each party immediately following the alleged incident.

"Mr. Smith didn't run away," Harper said. "He didn't leave, but went down to the front desk and waited for the police." Then he'd been "more than happy to allow them to search his apartment." He'd signed a voluntary waiver for them to do so. "He's more than willing to provide them with physical evidence and he even helps them to collect it as its being done."

And what does the KPD do with that evidence? *Nothing.* "Investigator Tipton tells you that they didn't submit that evidence to any sort of laboratory for testing.

"And what does Ms. Mack do after the police interview at the KPD? She tells the folks here in Knoxville that she'll see her doctor when she gets back to Georgia. That sounds reasonable, but she doesn't follow through. As far as we know sitting here today, she's never been to a doctor complaining about anything that occurred on October 24, 2011.

"You don't know things that you should about this case. That creates a reasonable doubt. Keep in mind that it is the state's burden to prove guilt *beyond a reasonable doubt.* If they have not done that, you have to find Mr. Smith *not guilty.*"

Harper returned to his seat beside his client at the defense table. Larry Lee was smiling now—a genuine smile—and nodding in agreement.

In the gallery, Sasha and the Band of Sisters inhaled deeply, bit their lips, and shifted in their seats in uncomfortable anticipation. Harper's summation had been effective: brief, concise and possibly the best he could have mustered in a case with no witnesses and no evidence to speak of. But had it been enough to sway the jury? Sure, his client had taken the stand against advice and self-destructed under cross-examination, but as Harper pointed out, the burden was on the state.

During closing arguments the state is allowed a rebuttal, and Nassios stood once again to address the jury. "I'm not going to belabor an argument because I know you are tired, but before you retire for your deliberations, I want you to think about the life that each of these two people bring to the table." Nassios paused for effect, allowing the jurors to look between Ayesha and Larry Lee.

"Ayesha is young, just a kid really, has been unsettled, vulnerable, homeless with marginal support. Smith, on the other hand, is *seasoned*—in his fifties with life experience. He knows what to do. It means nothing that he did not leave. Larry Lee Smith *knew* that he had to cooperate. He was trying to wrap his mind around the fact that he'd just messed up. That's why he went to the office before Ayesha. He *knew* he was in trouble."

She explained that once at the police station, Larry Lee's brain was racing. "He's throwing out everything he can, trying to excuse his behavior and get Patty Tipton going in different directions." Then Nassios reiterated Larry Lee's six versions of events for the jurors. "Only someone savvy and manipulative, very manipulative," would invent such a series of evolving scenarios.

Then there were his bizarre excuses related to the victim's DNA on his hands. "When he said, 'What she said happened, *happened,*' he meant: *Yeah, I had my hand in her vagina.* Now, I'm not telling you that is a *confession* to rape. It's an *admission* that he'd had sexual contact with her—which he could then later claim was consensual. There's a difference between admission and confession. But at that point it was reasonable to assume that he was going to claim *consensual* sex as his defense.

"So the DNA wasn't tested," the prosecutor admitted. "It probably should have been."

Then Nassios reminded the jury that the state had not claimed dire physical injuries for the victim. The sore neck and throat, the strained leg and groin muscles and the vaginal scratches had healed in a matter of days. "Ayesha didn't go to the doctor," Nassios acknowledged. "I don't know why. Maybe she felt she couldn't *afford* to go to the doctor. I have insurance; I go to the doctor. I bet you do, too. Maybe it's not so easy for some people."

On that final note, Nassios returned to her seat and Judge McGee began his instructions to the jury. At just past four in the afternoon, the panel retired to deliberate the fate of Larry Lee Smith.

Deliberations took under an hour. Sasha and the rest of the group had retired to her hotel to recharge on coffee and cookies and barely made it back in time. Just after arriving back at the courthouse, they were called into the courtroom. The twelve jurors filed in and the judge asked the foreperson, Mr. Donovan, if they had reached a verdict.

"We have, Your Honor," Mr. Donovan answered. The jury found the defendant guilty on all three counts. At the defense table, Harper showed no reaction while Larry Lee resumed his pursed-lipped expression and shook his head in seeming disbelief at the injustice of it all.

Tears streamed down Anita's cheeks. A young female juror with long, dark hair had turned to look at the group after the verdict was read. She observed Anita's tears. When her eyes met Sasha's, Sasha made a silent clapping motion of relief and agreement. Maintaining the posture of an impartial and silent juror, the young woman allowed herself a small smile. Her eyes communicated that she understood and that she too was relieved.

The judge set April 11, 2013, six weeks into the future, as the day of the defendant's sentencing hearing.

"Your Honor, I want to ask for a new lawyer!" Larry Lee blurted out. Judge McGee, in his characteristic gentle manner, advised him that this was neither the time nor the setting to address that matter. Harper gathered his notes and placed them in his briefcase.

Knoxville News Sentinel court reporter Jamie Satterfield was present for the second day of the trial. In the hallway, afterward, she talked to Nassios and asked for a statement from Anita. Her story ran on page 8A of the February 27, 2013, paper. The headline began with a signature Satterfield bang:

Prosecutor to seek life sentence after conviction

Knoxville police believe Larry Lee Smith got away with murder.

But Knox County Assistant District Attorney Leslie Nassios hopes to make sure he dies in prison anyway.

A six-woman, six-man jury on Tuesday took less than an hour before deeming Smith, 52, guilty of aggravated rape and aggravated kidnapping in an October 2011 attack on an 18-year-old woman.

Smith has a violent history that includes prior convictions for rape and kidnapping in two other states.

Because of that, Nassios has filed notice of her intent to seek a sentence of life without parole under a state law that targets the worst of the worst in the criminal justice system.

* * *

The article then moved through parts of Michelle's story and ended with:

Michelle Anderson's mother, Anita Anderson, attended the trial and wept when the verdict was announced.

31. <u>SOMETHING'S WRONG HERE</u>

Forty-four days later, on Thursday, April 11, 2013, the Band of Sisters again assembled in Knoxville for the sentencing of Larry Lee Smith. Amanda drove from her home on one side of Atlanta to Ayesha's on another, and they rode to Knoxville together. Katherine drove over the mountains from North Carolina with a friend, joining the rest of the group—Bert and Sasha; Anita; her sister, Janice; Ted; Anita's son, Doug; and Susan and her friend, Bobbi. They all met at the courthouse in the morning.

In the courtroom, multiple cases were being presented. Larry Lee, in his inmate uniform of faded-black and white stripes, sat alone, shackled and cuffed at the far end of the second row of the otherwise empty jury box. He continued to wear his thin, bushy, white-gray hair pulled back into a small ponytail and Sasha considered it, overall, an improvement. Although on this date, it looked messy and unkempt.

Just after the group took their seats, Mitch Harper entered the room with a stack of folders clutched under his left arm. As he made his way to a court-staff waiting room, he passed directly in front of his client without so much as a glance.

Several cases had to be heard before Larry Lee's, so the group sat and waited patiently. Sasha found herself engrossed in another proceeding when Anita gave her a nudge. Sasha looked at her and saw that she was motioning with her eyes toward Larry Lee. Sasha turned her head in his direction and was startled to see him glaring right at them. He seemed to be mouthing something to them from his seat thirty feet away. When he finished, he shook his head, adding emphasis to whatever it was he had just said.

"What is he doing?" Sasha asked.

"He just said something to us!" Anita responded. Neither Anita nor Sasha had been able to make out what he'd said, but Larry Lee seemed pleased with himself and turned his gaze back toward the middle of the courtroom. Whatever it was, Sasha thought he looked noticeably more smug.

Eventually, the courtroom cleared and Larry Lee's sentencing hearing began. Bound and encumbered by his shackles and chains, he struggled down from the jury box and shuffled across the courtroom to the defense table.

Nassios rose and went to a podium that faced the judge. Unlike at the trial, Larry Lee's malignant criminal history was fair game. Nassios cited his convictions for the 1981 kidnapping and rape in Florida of then-fourteen-year-old Katherine McWilliams and the 1989 kidnapping and assault in Georgia of then-eighteen-year-old Amanda Sanders, both incidents facilitated by his offering of assistance to the girls before using his signature throat-choking move to overpower them. She maintained that Larry Lee was a *violent repeat offender* who met the criteria for life in prison without the possibility of parole

Judge McGee considered and reviewed the facts of the case aloud. Then he expressed his agreement with Nassios' recommendation: a life sentence.

And like that, it was over.

The Band of Sisters barely had time to register what had happened. Then there was a flood of relief and rejoicing in the gallery as members broke into smiles and squeezed each other's hands in triumph. Sasha spontaneously pumped both fists into the air, which drew the ire of the bailiff from across the courtroom, who shot her a look of disapproval

Anita sighed deeply and looked at Ted. Perhaps for the first time since her daughter's disappearance and death twenty-six years before, she did not cry. Larry Lee had seemingly gotten away with the kidnapping and murder of Michelle, but there had finally been recognition, validation, even a justice of sorts for Anita and her family. During his trial, every newspaper story that covered it had revisited the account of Michelle's assumed fate at Larry Lee's hands. In the court of public opinion, he had been accused and, no doubt, convicted by many.

Knoxville News Sentinel court reporter Jamie Satterfield covered the sentencing hearing. Her final story about Larry Lee would appear on page 7A the next morning under the headline:

Man gets life term in prison for 2011 rape

A serial rapist suspected in a decades-old slaying of a teenage Knoxville girl offered up Thursday not an apology to his latest victim but forgiveness...

"I understand I have a messed-up life," Larry Lee Smith, 52, said before turning toward the young woman. "I forgive you for this because I know I didn't do anything to you. Something's wrong here."

At the time, the Band of Sisters, sitting all around Ayesha, turned to look at her as soon as Larry Lee uttered those words. Tears welled in Ayesha's eyes as feelings of shock and outrage moved through her. The women on either side of her put their arms around her. Sasha, sitting directly in front of her, reached back, touched her on the leg, and mouthed, *It's okay.*

The victim, too, was given an opportunity to have her say. Although shaking with hesitation, Ayesha made her way to the podium. "I've had a hard time," she said softly into the microphone. "This has hurt me a lot."

As Larry Lee was led from the courtroom to the bus carrying prisoners back to the county jail, those who'd been in attendance at the hearing began emptying into the hallway outside. Sasha caught Leslie Nassios as she exited the courtroom. "You're our new hero," Sasha told her.

"Just look at how many people one man impacted," Nassios observed, looking over at the gaggle of folks chattering and milling about. "All those victims."

"Even he's a victim," Sasha observed.

"I don't know about that!" the prosecutor retorted.

The courthouse began to empty as staff, including Nassios and her team, left for lunch. The group of twelve, however, lingered about. They'd come together hoping—praying—to see Larry Lee put away for life, and they'd gotten their wish. But there can be no real celebration associated with the saga of Larry Lee Smith and the lives he's harmed, including his own, but there was a sense of relief and quiet celebration of a battle fought, and on more than one front, won. Faces flashed smiles, voices laughed and chatted, cameras clicked and preserved priceless moments.

With the building nearly empty, the group was free to pose almost anywhere they chose. They lined up along the wine-colored, burlap-textured wall, just under the large, gold letters spelling out Criminal Court Div. III. The Band of Sisters—Sasha, Anita, Katherine, Amanda, Ayesha, and

Susan—gripped each other's hands and raised them high in a unified declaration of triumph.

"Look at those happy faces!" Joe DeVuono would observe a few days later after Sasha emailed him the photo.

Outside the upper level of Knoxville's City-County Building, on an open crosswalk looking into the downtown, Bert captured an image on his camera that Sasha had been imagining for some time. In her efforts to tell this story, she'd kept Larry Lee's victims couched to some degree in anonymity. In doing so, she had envisioned a photograph of the women linked arm-in-arm, united and strong, bound together by this strange saga, but taken from behind to preserve their identities and the new lives they've made for themselves.

Bert centered his lens on a clock tower in the distance. Tall historic city buildings peeked through blooming green branches on this sunny spring day. Ayesha stood in the middle, her newly-trimmed dark hair short and tapered, bangs pulled to one side. To her left stood Amanda with her long, wavy blonde tresses flowing across her back. On Ayesha's right stood Katherine, her auburn-brown hair cut short and stylishly angled. On either end were Sasha, with her blonde-brown highlighted bob, and Anita in her short, dark curls, framing the women who'd come together to form this Band of Sisters.

As the group slowly pulled apart, exchanging hugs and thank-yous and promises to stay in touch, the out-of-towners prepped for their half-day drives and the in-towners headed home to relax and reflect upon all that had come about. In the coming weeks and months their focus would shift back to the immediate realities of their respective lives, but the experience had changed each one of them.

For Anita, the Band of Sisters had been a healing force: she (and Michelle) were so much less alone. For Ayesha, who'd now transitioned from fast-food employment to a Monday-to-Friday day job and had bought her first car, Larry Lee's conviction and sentencing had been an affirmation of her worth and her power, one she sorely needed.

Amanda and Katherine had traveled from decades past to give their life-changing gift of support to both Anita and Ayesha. Even Michelle's brother, Doug, smoking a cigarette outside during a court recess, had shared some feelings with Katherine, a significant step for him.

The next day, Friday, April 12, 2013, Sasha got an email from retired KPD Investigator Randy York. He'd been across the country for his daughter's wedding:

> I heard Larry Lee got life. I wanted to be there.... I did all I could do, and I thank you for your help and input in this matter. I'll not forget you.

"Band of Sisters"
L-R: Anita, Amanda, Ayesha, Katherine and Sasha

32. <u>IN CLOSING</u>

Just after the sentencing hearing in mid-April 2013, Sasha received another email from York, which contained an intriguing element of mystery:

> Hold off on the end of your book; can't explain now but will keep you updated.... You'll be the first to know if all goes well. Don't write the last chapter yet.

In the meantime, over at the KPD, Investigator Jeff Day tied for Officer of the Year in recognition of the high number of cold cases he'd solved. DNA was kind of magical in that way. Sasha sent him an email message of congratulations, to which he responded:

> I will be in touch soon regarding Michelle's case. May have some info... Can't say more right now. And thanks for the other email, I appreciate it. I would trade all those cases to solve Michelle's case. I will be in touch. Jeff.

What was happening? Was Larry Lee *talking?* Had he

finally shared some kind of revelation—a *confession?* As much as Sasha wanted it to be true, her observance of Larry Lee's performance on the witness stand had illuminated his devious methods of defense and defiance. The way he'd called Ayesha out at his sentencing—saying he forgave *her* for his fate—showed that he was heavily invested in the charade—in the con. *Guilt,* it seemed, was not a standout feeling on Larry Lee's emotional palette.

Still, the press coverage during the trial and sentencing—the four newspaper articles—had no doubt generated as much pressure as Larry Lee had ever faced regarding his role in Michelle Anderson's disappearance and death. In each of the four articles his latest mug shot was featured along with his name. *Could this press exposure, coupled with his life sentence, have pushed him over the edge?* It was an intriguing notion, especially after all this time, but all Sasha could do was wait.

Eventually, additional bits of information floated Sasha's way, and a clearer picture began to coalesce. Some interesting events *had* been unfolding at the jail: Larry Lee had allegedly been talking to a cell mate, revealing that he'd sexually assaulted Michelle. After he'd dropped off Chas that night, he reportedly claimed he'd driven up Cherry Street, to a spot where prostitutes and addicts sometimes gathered, just off the interstate. There he'd assaulted Michelle, raped her, and tossed her personal items up the hillside. He did not admit anything beyond that. No murder. No dumping of the body.

Upon getting this report, Investigator Day and a forensic team scoured the area. Highway ramp reconstruction had altered the lay of the land there, but Jeff Day told Anita that they'd found a weathered purse and an 80s model Kodak camera. As he described the purse to Anita, it didn't sound like the Davey's bag Michelle had carried that night, but he said he'd bring a picture by her office just in case. In the meantime, he would continue searching for a connection between Larry Lee and the Crossville area where Michelle's body was found.

After Day's visit, Anita had driven over to the spot off Cherry Street, beside the interstate. It was a large expanse behind a car-parts company with a dead-end drive leading in.

"It looked real sketchy," Anita told Sasha. "Shacks. Not a good area at all. So I didn't want to be there alone. Haven't been back again."

Anita thought a break in the case was imminent, that the file was being submitted to Nassios, that charges would be brought any day. But now that a period of time had passed and again nothing new had occurred, Anita felt the weight of one more disappointment. She told Sasha that she felt like an emotional yo-yo: up whenever there were new developments—or the possibility of new developments— then plunging back down when the anticipation was followed up by nothing.

As soon as Sasha got wind of the "confession" and the possibility of new charges against Larry Lee, she had more questions than answers. To begin with, how could physical evidence survive twenty-five years out in the open, exposed to the elements, in an area that had been through a major reconstruction?

But regarding the purported new disclosure itself, Sasha could imagine it being true, at least in part. After dropping off Chas at the corner of Cherry and Jefferson, Larry Lee and Michelle would have been traveling north on Cherry Street, headed toward I-40W, which would have taken them to the Broadway Street exit in the direction of Michelle's Tacoma Trail home.

But before getting on I-40W, Larry Lee would have been excited, impatient, *anxious*—as he was in all his impulsive attacks—to take control of this lovely, inebriated young girl who'd found herself caught in his snare. A secluded spot off Cherry Street would have been the ideal place for an assault, a rape, even a murder. And his claim of tossing Michelle's things on the hillside by the interstate would account for the missing shoes, socks, underwear and purse when her remains were found two years later.

But following these reports of a confession, more than a year passed with no further updates from Larry Lee. Jeff Day did come upon a note in the TBI file in which a former employer stated that Larry Lee had delivered car parts in the direction of Crossville and would, therefore, have knowledge of the area. Sasha had also informed Day of Marci's theory that Michelle, in her drunken state, had insisted on going to see Marci's brother at the juvenile detention facility near Crossville. Larry Lee would have been only too happy to oblige, opening up an opportunity to assault, rape, and murder her somewhere along the way. But as with everything else, this was all conjecture. Day needed evidence. He was having meetings with Nassios so she could provide advice about what was needed to move forward with a solid case against Larry Lee, but the outcome remained uncertain.

To this day, the forensic evidence taken from the Michelle Anderson crime scene and York's investigative file have not been found. And neither Sasha nor Anita ever learned the results of the DNA tests done on the nails provided by Dr. Bass (or if the nails were even sent for testing). Chas seems to have dropped back off the radar, but Day's investigation remains focused on Larry Lee. Several people familiar with the case, including Sasha and Anita, believe Chas lied about what happened upstairs in Larry Lee's apartment that night, but have presumed him to be the less likely suspect based on Larry Lee's criminal history and pattern of kidnapping and rape. As Nassios stated, the possibility that Larry Lee operated in conjunction with Chas seems unlikely, but the unresolved nature of the case makes Chas's involvement part of the mystery that remains.

In May 2013, Larry Lee Smith filed an appeal for a new trial in the kidnapping and rape of Ayesha Mack, arguing that his attorney, Mitch Harper, had failed to properly represent him and that he had been denied a fair trial due to the questioning about his prior felonies. In April 2014, after several delayed motions, Judge McGee denied a new trial, sending the State of Tennessee vs. Larry Lee Smith further along on its journey through the appeals channels of the legal system. These channels offered the serial offender a faint chance of hope—a connection, a distraction. The next stop would be the Tennessee Criminal Court of Appeals.

Sasha contacted Nassios and asked if Larry Lee could, in fact, get a retrial someday. Anything's possible, Nassios told her, but then she informed Sasha that an appeals court would have Larry Lee's entire criminal record on file. They'd know what kind of man he was, what kind of heinous crimes he'd committed. It was unlikely that he would ever walk free again.

Whatever the elements and experiences that had intersected, interacted and converged in the personality-building process of Larry Lee Smith, they had tragically amalgamated to produce an impulsive predator who looked for the right opportunity to overpower, dominate, and rape vulnerable young women. The community could not control him, and he could not control himself.

Someone posted a collection of family photos on Ruby's obituary website when she passed away in the summer of 2010. One was of a shoreside family scene, taken on a beach blanket in the mid-1960s, with a late-thirtyish Ruby, a teen-age Nancy, a pre-teen Brad and preschooler Larry Lee. Absent from the photo was Bonnie. Was she the one taking the picture? Or had she already taken her life?

Little Larry Lee was making a *g-r-r-r* face in the direction of the photographer. He had his small hands clenched like claws and his body positioned to strike—a little pretend monster. Did the small boy in that picture still have a chance? Had the collision of forces derailing his life to one of obsessed predator already occurred, or had they just begun in this family set to implode?

Clearly, somewhere between the nature and the nurturing of Larry Lee, things had gone seriously awry. Family systems theories would likely label him a *mascot*, the youngest member of a dysfunctional family who was never allowed to grow up, was never independent of his mother, was never held accountable and didn't really fit into the world at large. His awakening sexuality merged with his already-developed insecurities, his feelings of inadequacy, his suppressed anger, leading to fantasies of control and domination. He became pathological in his compulsions: the kidnappings, assaults and rapes.

Just how and when events in Larry Lee's life and mind had collided to create the compulsive sexual predator he'd become would never be clear. Yet it had happened; it could not be denied. Just as he had stated at his most recent sentencing hearing: "I know I have a messed-up life," just before he looked at Ayesha and denied his assault of her one last time.

Spring had arrived in full, lush bloom at Sasha and Bert's mountaintop cottage. A breeze blew in through the slatted bamboo shades over the windows. On the north-facing porch, vividly colored flowers spilled out of large red pots. Perched on a branch in the large pecan tree just outside the office window, a bird chirped a short two-tone refrain, over and over: the first note climbing, the second one flat and low. Sasha stopped her typing to listen. Between the warbling of birds, the croaking, guttural chorus of nearby frogs, the crow of a neighboring rooster, and the eerie late-night howls of coyotes, she and Bert were surrounded by a symphony of nature that serenaded Sasha as she scrutinized the nearly-complete manuscript.

Was Larry Lee a victim before he became a perpetrator? Sasha wondered this as she sat at her laptop. What were his thoughts during moments of quietude? Did he ponder the state of his life and wonder about the source of the impulses that had controlled him and victimized others? Did he experience remorse and regret, not just for getting caught, but about his actions?

As his case entered the appeals process, Larry Lee was in his fifth decade. Of his thirty-five adult years—from age eighteen to fifty-three—he'd spent approximately ten years as a free man. The remaining twenty-five years had been lived as a resident of a state penitentiary: first Florida, then Georgia, and now in his home state of Tennessee.

All along this path, he'd lied. While his victims pointed fingers, while law enforcement collected evidence and juries found him guilty, he'd made excuses, denied guilt, blamed others, called his accusers the real liars.

But what did he tell himself about the state of his affairs? Sasha wondered. She would welcome the opportunity to talk one-on-one with Larry Lee; she'd wanted to interview him for years. Since Sasha had been researching and writing about his crimes and victims, she'd tried multiple times to reach out to him, but he'd never responded, as she'd expected.

On the day of the most recent assault, as he paced the interview room at the KPD after he'd shown Investigator Patty Tipton the photos of women bound with the ties on his bed, and she'd gone to his apartment in search of evidence, the camera in the upper corner caught him saying to himself aloud: "They're going to put me away for life."

It was a premonition that came true. Yet even in the face of strong state's evidence, Larry Lee never waved the white flag, never said, *Okay, you've got me.* Even when he'd already made compromising statements, he'd backtracked, changed his story, said he didn't mean the very thing he'd already said.

But now that he is in his fifties and imprisoned for the remainder of his life—if his appeals are unsuccessful, and statistically speaking, the odds are against him prevailing—does he still hold onto the faint hope he might someday be free again? Even if each shot at freedom had ended the same? After two decades in the slammer—going in as a man in his twenties and leaving in his late forties—Larry Lee was still not able to control his deviant behavior, not even to remain free. When that monster inside of him perceived an opportunity, the more rational side of Larry Lee disappeared. Those compulsions, they are something else! And now, here he was, in prison again.

Sasha wondered about the psychic defenses employed by the personality of the prisoner. Did Larry Lee's eyes really become watery when Investigator Day questioned him about Michelle? Or was that all a show? Did he know the pain of his victims? Or had he always reasoned to himself that in some way they asked for it, or that they enjoyed it once he had overpowered them into submission? Did he see his need to dominate as just a quirk, an eccentricity—sort of like his new fictional hero, *Christian Grey?* Had he rationalized his compulsion to rape as merely a personal preference, a kind of problematic *fixation,* admittedly a bit difficult to control?

Yet now that he was a registered sex offender, now that his mother was gone, now that he'd failed in his efforts at normality in the free world once again—having assaulted and raped another girl—had he begun to reflect on his "problem" a little differently?

Did he finally feel the direness of his disorder more clearly?

What if Larry Lee understood that peace of mind will not be found in pursuing his likely-unattainable physical freedom, but by his psychological *acceptance* of his predicament in this life—that predicament being his psychological and sexual disorder, his compulsion to forcibly rape young women? Larry Lee could claw at the confinement of his captivity through appeals, hoping for a miracle reprieve. But given his options at this juncture of his life and status of his incarceration, it seemed to Sasha that now there is only one choice that holds the promise of *real* peace for Larry Lee Smith—the *truth*.

Sasha imagined the mental freedom to be gained by Larry Lee at this stage of his saga, if instead of battling unlikely appeals by perpetuating more of his lies, he simply *stopped* and told the truth. Like an addict taking that first step toward getting clean: admitting there's a problem, a powerlessness, an unmanageability. And then, having owned "the problem," he would acknowledge the harm he had done to his victims, their families, his family, even to himself.

And if he were sincere, he would make amends, where possible, starting with the family of Michelle. He would come clean about that crime. Her family deserves to know; they *need* to know, no matter how upsetting the details.

One might suppose, for the very welfare of his own soul, Larry Lee *needs* to tell that truth, at long last.

Having nothing left to lose can be freeing in a way. The decisions become less difficult, less complicated. If Sasha Reynolds had the ear of Larry Lee Smith, she would tell him that.

EPILOGUE & ACKNOWLEDGEMENTS

I don't know if it was *destiny* that I tell this story; I don't know if I was *supposed* to write this book, but it has often seemed so. Doors opened, people talked, reports and records came my way. A passion began to burn somewhere within.

At times the journey seemed to propel itself, and I merely rode along like a passenger delivered to the next information stop on a human conveyer belt. As I connected events and people across states and decades, I began to get a clearer sense of what likely happened to Michelle, a fifteen-year-old girl from my old neighborhood who'd failed to return home one cold Friday night twenty years before. Pressing long-forgotten pieces of the puzzle into place, a picture began to take shape in my mind.

I learned that on that Friday night she'd run into a man named Larry Lee. And it turned out she wasn't the only one.

* * *

From the beginning of this seven-year-plus undertaking, I experienced immense gratitude for the kindness, interest, cooperation, collaboration, support and feedback this book project received from so many:

Dr. William Bass – Stumbling upon the talk to be given by Bill Bass and his coauthor *Jon Jefferson* (pen name, Jefferson Bass) in Guntersville, Alabama, on that fall afternoon in 2007, marked the beginning of this compelling expedition. Bass's forensic report and the related newspaper articles, which he generously mailed to me, laid the foundation for my ongoing quest.

Randy York – York's interest and cooperation in the exploration of this cold case gave life to my research. The commitment of this retired KPD homicide investigator, who initially came on board the case two years after Michelle's disappearance, is exemplary. No one worked harder to solve this crime than he did.

Grey Steed and *Joe DeVuono* – It was through a chance meeting over twenty years ago that the local FBI became involved in investigating Michelle's disappearance at all. Working purposefully behind the scenes, Special Agents Steed and DeVuono assisted York and the KPD in an effort to solve the crime. When I reached out to the agents not long after their retirement from the FBI, they generously offered much valuable perspective and insight on the history of the case and about their investigation that had gone on before.

KPD Lieutenant Jeff Stiles and *Investigator Jeff Day* – A corner was turned in the efforts to revive the investigation into the cold case of Michelle Anderson's disappearance and death when Lt. Stiles learned of its existence. Any progress that unfolded through the KPD afterward followed Stiles' assignment of cold-case Investigator Jeff Day. It was Day's work, through his Channel 6 News feature, that brought the story back into the public eye. I applaud the efforts of both of these officers.

And I am also grateful to *Detective Jeff McCarter* in Sevier County for meeting with me and openly and honestly describing the challenges and parameters of managing a caseload of registered sex offenders.

Assistant District Attorney Leslie Nassios – It was gratifying to experience the entrance into the story of this prosecuting attorney in Larry Lee's latest attack on a young female. I was far outside any official loop of information-sharing on this case, so I just played my cards as opportunity allowed. And suddenly opportunity allowed for me to have an audience with this skillful litigator. Nassios has an astute mind, and I got to spend over an hour gleaning bits of legal wisdom from it. I can't thank her enough for giving me that time and for the stellar job she subsequently did in the courtroom.

And I remain indebted to Nassios' assistant, *Kim Strike,* who made sure her busy boss laid eyes on my timeline containing the history of Larry Lee.

Jim Balloch and *Jamie Satterfield, Knoxville News Sentinel* – We'd come so far. The cold case had been reopened, the survivors had banded together, the victim of Larry Lee's latest assault was following through, and the trial was about to begin. But few in the city knew of that pending trial or the story of Larry Lee; his latest attack hadn't made the news, even if his bail was set high enough that he'd remained in jail for the fourteen months leading up to the trial.

Chance led me to reach out to Jim Balloch, and through him, Jamie Satterfield: both were reporters at the newspaper. Media coverage fell into place smoothly with a front-page story leading into the trial and coverage of it each day. We couldn't have wished for more.

The Survivors – Of course, the central survivor in this story is *Anita,* a mother without a clear answer about her daughter's death. She is a private woman who agreed to talk to me, because, more than anything, she wants and needs to know. Still, it took time for her to trust. I wanted to tell her private story in a public way.

When I went looking for the story of what happened to Michelle that night, I ultimately found the stories of the others: *Katherine, Amanda, Ayesha, Sara, Maryanne* and

Jenny. The first three, along with Anita and myself, became the *Band of Sisters.* Each survivor shared a piece of themselves in the telling of this story, most importantly with each other and especially with Anita and Ayesha. It was an honor for me to be allowed into their respective lives.

Joey and Jenny – I know that communicating with me was not a straightforward decision for either of them, each for different reasons. Yet they did, freely and voluntarily, let me into their familial world just long enough to get a glimpse of the inside through their eyes. And that matters, a lot, because every story is personal and complicated and experienced individually by those in disparate roles. The stories of Joey and Jenny enriched and enlightened the narrative of this saga. I thank them.

In addition to the officials who played major roles in the investigation and prosecution of Larry Lee, there were myriad individuals who also assisted me in my effort to accurately capture this tale, including court and records clerks whose phones I rang off and on, sometimes over a couple of years. Also among the people I want to thank is *Ms. Ellen Barnes,* retired court reporter from DeKalb County, Georgia, who allowed me to purchase the entire transcript from Larry Lee's Georgia trial. She and her grandson were a delight to meet.

Numerous folks read test chapters and sections of this book manuscript, which expanded, contracted and evolved over a period of years. And they provided valuable feedback to me. Among those willing souls, to whom I am immensely grateful, are *Alex, Angela, Celesté, Dolly, Glenda, Herb, Judy, Karen, Kristen, Marianne, Max, Nancy, Nkechi and Rebecca.*

A sometime partner in my pursuit of the story was not a person but a place. Well, actually a person at a place, the general manager at the *Hampton Inn* in historic downtown Knoxville, *April Lane.* The hotel sits at the corner of Main and Henley, facing the same direction as the City-County Building on their shared street. The façade of this pleasant downtown hotel is designed to fit in with the historic surroundings, and it does so nicely.

Ms. Lane believed in this book project, and, over my numerous trips to Knoxville, she and I worked out a number of dollar-saving deals. Many of my interviews were conducted in its comfortable suites. I give Knoxville's classy downtown Hampton Inn five stars.

Clint Cargile – Editor of *Similar Transactions.* I first met Clint when he was an English major at the University of Alabama. He wrote features for a regional publication my husband and I were involved with at the time. His writing was outstandingly clever and entertaining. We had no doubt this guy would find his way.

After graduating from UA, Clint earned an MFA in creative writing from Southern Illinois University and an MA in history from Northern Illinois University, where he directs a creative writing camp each summer with his wife, Gillian, also a writer. In addition to teaching, Clint is a busy freelance writer and editor.

When he agreed to take on *Similar Transactions,* my husband and I shared a collective sigh of relief. We knew his work; we trusted his judgment; we needed his mastery. We needed an interested yet objective professional eye with a ready and willing red pen. Clint understood the story and its genre. Like a sculptor with a carving tool, he expertly trimmed and gently reshaped parts of the long narrative to which I'd become far too close to know where it had grown too fat and where it was too lean.

The result, we believe, is a compelling and entertaining read that contains more than a few meaningful messages within.

"Bert" in the book is my husband, my partner, and my collaborator in all ways on this book project. Although I put most of the words on paper and conducted the research, Bert accompanied me to other states, sat in on interviews, listened to each written word read aloud over and over, made edits, assisted in making decisions and became as committted to and entranced by this saga as did I. And, aside from its front cover, he designed and laid out the entire book, the look of which reflects his clean, precise style.

As the manuscript of this book grew on my laptop, ideas for art, including the cover and an online presence, began to percolate in our minds—and in the minds of a few fellow creatives. We are indebted to *Tramayne Wright* of Studio 5 Agency, *Andrew Higdon* of BR&HQ, *Michael Palmer* of Palmer's Almanac, and *Charles Lange* of Lange Media.

One more thing – In the book I don't write in the first person, although in the many early drafts of the manuscript, I did. But as the story grew, it seemed that my part would be better told told from the same third-person perspective as the others. It made for a smoother read, we decided.

If you've reached these latter pages, I surmise that you've read what came before. Thank you. *And many thanks again* to the dedicated and brave souls who shared their stories, who pursued justice, who cared enough to come forward.

Gratefully,
S. R. Reynolds